R. David Edmunds

Tecumseh

and the
Quest for Indian Leadership

Second Edition

THE LIBRARY OF AMERICAN BIOGRAPHY

Edited by Mark C. Carnes

New York   Boston   San Francisco
London   Toronto   Sydney   Tokyo   Singapore   Madrid
Mexico City   Munich   Paris   Cape Town   Hong Kong   Montreal

For Gail,
the second-best forward to ever play for
the Blue Mound Knights

Executive Editor: Michael Boezi
Executive Marketing Manager: Sue Westmoreland
Production Manager: Donna DeBenedictis
Project Coordination and Electronic Page Makeup: Integra Software
    Services Private Limited
Cover Designer/Manager: John Callahan
Cover Illustration: Tecumseh (1768–1813) (colored engraving), American
    School (19th century)/Private Collection, Peter Newark American
    Pictures/The Bridgeman Art Library International
Photo Researcher: Rona Tuccillo
Manufacturing Buyer: Roy L. Pickering, Jr.
Printer and Binder: R.R. Donnelley & Sons Company/Harrisonburg
Cover Printer: Phoenix Color Corporation

Library of Congress Cataloging-in-Publication Data

Edmunds, R. David (Russell David), 1939–
    Tecumseh and the quest for Indian leadership / R. David
    Edmunds. —2nd ed.
        p. cm.—(The Library of American biography)
    Includes bibliographical references and index.
    ISBN 0-321-04371-5 (alk. paper)
    1. Tecumseh, Shawnee Chief, 1768–1813.   2. Shawnee Indians—
Kings and rulers—Biography.   3. Indians of North America—Wars—
Northwest, Old.   4. Indians of North America—Wars—1812–1815.
I. Title.   II. Series: Library of American biography (New York, N.Y.)

E99.S35T136 2006
974.004'973170092—dc22 [B]

                                                          2006015436

Please visit us at www.ablongman.com

ISBN 0-321-04371-5

1 2 3 4 5 6 7 8 9 10—DOH—09 08 07 06

Contents

Editor's Preface

This is an unconventional biography. Tecumseh, the Shawnee warchief, did not write memoirs, nor did those who knew him best leave letters and reports to be filed in the archives. Because of a dearth of usual sources, R. David Edmunds, author of this study, approaches this biography differently. In addition to mining sources compiled by Tecumseh's British and American enemies and sometime allies, Edmunds enlists ethnographic studies of Native American societies and culture.

But much of Edmunds's art is in the approach itself. He holds a lens up to his subject and then manipulates the lens deftly, causing different figures and issues to move in and out of focus. Now young Tecumseh comes into view, a "wiry, muscular boy who matured quickly" and excelled at hunting games. Edmunds adjusts the lens, and now the Prophet, Tecumseh's alcoholic brother turned religious visionary looms large; another adjustment, and Shawnee war and peace leaders fill the foreground, while U.S. government agents skulk in the shadows, conniving to acquire more Indian land; now the adult Tecumseh and the Prophet rally the tribes of the Midwest to challenge the steady incursion of white settlers. In the final pages, Edmunds holds the lens so close that the pages smolder. Abandoned by British and some of his Indian allies and surrounded by U.S. troops, Tecumseh, fighting from a dense thicket, is struck down in fusillade of bullets.

Edmunds, holder of a chaired professorship at the University of Texas at Dallas, has written many important books on Native American history. He has served as president of the American Society for Ethnohistory and of the Western History Association. He also has served as a consultant to several tribes who have sued to recover lands seized by local, state, and federal governments.

Edmunds points out that while Tecumseh was crushed, and his defeat became emblematic of the "vanishing redman" of nineteenth-century lore, the Native American population grew steadily during the twentieth century, increasing from 237,000 in 1900 to 4 million in 2000. Native Americans, once the only inhabitants of what is now the United States, have become an "integral part of the multi-ethnic fabric that comprises the larger history of the United States. Tecumseh's epic struggle is an important component of the broader American experience." Edmunds adds, "All Americans are richer for its inclusion." Readers of this book are also enriched by Edmunds, who has provided the spectacles with which to view clearly a subject whose past is both murky and compelling.

MARK C. CARNES
ANN WHITNEY OLIN PROFESSOR OF HISTORY
BARNARD COLLEGE, COLUMBIA UNIVERSITY

Author's Preface

Most Americans of the twenty-first century have only limited knowledge of the circumstances surrounding the War of 1812. Sometimes called "the Second War for Independence," the war often is given short shrift by academic historians enamored with the Revolutionary period, the intellectual grace of Thomas Jefferson, or the changes that swept through American society during the 1820's. Some of this lack of interest undoubtedly is due to the conflict's seemingly indecisive outcome: after three years of warfare, the Treaty of Ghent essentially reestablished the country's borders at their prewar locations. American designs on annexing Canada, however, were dealt a setback from which they never recovered.

Generally, the war did not go well for the United States. American invasions of Canada failed, and the British burned Washington, D.C. British impressment of American seamen ended after the conflict, but the British navy still controlled the seas, and many Americans, including future presidents, remained convinced that His Majesty's government had not relinquished plans for additional colonies on the North American continent. Indeed, the most singular U.S. victory in the conflict, the Battle of New Orleans, took place after peace had been signed, but before news of the accord could reach opposing British and American armies near the mouth of the Mississippi. Moreover, except for Andrew Jackson, whose victory over the British at New Orleans served as a springboard to the presidency, and perhaps Francis Scott Key, who penned the stanzas of what would become *The Star Spangled Banner* while watching the British bombardment of Fort McHenry, the war produced few heroes or individuals familiar to modern Americans.

If the outcome of the War of 1812 seemed confusing and indecisive for most Americans, it proved disastrous for the

Indians. For Native Americans, the end of the conflict signaled the end of a strategy developed by the tribes during the colonial period and maintained through the three decades following the American Revolution. For over a century, many of the tribes in the eastern half of the modern United States had attempted to maintain their political autonomy by shifting their allegiance between competing colonial powers. In an attempt to preserve their own independence, tribes such as the Shawnees had carefully assessed the strengths and strategies of colonial powers, first supporting the French against the British, then the British against the new United States. As long as two opposing colonial powers contested the region, the Shawnees and other tribes often could tip the balance in the contest, and the competing powers were forced to bid for their allegiance and services. During the American Revolution and in the years that followed, most Shawnees had maintained an alliance with the British, since they envisioned the Redcoats as a lesser threat than the American frontiersmen who invaded their homeland. But after the Treaty of Ghent, the Crown no longer promised arms, ammunition, or alliances. Thus Indians no longer could rely upon any outside assistance, and in any event, the nearest British agents were in Canada. After 1815, the Indians were forced to deal only with the Americans. The time-honored policy of balancing competing powers had ended.

In contrast to the relatively few American heroes associated with the War of 1812, Tecumseh emerged from the Indian ranks as one of the foremost Native American figures in American history. Universally admired by his Native American followers, his British allies, and even his American opponents, Tecumseh dominated Indian leadership during the conflict and held the Indian coalition together through the force of his personality. Unquestionably his energy and dedication transformed the religious revitalization kindled by his brother's visions into a formidable political and military movement that alarmed American leaders and temporarily halted American expansion in the lower Ohio Valley. In 1813 he was killed, and his movement was defeated, but following his death his reputation continued to grow, as even his enemies eulogized his passing. The circumstances of his life were rapidly encased in legend, and eventually the man and the myth became one. Tecumseh is part of American folklore, as well as American history.

In 1984, prior to the publication of the first edition of *Tecumseh and the Quest for Indian Leadership,* Glen Tucker's *Tecumseh: Vision of Glory* had been the standard biography of the Shawnee war chief. Published in 1956, Tucker's narrative was written in dramatic prose, but his cavalier use of sources resulted in a work of questionable accuracy. Indeed, while writing a tribal history of the Potawatomis during the late 1970s, I initially had relied upon Tucker's volume as a guide to the tribe's association with Tecumseh and his movement. I soon learned, however, that much of what Tucker had written was refuted by documentary evidence. Almost all contemporary documentation illustrated that the movement had originated from the religious teachings of Tenskwatawa (the Shawnee Prophet), Tecumseh's brother, not the Shawnee war chief. But those documents also illustrated that Tecumseh skillfully had transformed his brother's religious revitalization movement into the political and military confederacy that flowered between 1808 and 1813. I found Tecumseh's efforts to be a fascinating struggle against opponents, both Indian and American, who were blinded by their cultural biases and threatened by Tecumseh's statesmanship.

Yet why had non-Indian historians so readily accepted the myths and legends that had accrued to the Shawnee chief following his passing? I was determined to separate fact from fiction, and to write a biography of Tecumseh free from the apocrypha that enshrouded him. After considerable research and a careful evaluation of many sources, I found that the circumstances surrounding Tecumseh and his endeavors contained a remarkable saga; they did not need the embellishments of folklore and mythology.

Since 1984, other biographies of Tecumseh have been published. Some are longer and more detailed than the text that follows this preface. Several novels or works of fiction featuring Tecumseh also have been published, and at least two dramas or "docu-dramas" on Tecumseh and his role in the

War of 1812 have been produced for television. In addition, an outdoor pageant focusing upon Tecumseh's life offers repeated performances near Chillicothe, Ohio, every summer, much to the delight of local merchants and popular audiences. Some of these publications or productions offer increased details about Tecumseh's life, but they also illustrate that historians, film producers, and directors of historical dramas still have difficulty in separating the man from the myth. Tecumseh remains such a fascinating, admirable, historical figure that the temptation to embellish his career continues. As one author admitted, after being questioned about very questionable speeches supposedly delivered by Tecumseh to the Cherokees and Seminoles, "Well, if he didn't exactly say that, it's what he would have said."

Yet Tecumseh's life and contributions to both Native American history and American history stand on their own. As Gregory Dowd has illustrated in *A Spirited Resistance: The Native American Struggle for Unity, 1745–1815*, Tecumseh's efforts to organize a broad coalition of tribespeople had precedents in the efforts of Pontiac and Little Turtle, but they also foreshadowed pan-Indian political movements that have coalesced in the twentieth and twenty-first centuries. Like Tecumseh's confederacy, modern Native American coalitions such as the American Indian Movement also appealed to many younger individuals, transcended tribal lines, and sometimes were opposed by established tribal leaders. Some of these recent organizations also have relied upon charismatic leaders, although none of these spokesmen have approached Tecumseh's stature. Moreover, also unlike Tecumseh, few of these modern leaders have attracted the praise and admiration of their opponents.

But some things remain. Two centuries after Tecumseh's death tribal people still strive to protect their homelands. Contemporary Native Americans leaders also endeavor to both ensure and enlarge tribal autonomy. Indian communities endure, but their struggle continues.

This new edition of *Tecumseh and the Quest for Indian Leadership* contains study and discussion questions that focus upon Tecumseh, the Shawnee people, and their interaction with other Native Americans and non-Indians during the eighteenth and early nineteenth centuries. Additions to the "Note on Sources" provide further suggestions of books and essays published since 1985 which offer readers additional information upon Tecumseh and his times.

R. DAVID EDMUNDS
WATSON PROFESSOR OF AMERICAN HISTORY
UNIVERSITY OF TEXAS AT DALLAS

1

The Shawnees

October found the forests along the Ohio River bedecked in red and gold. The trees that shrouded the banks still clung to their foliage, partially concealing the large number of men who constructed a fortified camp at the confluence of the Ohio and Kanawha rivers. Across the Ohio, on the western shore, a Shawnee warrior watched from the shadow of the trees, assessing the strength of the soldiers. The warrior, Cornstalk, was a man much respected by his people. Not only was he a famous orator, but he also had led many raids against tribal enemies, and younger warriors were honored to be included in his war parties. But on this day, October 9, 1774, Cornstalk's heart was heavy. He knew he soon would be forced to attack the Virginians, a people whom he had befriended during much of his lifetime.

Making friends with the white men had never been easy for the Shawnees. The Master of Life had led his people to the Ohio Valley, but Cornstalk knew the Virginians also wished to settle there. In fact, the valley was a fertile region which always had attracted strangers. In the distant past, when the Shawnees' forefathers had first occupied the area, they had built villages along the many tributaries that joined the Ohio as it wound its way toward the Mississippi, the great river of the West. Here the old ones had prospered, forming part of the Fort Ancient Aspect, a culture that dominated the central Ohio Valley during the late pre-columbian period.

Although the Fort Ancient people adopted cultural traits from several areas, they were heavily influenced by the

1

Mississippian culture, a way of life that flourished in the Mississippi Valley and across the southeastern states in the three centuries prior to the European invasion. The Fort Ancient people were farmers and hunters, growing crops of corn, beans, squash, and sunflowers in small fields scattered along watercourses. They supplemented their horticulture with game—primarily deer, elk, and smaller animals—and also caught large numbers of fish from nearby streams and rivers. A village people, they lived in houses constructed of poles and covered with bark, cattail mats, or daub and wattle (sticks and dried mud). These villages were often arranged in rows around a central plaza, and sometimes were enclosed within earthen and log fortifications, a trait which gave the culture its particular name. The Fort Ancient people were skilled craftsmen who molded squat, rounded, broad-mouthed pottery and shaped small ceramic animals and other effigies. They worked in stone, pressure-flaking long, narrow projectile points, flint knives, and scrapers. Other utensils were manufactured from wood, bone, or antlers.

The Fort Ancient people flourished from around 1200 A.D. to about 1650, then their culture seemed to decline as the population in the Ohio Valley dwindled. Although some of their former village sites were occupied intermittently after the early seventeenth century, many of the new residents were a foreign people, more closely tied to the tribes of the Northeast than to the prehistoric cultures of the Ohio and Mississippi valleys. Meanwhile, some of the Fort Ancient people moved west, following the Ohio Valley. Others fled south, probably seeking refuge among the remnants of the crumbling Mississippian cultures. The reason for their dispersal remains unknown, although new diseases introduced along the East Coast and transmitted across the Appalachians may have contributed to their migrations.

Most ethnologists believe the Shawnees formed part of the Fort Ancient Aspect and participated in the dispersal. In 1673, when Marquette descended the Mississippi River, Illinois tribesmen informed him that the Shawnees lived to the south and east, in villages scattered along the Ohio. Nine years later a French map based upon La Salle's expeditions indicated that most of the Shawnee villages north of the Ohio River had been destroyed or abandoned, and that many of the Shawnees had established towns on the Cumberland River in western Kentucky and northern Tennessee. In the 1680s, when the Iroquois invaded the Ohio Valley, the Shawnees again scattered to the west and south. During 1683 several hundred Shawnees fled to Illinois, where they sought refuge near Fort St. Louis, a French post at Starved Rock on the Illinois River. Most of the other Shawnees moved to the southeast, erecting villages along the Savannah River in Georgia and South Carolina. There they became the dominant tribe in the region, assisting the British against the Westoes, Cherokees, and other Indians.

The Shawnees did not remain in their new homes for long. When the Iroquois threat diminished, the tribesmen in Illinois accepted an invitation from the Delawares, and in 1692 they returned to the East, establishing a new town in Pennsylvania on the lower Susquehanna River. Led by Martin Chartier, a French deserter from Fort St. Louis, these Shawnees attached themselves to the British. In 1694 they were joined by a small band of their kinsmen who had remained in the Ohio Valley, and in the next two decades most of the southern Shawnees also moved to Pennsylvania. Some arrived as early as 1707, but others fled to the north in 1716, escaping the devastation of the Yamasee Wars.

The years in Pennsylvania were a time of mixed blessings. Although the Shawnees lived peacefully with their British and Delaware neighbors, they continued to suffer at the hands of the Iroquois. The Six Nations no longer made war upon them, but they treated both the Shawnees and Delawares as vassals, demanding tribute and the right to negotiate for the two tribes with the colonial government. Unfortunately, British officials agreed to the Iroquois position and treated the Shawnees as subjects of the Six Nations. Although the Iroquois subjugation caused little hardship, it was humiliating and it complicated the Shawnees' relationship with the British.

Shawnee-British relations deteriorated throughout the first half of the eighteenth century. Some of the problems arose over land. Since Pennsylvania was established as a haven for religious refugees, the colony began to attract large numbers of Europeans fleeing religious oppression on the Continent. In 1711 Mennonite settlers moved into the lower Susquehanna Valley in such numbers that the Shawnees were forced to move their villages further up the river. During the next two decades, similar intrusions occurred, and by the late 1730s most of the tribe had migrated west, settling on the headwaters of the Ohio. There they quarreled with British traders and in 1745 a party of warriors seized some trade goods, then fled west seeking safety at new Shawnee villages in Ohio. Some members of the tribe sought temporary sanctuary among the Creeks in Alabama, but by mid-century most of the tribe had reoccupied the old homeland in the Ohio Valley. On the eve of the French and Indian War, Shawnee villages stretched from western Pennsylvania to the mouth of the Cumberland, but Logstown, located about twenty miles downstream from the forks of the Ohio, and Lower Shawnee Town, at the mouth of the Scioto, were by far the largest settlements.

Shawnee participation in the French and Indian War was, at best, half-hearted. Although they had become estranged from British officials, the Shawnees held little affection for the French, and their ties to New France had always been tenuous. As both the British and French moved toward war, the Shawnees attempted to remain neutral. Yet they still traded with certain British merchants, and French officials resented the presence of these traders in the Shawnee villages. Since French wares could not compete with the more durable and less expensive goods provided by the British, French officials sent several armed expeditions into the Ohio country, destroying British trading centers and killing British traders. In 1750 one of these raiding parties attacked a Shawnee village, and in the ensuing melee several lives were lost. Angered, the Shawnees appealed to Pennsylvania for assistance, but the colonial legislature generally ignored their pleas. Embroiled in a dispute with Virginia over which colony should dominate the trade of the Ohio country, the Pennsylvanians seemed more concerned about the Virginians than about the French.

Rebuffed by the British, the Shawnees had little choice but to come to terms with New France. As French military strength in the Ohio Valley increased, the Shawnees wisely accepted the new balance of power, and in 1754, when the French erected Fort Duquesne at the forks of the Ohio, the Shawnees seemed securely in the French alliance. Shawnee ties to the French were temporarily strengthened by their participation in Braddock's defeat. On July 9, 1755, Shawnee warriors joined with other Indians and French troops to ambush General Edward Braddock's ill-fated column as it approached Fort Duquesne. The resulting victory not only provided the Shawnees with plunder, it also seemed to release a flood tide of resentment toward the British that had accumulated through years of slights and frustration. Between 1755 and 1758 Shawnee war parties periodically attacked the frontiers of Pennsylvania and Virginia, burning cabins, taking scalps, and stealing livestock. Some of the older warriors remained in their villages, but many of the young men vented their anger against those white men with whom they were most familiar.

The catharsis did not last long. Although the French needed their Indian allies, they were hard pressed to support them, and by late 1757 the Shawnee villages in eastern Ohio were short of food and ammunition. Meanwhile, the British slowly regained the ascendancy, and in November 1758 General John Forbes captured Fort Duquesne, raising the Union Jack again over the forks of the Ohio. Once more the Shawnees scrambled to accommodate to the changing circumstances. Some of the more ardent Francophiles withdrew to the Scioto where they avowed their neutrality, while those warriors who had refused to join the French now met with the British. Although they asked British officials to keep settlers east of the Appalachians, they agreed to cooperate with the colonial governments, and in 1760 Shawnee warriors assisted the Virginians in their campaign against the Cherokees.

Unfortunately, the Shawnee-British rapprochement was of short duration. The Shawnees believed that the British occupation of the forks of the Ohio was only temporary.

They assumed that British troops, like their French counter-parts, had come only to fight the war, and since the conflict was ending, the Redcoats would soon withdraw east of the Appalachians. But when the British rebuilt the post and renamed it Fort Pitt, the Shawnees began to question the Crown's intentions. Their suspicions were further aroused when other contingents of British troops garrisoned former French posts on Lake Erie, then sailed on to occupy Detroit and other forts in Indiana and Michigan. Of course the French had kept small garrisons at some of these western posts, but the British occupation seemed to presage a much more extensive European presence.

If the Shawnees were concerned about too many Redcoats, they complained that the parties of British traders who visited their villages were too few. Following the French withdrawal, the Shawnees were desperately short of trade goods and pleaded with British officials to allow frontier merchants to enter the Ohio country. But in 1760 British Indian agents informed the Shawnees that the Indian trade would be conducted only at British posts, where it could be supervised by British officers. Concomitantly, the British Indian Department restricted the licenses of traders, sharply reducing the number who were permitted to trade with the Indians. The officials assumed that the new regulations would curtail the rum trade and other bartering practices detrimental to the Indians, but in reality the policies caused innumerable hardships for the tribespeople.

Sir Jeffery Amherst added insult to injury. In 1761 Amherst, who served as commander in chief of His Majesty's Forces in North America, ordered all British Indian agents to put severe limits on the amount of ammunition and provisions that they furnished to the tribes. Obsessed with reducing the Crown's expenses, Amherst disliked Indians and believed that they could easily live by hunting. If they needed arms and ammunition, let them purchase such commodities through the fur trade. Ignorant of frontier diplomacy, Amherst failed to realize that gifts had always played a central role in European-Indian protocol, and that any British parsimony would be interpreted as an insult by the Indians.

Although experienced agents such as Sir William Johnson and George Croghan warned Amherst against these policies, the general had his way, and the results were as Johnson and Croghan had predicted. The Shawnees and other tribesmen were incensed. The Shawnees were a communal people who shared their possessions with those members of their villages who needed such supplies. To have wealth and refuse to share it violated fundamental precepts of Shawnee society. Even the French, perennially short of provisions, had always apportioned part of their meager stores to the tribesmen. But now the British, who possessed a virtual cornucopia of supplies, refused to share them amicably. Embittered, the Shawnees met around their campfires and complained to each other about the Redcoats' callousness.

They also complained about British demands that they surrender all white "prisoners." During the recent warfare the Shawnees and other tribesmen had taken dozens of captives whom they had carried back to their villages. Assuming that these individuals were being subjected to "untold hardships among ye savages," officials insisted that the Indians bring them to British posts. The Shawnees were perfectly willing to surrender all those prisoners who wished to return, but some of the captives had formed strong attachments to the Indians and preferred to remain in the Shawnee villages. Several former prisoners of both sexes had taken Shawnee spouses, and some were raising mixed-blood families. Others, even though they had no formal family ties, found life among the Shawnees preferable to the drudgery of the colonial frontier and refused to be repatriated. The Shawnees were understandably reluctant to send these people back to the British, but in 1762 they reluctantly agreed to bring the former prisoners to British posts. Ironically, although British troops attempted to restrain the expatriates, many escaped, and when the Shawnee delegation returned home, they found several of their former prisoners already back in the Shawnee villages.

If the Shawnees welcomed their former prisoners, they resented other British settlers who now spilled over onto their lands. In 1758, following Forbes's capture of Fort Duquesne,

some British settlers had erected cabins along the lower
Monongahela, and in the years that followed the influx of
white frontiersmen increased. At first British officials attempted
to keep the settlers east of the mountains, but the frontiersmen
arrived in such numbers that Colonel Henry Bouquet and other
officers at Fort Pitt seemed powerless to stop them. Shawnee
anger over the intrusion was focused upon the settlers' hunting
habits. Most tribesmen were willing to tolerate the small British
farms that hugged the river valleys, but they were infuriated at
white hunters who ranged far into Ohio and Kentucky, slaugh-
tering deer and other animals. In retaliation, they waylaid
lonely hunters, taking their scalps but leaving their bodies concealed in the forest. Delegations of white settlers complained,
but British officials turned a deaf ear and the hunting
temporarily subsided.

The mounting tension between the Shawnees and the
British ensured the tribe's participation in Pontiac's Rebel-
lion. In June 1763, when messengers brought news that the
Ottawas and their allies had risen at Detroit, Shawnee and
Delaware warriors joined to scourge the western frontiers of
Pennsylvania. Throughout the summer Shawnee war parties
ranged as far east as their old homes on the Susquehanna,
taking scalps and burning cabins. In July the devastation
spread to Virginia as bands of warriors ascended the
Kanawha to strike at settlements in the Shenandoah Valley.
But Shawnee and Delaware assaults upon Fort Pitt ended in
failure. Well supplied with food and ammunition, Captain
Simeon Ecuyer withstood their siege and the Redcoats
remained at the forks of the Ohio.

By autumn 1763 the Indians' fate was sealed. Although
they had won a series of initial victories, the tribesmen had
neither the will nor the resources to fight a prolonged conflict. In mid-August Colonel Bouquet and mixed forces of
British and colonial troops relieved Fort Pitt. The Shawnees
and their allies had attempted to oppose Bouquet's march
across Pennsylvania, but he had defeated them at the Battle
of Bushy Run, and the Indians had retreated into Ohio.
Three months later Pontiac abandoned his siege of Detroit
and most Indian resistance ended.

Eager to reassert their authority, the British made a show of force in the west. During the summer of 1764 Colonel John Bradstreet sailed along the southern shore of Lake Erie, where he met with some Shawnees and Delawares who promised him they would remain at peace. In October Bouquet marched west from Pittsburgh, and discounting earlier Shawnee promises, summoned other Shawnees and Delawares to the Muskingum River. Forgoing the usual formalities, Bouquet demanded that the Indians relinquish all their prisoners. Otherwise, his army would sweep through their villages, destroying their crops and killing their families. Intimidated, the Indians agreed. After surrendering all captives in their possession, the Shawnees promised that six warriors would be given to the British as hostages until prisoners held in distant villages could be brought to Fort Pitt.

Bouquet's efforts brought a decade of peace to the upper Ohio, but the years were unhappy ones for the Shawnees. Although the British again distributed presents as part of their diplomacy, their economic policies created chaos in the Indian trade. At first the Crown attempted to restrict trade to British posts and to standardize the price of all trade goods. Such policies meant that the Shawnees and other tribes would have to travel to Fort Pitt to barter their furs for ammunition and provisions. The policy angered the Shawnees and many colonial traders, who saw the regulations as an infringement upon their right to conduct business with the Indians. Consequently, many merchants illegally entered the Indian country and sold their wares in the Shawnee villages.

Unable to enforce their policies, the British government abandoned such restrictions in 1768 and relinquished the regulation of the trade to the colonies. In theory, each colony was to license and control all trade conducted by its citizens with the Indians. In actuality, the colonies did nothing. Shawnee chiefs who earlier had complained about a shortage of traders in their villages now found their towns overrun by unscrupulous merchants, each trying to gain an advantage with the tribesmen. One unfortunate result of such competition was the burgeoning use of alcohol as a trade item. After 1765, when Americans began to boycott British manufactured goods, many items popular in the Indian trade became both scarce and expensive. But whiskey could be distilled locally and was in good supply. Many traders therefore relied more heavily upon alcohol as a trade commodity and offered the Shawnees fewer British goods. The traders' profits increased, but so did the misery in the Shawnee villages.

Although Shawnee chiefs worried about the whiskey trade, they were more concerned about the continued infringement upon their hunting lands. Following Pontiac's Rebellion, the Crown had forbidden British citizens to settle west of the Appalachians, but frontiersmen in Pennsylvania ignored the edict and established homes in the Monongahela Valley. British troops forced many back over the mountains, but settlers from Virginia outflanked the Redcoats and passed through Cumberland Gap to build cabins in West Virginia and Kentucky. The Shawnees maintained no villages in this region, but they hunted south of the Ohio and considered the region as their own.

The Iroquois contributed to the tension. Envisioning themselves as the dominant tribe in the East, the Iroquois still claimed hegemony over the Shawnees. In 1765, following Pontiac's Rebellion, the Iroquois had tentatively agreed to cede all of Kentucky east of the Tennessee River to the British. No formal agreement was negotiated until 1768, when Iroquois delegates signed the Treaty of Fort Stanwix, giving their formal consent to the cession. Iroquois claims to the region were specious at best, for they neither occupied it nor hunted in it; but since the British still recognized their dominion over the Shawnees, the Crown considered the treaty to be valid.

The Shawnees disagreed. By the 1760s almost all the Shawnees were living in the Scioto Valley, but they hunted south of the Ohio River, in the Bluegrass region of Kentucky. Although they earlier had been tied to the western Iroquois, they no longer considered themselves subservient to the Six Nations, and they bitterly resented the latter's cession of their lands. The Shawnees had no intention of giving up

Kentucky and were determined to defend it against white settlers. Believing themselves betrayed, the Shawnees severed their ties with the western Iroquois and sought new alliances with other Indians in the west. These tribes, such as the Miamis, Mingos, and Wyandots, also hunted in the Ohio Valley and shared the Shawnees' apprehension that Kentucky might be overrun by frontiersmen.

Their fears were well-founded. Although the Proclamation of 1763 forbade British subjects from settling in the transmontane west, the proclamation was ignored. Frontiersmen envisioned Kentucky as a logical region for settlement, and during the early 1770s hunters and surveyors crossed the mountains searching for future homes and town sites. Lord Dunmore, Governor of Virginia, gave lip service to London's demands, but privately he encouraged the frontiersmen in their explorations.

The land speculators were supported by some of the most prominent families in Virginia, and in the spring of 1774 John Floyd led a party of surveyors representing George Washington, Patrick Henry, and several other Virginians into Kentucky to stake out lands along the Ohio River. The Shawnees had repeatedly warned British officials that they would oppose such trespassers, and in April they captured several members of Floyd's party. After destroying all the surveyors' equipment, they released the white men unharmed, but warned them not to return. Meanwhile a war party of Cherokees attacked some Pennsylvania traders on the Ohio, killing one man and wounding two others. At Pittsburgh, John Connolly, who led the local militia, accused the Shawnees of the attack and urged frontiersmen to retaliate. Following Connolly's directive a small party of frontier ruffians led by Michael Cresap surprised several unsuspecting Shawnees, and in two encounters they killed three Indians and wounded several others.

Angered by the murders, Shawnee leaders still tried to maintain the peace. Once again they failed. This time, however, the victims were Mingos. The Mingos were former Iroquois who had relocated on the upper Ohio and had gradually severed their ties with the Six Nations. Associated with the Shawnees and Delawares, they too had been forced west from Pennsylvania. During this period they lived in Ohio, east of the Muskingum. Most prominent among the Mingo chiefs was Logan, famous as an orator and well known for his friendship toward British settlers. Logan's village was located at the mouth of Yellow Creek, near modern Steubenville, Ohio.

On the morning of April 30, 1774, a small party of Mingos from Logan's camp crossed the Ohio to purchase some milk from a settler who lived just opposite the Indians, on what is now the West Virginia shore. Included in the party were Logan's father, his brother, his sister, and her infant son. When they reached the farmhouse, they found it occupied by a party of frontiersmen led by Michael Greathouse, who promptly offered them a quantity of whiskey, then engaged them in a shooting match. Some of the Mingos became so intoxicated they couldn't hold their muskets, but others, eager to prove their marksmanship, readily agreed to shoot at a designated target. Yet the contest was a ruse; when the Indians had discharged their weapons, the whites turned and fired upon them, killing both men and women indiscriminately. Greathouse and his companions then bludgeoned those Indians too intoxicated to escape, and hid the bodies of the victims. Other Indians, including some Shawnees, who crossed the river to investigate the firing were also ambushed, and by sunset about a dozen Indians lay dead in the thick underbrush along the Ohio. Among the slain were most members of Logan's family. Only the infant had been spared, but he had been carried back to the settlements.

Incensed by the slaughter, Logan vowed to seek justice in the traditional Indian manner: he would kill a similar number of Virginians. Yet he first assured British officials that he wanted no general war with the colonists. When he had ful-filled the vendetta, the killing would stop. During May and June the Mingo chief led a series of raids against isolated set-tlements in Virginia. A few Shawnees, those whose relatives had been killed by Cresap, accompanied Logan, but the vast majority of the tribe remained at peace. At his town on the

Hocking River, Cornstalk protected several Pennsylvania traders from hostile warriors and even provided an escort to accompany the frightened merchants back to Pittsburgh. Still hoping to avoid a confrontation, Cornstalk wrote to Indian agent Alexander McKee asking him "to present our good Intentions to the Governors of Virginia and Pennsylvania, and request that a stop may be put to such Doings in the Future. . . . I have with great Trouble . . . prevailed upon the foolish People among us to sit still and do no harm till we see whether it is the intention of the white people in general to fall upon us." Meanwhile Logan ceased his raiding and informed the British that justice had been done. The killing was over; the Indians were satisfied.

But not John Connolly. At Pittsburgh the militia officer remained eager for war and tried to arrest the Shawnee delegation that had escorted the traders from the Indian country. The traders interceded and warned the Indians to flee, but Connolly sent a party after them. These pursuers fired upon the Shawnee camp as the Indians lay sleeping. Luckily, the Shawnees suffered only one warrior wounded, but Connolly's actions convinced them that the Virginians could not be trusted, and when they returned to their villages, they too spoke for war.

While his troops were pursuing the Indians, Connolly wrote to Lord Dunmore, falsely accusing the Shawnees of initiating the slaughter. Goaded on by Connolly's message, Dunmore mobilized part of the Virginia militia for a war against the Shawnees. He envisioned a three-part campaign. Four hundred men led by Major Angus McDonald were to advance toward Wapatomica, the Shawnee town on the Muskingum; 1,000 men under Colonel Andrew Lewis planned to march to the mouth of the Kanawha, where they eventually would be joined by another 1,200 troops assembled by Dunmore at Pittsburgh. Dunmore's and Lewis's forces would then cross the Ohio and attack the Shawnee towns along the Scioto.

Aware of the British preparations, the Shawnees made plans of their own. Emissaries were sent to the Great Lakes tribes and to the Iroquois, seeking allies against the Virginians. Other messengers visited the Chickasaws and Creeks, attempting to bring the southern Indians into the confederation. But the Shawnee efforts produced few results. The British Indian Department intervened to keep the Shawnees isolated. In the north Sir William Johnson and his nephew Guy Johnson used their influence to prevent the Senecas and the Great Lakes tribes from providing any assistance, while British Indian agent John Stuart effectively neutralized the southern Indians. Left on their own, Cornstalk and other Shawnee leaders decided to strike the British before Lewis's and Dunmore's forces could join together. In early October Cornstalk mustered 300 warriors and led them to the Ohio, opposite the mouth of the Kanawha. There they awaited the arrival of Lewis's army.

* * *

As Cornstalk stood watching the Virginians across the Ohio, he formulated a plan of attack for the following morning. He would divide his warriors into two groups, leading the larger force across the river to attack the Long Knives at sunrise. The second party, comprised primarily of old men and adolescents, would remain on the western bank of the Ohio to cut down any of the Virginians who attempted to flee across the river. To ensure they would not be discovered, Cornstalk led the main body of warriors about six miles upstream, where they constructed rafts of driftwood. During the night they crossed the Ohio and proceeded along the eastern bank until they were within two miles of the sleeping Virginians. There Cornstalk halted his force and waited for several hours, then led his warriors forward, intending to strike the Virginians just before sunrise.

In the British camp most of the frontiersmen slept peacefully, unaware of the approaching Shawnees. Guards had been picketed during the night, and shortly before dawn two Virginians, James Robertson and Valentine Sevier, left the camp to hunt turkeys. As the hunters proceeded north up the river valley they encountered the rapidly approaching Indians. Both white men fired their weapons, then fled back to camp where they sounded the alarm, arousing the sleepy

Virginians. Lewis immediately sent two columns of troops to meet the Shawnees, whom they encountered about three-quarters of a mile from the camp. The Indians fired first and the Virginians fell back, but soon reinforcements rushed forward from the bivouac.

At first the warriors held a marked advantage. The river bottom was strewn with fallen trees and overgrown with dense vegetation, and the Shawnees took advantage of the cover to conceal themselves while pouring in a deadly fire upon the Virginians. Several militia officers were killed or wounded in the initial attack, but the Virginians soon adapted to the terrain and also took advantage of the underbrush. The battle raged throughout the day, while Cornstalk, Logan, and other chiefs passed along the Indian lines encouraging their warriors. Although, as the Virginians later admitted, "Never did Indians stick closer to it, nor behave bolder," by evening most of the warriors had exhausted their ammunition. Shortly before sunset, they slowly withdrew from the action and crossed over into Ohio. The Battle of Point Pleasant was over.

Although the Indians suffered fewer casualties (the Virginians lost 81 killed and 140 wounded), they failed to rout their enemy and the British claimed the victory. Across the Ohio the Shawnees and their allies regrouped, then retreated to the Scioto where they met in council. There they learned that Wapatomica, the Shawnee town on the Muskingum, already had been destroyed by McDonald's forces and now their villages in central Ohio were vulnerable. Cornstalk addressed the assembled warriors, reminding them that he earlier had argued for peace but they had asked him to lead them against the Long Knives. Since they had failed to defeat the Virginians, did they wish to continue the war? Were they willing to attack Dunmore's army before it reached their villages? When he received no reply, the Shawnee chief announced that he would try to make peace with the enemy.

While the Shawnees met on the Scioto, the Virginians were marching toward the Indian villages. By this time Dunmore had left Pittsburgh and had proceeded down the Ohio to the mouth of the Hocking, where he was informed of the recent battle. He immediately led his army into Ohio, attempting to intercept the retreating Shawnees before they reached their villages. Meanwhile, Lewis and the survivors of Point Pleasant followed in the Shawnees' wake. By October 16 Dunmore's troops had reached modern Hocking County, Ohio, where a messenger from Cornstalk informed them that the Shawnees wanted to make peace. There the Virginians halted, established a fortified camp, and prepared to meet with the Indians. Dunmore also sent messengers to Lewis, ordering him to stop his advance upon the Shawnee villages.

After some preliminary negotiations, Cornstalk and seventeen other warriors entered the Virginians' camp. Attempting to defend the Indians' position, Cornstalk detailed past British injustices and charged that the British were responsible for the recent bloodshed. But both Cornstalk and Dunmore knew that the British now held the upper hand, and the Shawnee's speech had little impact. The council lasted several days, but when it ended the Indians reluctantly signed an unofficial treaty through which they agreed to relinquish their hunting lands in Kentucky. They also promised to surrender all prisoners and stolen property, and to permit the British to travel unmolested on the Ohio River. In return, Dunmore agreed that British settlers should not hunt north of the Ohio. He also promised that traders again would be sent into the Indian country, but the Indian trade would be closely controlled by the government. The Shawnees would be forced to abide by these regulations.

The agreement was a bitter pill for the Shawnees to swallow, yet they had little choice. The British army sat poised to strike their villages. If they refused Dunmore's offer, there would be further bloodshed and this time their women and children would suffer. Many of the warriors muttered among themselves, vowing never to surrender Kentucky to the Long Knives, but for the present they would make their sign on the document. Soon the British army would retreat over the mountains and their families no longer would be threatened. If other Virginians dared to enter Kentucky, let them come. The Shawnees had always excelled at war in the forests, and with the army gone, isolated settlements in the Bluegrass country would be no match for Shawnee war parties.

CHAPTER

2

Learning the Warrior's Path

In 1768, while the Iroquois were selling Shawnee lands at the Treaty of Fort Stanwix, a Creek woman married to a Shawnee man gave birth to a son at Old Piqua, a Shawnee village on the Mad River in western Ohio. The woman had a difficult labor before giving birth in the small lodge especially constructed for that purpose, some distance from the family's wigwam. The mother, Methoataske (Turtle Laying Its Eggs), had grown up among the Creek villages in Alabama and had met her husband when some of the Shawnees sought refuge among the Creeks during the 1750s. The father, Puckeshinwa, remained with his wife's people until about 1760, when the family left Alabama and migrated to Ohio.

There were other children in the family. Before leaving Alabama, Methoataske had given birth to a son, Chiksika. A girl, Tecumpease, and a boy, Sauwauseekau, were born on the family's prolonged journey to Ohio. After arriving among the Shawnees, the couple produced another daughter, making Tecumseh, the little boy born in 1768, the fifth child in the family. In the years that followed other children were born to the union. A third daughter, Nehaaeemo, was born around 1770, and in 1775 Methoataske gave birth to triplets. One of the three infant boys suffered from a birth defect and soon died, but the other two, Lalawethika and Kumskaukau, were healthy and survived.

The triplets were born following the death of their father. After returning from the South, Puckeshinwa had taken up the war club; during Pontiac's Rebellion he had joined with other

17

Shawnees to scourge the frontiers of Virginia. His medicine had been good, and within a decade he had emerged as one of the leading war chiefs among the Shawnees in Ohio. An admirer of Cornstalk, Puckeshinwa readily joined with other warriors when Cornstalk asked his people to attack Lewis's army at Point Pleasant. In 1774 Chiksika, Puckeshinwa's oldest son, was already fourteen years old, and the youth was allowed to accompany the Shawnee war party. Although some of the younger warriors were stationed on the west bank of the Ohio to cut off any Virginian retreat, Puckeshinwa encouraged his son to accompany him across the river, where the young warrior could participate in the battle. But the fighting did not go as planned; as the Shawnees retreated toward the Ohio, Puckeshinwa fell, mortally wounded by British gunfire. His kinsmen carried him across the river, where the dying warrior called Chiksika to his side and made him promise that he would never make peace with the Virginians. Chiksika also assured his father that he would care for his younger brothers and supervise their training as warriors. Afraid that the Virginians might follow them across the Ohio, the retreating Shawnees hurriedly made preparations to carry Puckeshinwa back to his village, but before a litter could be constructed the warrior died. He was buried secretly in the forest.

The death of Puckeshinwa left a great void in his family's life. Although Chiksika attempted to hunt for the family, he was hard pressed to provide enough meat, especially after the triplets were born in early 1775. Fortunately, other Shawnees shared their resources with the family. Many of Puckeshinwa's relatives provided fish and game for Methoataske and her children, and Blackfish, a war chief from Chillicothe, a neighboring village, also supported the family.

But the times were hard. By 1776, less than two years after Puckeshinwa's death, war had erupted between Great Britain and her colonies and the conflict soon spread to the Ohio Valley. Envisioning the war as a struggle between two groups of white men, many Shawnees at first remained aloof from the contest. Unfortunately, their efforts at neutrality failed. Although few Shawnees accompanied the first Mingo raids into Kentucky, American frontiersmen openly accused the tribe of hostilities. In the autumn of 1777 Cornstalk, who continued to urge Shawnee neutrality, journeyed to Fort Randolph, the new American post at Point Pleasant, where he agreed to assist some cartographers who were drawing maps of the Ohio Valley. While Cornstalk was in the fort, an American settler was killed by Indians on the Ohio. Although Cornstalk and his party obviously had nothing to do with the murder, local frontiersmen accused them of the crime. While the Shawnees were in the fort, a mob murdered Cornstalk, his son, and three other warriors.

News of Cornstalk's death reverberated through the Shawnee villages. Shocked by the treachery and goaded on by British Indian agents, the Shawnees fell upon Kentucky with a vengeance. In May 1778 over 400 Shawnee and Mingo warriors surrounded Fort Randolph, then marched up the Kanawha Valley burning farms as they went. During the summer smaller parties infested the Bluegrass country, and in September Blackfish led another army of over 400 warriors against Boonesborough, besieging the settlement for several days and spreading havoc through the neighboring countryside. But the Kentuckians were not willing to remain in their stockades, and in May 1779 they retaliated. Leading a force of mounted militia north across the Ohio, Colonel John Bowman attacked Chillicothe, the Shawnee town on the Mad River. The Americans quickly retreated, and they suffered more losses than the Indians, but the raid proved that the Shawnee villages were vulnerable.

Bowman's attack upon Chillicothe markedly affected Puckeshinwa's family. Evidence suggests that Chiksika and perhaps Sauwauseekau helped to repulse the Americans, but Methoataske and the younger children were terrified. Their concern was shared by many Shawnees, especially those less hostile to the Americans, those who still wished to remain neutral. Fearful that they would be subjected to further incursions, about 1,000 Shawnees, over one-third of the tribe, abandoned their villages in the summer of 1779 and migrated down the Ohio Valley, passing through Indiana and Illinois before settling in southeastern Missouri. Included in the emigration were Methoataske and her second daughter, the first child born after the family arrived from the South. The other children remained in Ohio.

Methoataske's separation from her children seems strange, especially among a people who valued family ties so highly. But her flight from Ohio did not represent a complete abandonment of her children. The Shawnees were a patrilineal people, and members of her husband's kinship group were obligated to help care for the family. In addition, by 1779 Tecumpease, the oldest daughter, had married a Shawnee warrior, Wasabogoa (Stands Firm), and she offered to take the younger children into her wigwam. Unquestionably their mother's departure was painful for the Shawnee children, but it was much more traumatic for the two surviving triplets than for the eleven-year-old Tecumseh.

Other family members stepped in to take the mother's place. Tecumpease always had been close to Tecumseh, and after Methoataske's departure the relationship between the brother and sister deepened. Although Tecumpease and her husband provided adequate food and shelter for the two triplets, she lavished her affection upon Tecumseh. The Shawnee boy already was much admired by his peer group, and his sister urged him to assert his leadership. He did not need much encouragement. Always a popular child, Tecumseh evidently possessed most of the qualities deemed important for a young Shawnee. A wiry, muscular boy who matured quickly, he excelled at the games and skills practiced by the boys of his village. According to his contemporaries, at an early age he became an excellent marksman with both a bow and a musket. He often led his boyhood companions on hunting forays in the nearby forests, where they killed rabbits, turkeys, and other small game, and he was especially fond of emulating Shawnee warriors. Stephen Ruddell, a captured white youth who became a friend of the young Shawnee, reported that Tecumseh frequently organized sham battles, dividing the village boys into two groups, then leading one party in a series of raids, ambushes, and counterattacks. Notwithstanding the loss of his parents, Tecumseh had a very successful childhood.

Chiksika also contributed to his success. Like Tecumpease, he seemed to have a special affinity for Tecumseh and took particular care to teach him the ways of a Shawnee warrior. He generally ignored the two triplets, but he allowed Tecumseh to accompany him on hunting trips in which the two brothers were absent from the village for weeks and sometimes months at a time. During the late 1780s, for example, Tecumseh joined Chiksika and several other Shawnees in a hunting expedition that traveled through southern Indiana, then crossed over into western Kentucky, where the warriors hunted some of the few remaining bison in the state. The chase was particularly exciting to the adolescent Tecumseh, but while racing after the fleeing animals his horse fell, throwing Tecumseh and breaking the boy's leg. Chiksika and his friends set the broken limb and then remained in the same camp for several months so that the leg might heal properly. Unquestionably, Chiksika was fond of his younger brother, and since he was about ten years older than the boy, it was only natural that Tecumseh, in turn, would idolize him; but the relationship between the brothers seemed to transcend all usual kinship ties, and the two remained close until Chiksika's death in 1788.

With the Shawnees besieged on all sides, it is surprising that normal family relationships were not more disrupted. Bowman's raid against Chillicothe was only the first of several American incursions into the Shawnee homeland during the Revolutionary period. In both 1780 and 1782 George Rogers Clark and Benjamin Logan led expeditions against the Shawnee villages on the Mad and Great Miami rivers, and in June 1782 the Shawnees joined with other tribesmen to repulse an attack by Colonel William Crawford upon the Indian towns along the Sandusky. Crawford's expedition ended in disaster as the Indians turned back the invaders, killing over seventy Americans.

The Shawnees also carried the war to Kentucky. In 1780 they accompanied Captain Henry Bird and a force of British soldiers who attacked and captured several small American posts just south of the Ohio, and in 1781 they ranged across Kentucky to the Clinch and Holston rivers in Tennessee, burning cabins, taking scalps, and stealing horses. They also fired upon American shipping on the Ohio River, and in August 1782 Shawnee warriors formed part of the multi-tribal force led by William Caldwell, Alexander McKee, and other British Indian agents who unsuccessfully attacked Bryant's Station. When American frontiersmen pursued the retreating raiders, the Shawnees and their allies ambushed them on the Licking River, and the resulting Battle of the Blue Licks was a significant victory for the British and Indians.

Growing up admist the chaos of war, the young Tecumseh was profoundly influenced by his experiences in these years. The Shawnees always had venerated warriors, but the prolonged conflict maximized the role of the war chiefs, giving them an increased authority within the framework of tribal politics. To a maturing adolescent, warriors such as Blackfish and Chiksika seemed larger than life. And Chiksika's veneration of their fallen father, a man who had died defending his people's homeland, reinforced the image of the warrior as a role model for Tecumseh. Of course not all Shawnees were as anti-American as Tecumseh's friends and family. Cornstalk's memory was still respected by many tribal members, but from Tecumseh's perspective Cornstalk had attempted to befriend the Long Knives and eventually had paid with his life. The Missouri Shawnees still tried to remain neutral in the conflict, but Chiksika and others openly denounced their flight from Ohio as cowardice. For Tecumseh the choice was clear. A Shawnee man's role was that of a warrior. Warriors did not compromise with the Long Knives.

For a young man so committed to the warrior's path, Tecumseh's first military encounter was an inglorious one. In 1782 he accompanied Chiksika in an attack upon the invading Kentuckians. During November of that year George Rogers Clark and Benjamin Logan crossed the Ohio intent upon avenging American losses at the Battle of the Blue Licks. Following a familiar route, the frontiersmen marched up the Great Miami Valley toward Shawnee villages north of modern Dayton. Since the American army numbered over one thousand, the Shawnees did not attempt to stop the expedition, but they did harass Clark's forces as the Kentuckians approached the mouth of the Mad River. Now almost fifteen years old, Tecumseh was allowed to join a war party led by his brother which fired upon an advance party of the enemy. Although the skirmish did not involve large numbers of men, the fighting was fierce, and in the first exchange of gunfire Chiksika was slightly wounded. Momentarily confused and shocked by the bloodshed, Tecumseh abandoned his position and fled panic-stricken through the forest. He later rejoined his brother's party, and although his flight was excused, he was humiliated.

He soon redeemed himself. Throughout the war much of the Shawnee effort had been focused upon American shipping on the Ohio River. During 1783, in the final days of the conflict, Tecumseh joined a small war party intent upon ambushing American flatboats carrying emigrants or merchandise to the settlements in Kentucky. In modern Brown County, Ohio—opposite what is now Maysville, Kentucky—scouts reported that several flatboats loaded with supplies were descending the Ohio, evidently destined for the mouth of the Licking River. The specifics of the encounter remain unknown, but contemporary sources indicate that Tecumseh made special efforts to vindicate himself and "behaved with great bravery and even left in the background some of [the] oldest and bravest warriors." The Shawnees captured one of the flatboats, killing the crew except for one hapless survivor who was carried ashore by the war party and then forced to march several miles inland. There the party stopped, kindled a fire, and burned their prisoner. Although Tecumseh had been in the forefront of the attack, he evidently felt great compassion for the captive. He failed to intercede on the latter's behalf, but when the fire subsided he "expressed great loathing of the deed" and vowed that he would never again remain idle if his intercession could save a prisoner.

Although the Treaty of Paris, signed in 1783, officially ended the American Revolution, in the West the bloodshed continued. Both the British and the Americans contributed to the problem. In the treaty the British relinquished all claims to the territory west of the Appalachians. But when British Indian agents met with the Shawnees and other tribesmen to discuss the treaty, they declared that the Indians still owned their lands. According to the agents, the Crown had only given up political control over the territory; the actual ownership of the region remained vested in the Indians. Therefore, although the United States now exercised theoretical political hegemony over the Ohio Valley, the new government had no right to occupy any of the Indians' lands.

British policy in this instance was obvious. Still smarting from Cornwallis's surrender at Yorktown, the Crown was eager to keep the Shawnees and other Indians alienated from the United States. Many British officials believed that the new American government was too weak to assert itself, and the Indians could successfully resist any American incursions. Moreover, the Crown hoped to retain control of the fur trade and sought to keep the tribesmen economically tied to British traders. Arguing that American merchants had failed to pay their debts to British creditors, British officials refused to vacate forts at Detroit and Michillimackinac. If the new government collapsed, the Crown could use such posts as a base to regain control over the interior.

While the British encouraged Indian resistance, the Americans goaded the tribesmen into acts of violence. Heavily in debt, the new American government saw the lands in Ohio as a source of revenue. American officials hoped to sell parts of Ohio to settlers and land speculators, and to use other sections as military bounty lands for veterans of the American Revolution. They argued that the Indians had no legitimate claims to the region, but they were willing to provide the tribes with nominal payments in return for the Indians' acquiescence in an American occupation of the territory. By the end of the 1780s American agents had arranged a series of questionable treaties designed to legitimize American expansion. Negotiated at Fort Stanwix (1784), Fort McIntosh (1785), Fort Finney (1786), and Fort Harmar (1789), the treaties were signed under extremely dubious circumstances. In several instances the Indians who attended the conferences had absolutely no legitimate claims to the lands in question, and more often the warriors who made their marks on the documents were, at best, minor chiefs who did not represent the wishes of their people. Although the government claimed that the treaties were valid, most Shawnees regarded them as a travesty and had no intention of abiding by them.

From the Shawnees' perspective, they had not been defeated in the American Revolution. Of course their villages had been invaded, but they had created similar havoc in Kentucky, and at the war's end American settlement had not advanced north of the Ohio River. The Shawnees still regarded the lands in Ohio as their own and intended to retain them. Confused by the new American claims to their homeland, the Shawnees watched in dismay as frontiersmen began to clear farms on the north bank of the river. Yet they seemed unsure of their response, and when Mingo and Cherokee war parties swept through Kentucky, Shawnee warriors did not join them.

Angered by the attacks, the Kentuckians blamed their old enemies, the Shawnees, and in September 1786 Clark and Logan again struck at the unsuspecting Shawnee towns on the Great Miami River, killing many Indians. Among the dead was Melanthy, and old chief friendly to the government who had participated in the Treaty of Fort Finney. Believing that the Kentuckians must have mistaken the Shawnee villages for those of a hostile tribe, Melanthy had approached the advancing frontiersmen carrying an American flag given to him at the recent treaty. But the Stars and Stripes held little protection, and the old Shawnee was first captured by the Kentuckians, then murdered.

The Shawnees struck back with a vengeance. This time, the maturing Tecumseh took an active part in the warfare. In 1787 he enlisted in a small war party led by Chiksika which journeyed into the South, where it joined with some Cherokees to raid American settlements in Tennessee and southern Kentucky. During the summer of 1788 the Indians made plans to attack Buchanan's Station, a small post in east-central Tennessee. Contemporary sources indicate that, several days prior to the attack, Chiksika experienced a vision that led him to believe he would not survive the approaching encounter. Although he informed the other warriors in his party of his premonition, he still insisted upon participating in the action, vowing that his father had fallen in battle and he too preferred to die as a warrior rather than succumb to the infirmities of old age. On the day of the attack, the Indians rushed the stockade, and during the assault Chiksika was mortally wounded. Carried from the battlefield, the dying warrior asked Tecumseh not to have him buried, but to leave him on a hill "where the fowls of the air could pick his bones."

Disheartened by Chiksika's death, the Indians abandoned the attack and withdrew to the Cherokee villages. There most of the Shawnees decided to return to Ohio, but Tecumseh and a few other warriors remained behind, evidently seeking vengeance for the loss of Chiksika. During the next two years they ranged across Kentucky and Tennessee, sometimes hunting and occasionally attacking white settlements. These were pivotal years for Tecumseh. His brother's death must have affected him deeply. Chiksika had served as both a father and a brother, and for the past few years the two men had been inseparable. But until 1788 Tecumseh had always stood in Chiksika's shadow, the up-and-coming younger brother of an already prominent Shawnee warrior. Now Tecumseh was forced to stand on his own. Unquestionably the experience hardened him toward the Americans; but, more importantly, the two years spent in the South following Chiksika's death gave the young Shawnee warrior an opportunity to exert his leadership. He earlier had led other Shawnee boys at games, but now he led the small party of warriors. In 1787, when he left Ohio, Tecumseh had followed his brother. In 1790, when he returned, he was a war chief.

While Tecumseh was in the South, more blood had been shed in his homeland. Following Benjamin Logan's destruction of the Shawnee villages along the Mad River, the tribe had relocated further to the north and west, building new towns in the Auglaize-Maumee watershed. These villages were clustered near Miami, Wyandot, and Ottawa settlements. This concentration of Indians in northwestern Ohio and northeastern Indiana gave the tribesmen better access to British supplies at Detroit, and it enabled them to assist each other if any of their villages were threatened by American expeditions.

The consolidation of the tribal villages along the Maumee waterway also reflected attempts by the Shawnees and other Indians to form a political alliance to counter American aggression. Encouraged by the British, the tribes met several times during the late 1780s, trying to reach a consensus of opinion about the United States. But unity was difficult for a people tied to tribal ways, and although they were unanimous in their opposition to the Americans, they disagreed over particulars. Much of the argument focused upon just where the boundary between Indian and American lands should be drawn. The Delawares and Wyandots, tribes still claiming lands in eastern Ohio, were reluctant to give up any of their territory; but since they were most vulnerable to American military expeditions, they hesitated to oppose the Long Knives adamantly. Most militant were the Shawnees, Miamis, and Kickapoos, who also claimed lands in the Ohio Valley, but who enjoyed more remote locations that offered some safety. The Shawnees and Miamis saw any compromise as ultimately endangering their claim to lands in western Ohio and Indiana, and they urged all the tribes to raise the hatchet against the Americans. In contrast, the Potawatomis, Ottawas, and Chippewas, whose villages lay near the Great Lakes, were willing to cede some lands in eastern Ohio. Since settlers already were pouring into the region east of the Muskingum, these northern Indians favored the recognition of American claims to that area. As political opportunists, the remnants of the Iroquois confederacy also favored the Potawatomi position.

Unfortunately, these disagreements played into the Americans' hands and enabled government officials to negotiate the series of treaties ending in 1789 with the Treaty of Fort Harmar. Insisting that the land cessions were valid, the government erected Fort Washington that year on the north bank of the Ohio, at the site of modern Cincinnati. Settlement soon spread into adjacent regions, and the Shawnees and Miamis were infuriated. Once again war parties descended upon the frontier, burning farms and attacking flatboats on the Ohio. At Fort Washington, Governor Arthur St. Clair of the Northwest Territory made one last attempt to seek a peaceful solution to the crisis. In the spring of 1790 American messengers were sent up the Wabash to the Miami villages carrying proposals for a conference, but the Indians threatened the emissaries' lives and rejected any new attempts at compromise. The Shawnees and Miamis remained adamant. There could be no permanent American settlement north of the Ohio River.

His peace overtures spurned, St. Clair turned to stronger measures. During the summer he assembled 320 regulars and 1,133 Kentucky militiamen at Fort Washington, and in late September General Josiah Harmar led the force north across Ohio toward the Miami towns near modern Fort Wayne, Indiana. Meanwhile, a smaller force under Major John Hamtramck ascended the Wabash from Fort Knox, at Vincennes. Shawnee scouts monitored Harmar's advance, and when the Americans reached the Auglaize, they found the Shawnee villages deserted. Although they destroyed a few cornfields, Harmar's troops encountered little resistance until October 19, when an advance party of about 200 men commanded by Colonel John Hardin was ambushed by a large war party of Shawnees and Potawatomis near the forks of the Maumee. The Americans suffered about 100 casualties, and in a similar exchange two days later a party of Shawnees, Miamis, Ottawas, and Delawares killed an additional 80 American troops. Since a total of 183 of his men had been killed, including one-fourth of his regulars, Harmar wisely retreated toward Fort Washington. Although Hamtramck's men encountered no Indians, they too abandoned the campaign and withdrew to Vincennes.

Tecumseh and his small party of warriors returned from the South in early November 1790, just after the American army had been defeated. He found that the Shawnees had reoccupied their villages along the Auglaize, and now seemed confident of their ability to defend themselves. Rather than crushing Indian resistance, Harmar's disastrous campaign had only rekindled the tribesmen's assurance that they could easily defeat the Long Knives. Tecumseh's anti-American sentiments, nurtured through his experiences in the South, blended in smoothly with the prevailing mood in the villages, and the young war chief found himself readily accepted as a spokesman for the more militant members of the tribe. Although the approaching winter precluded any further warfare, most Shawnees believed that the Americans would not accept the defeat. Tecumseh spent the winter months hunting, but he and other warriors expected that when the snow melted the Long Knives would return.

They were not disappointed. American officials had been humiliated by Harmar's defeat, and at Fort Washington Arthur St. Clair immediately began preparations for another expedition. In March 1791 Congress appropriated over $300,000 for a second campaign, and during the summer of 1791 St. Clair assembled approximately 2,300 men at Cincinnati. Unfortunately, St. Clair's preparations proceeded slowly, and his frontier army was plagued by shoddy equipment and inadequate provisions. Although he commanded two small regiments of infantry, the vast majority of his force was comprised of poorly trained volunteers and militia. The troops did not leave Cincinnati until September 17, and then proceeded slowly north toward the Maumee Valley. To add to St. Clair's burden, his army was accompanied by almost two hundred women, mostly prostitutes or camp followers.

The Shawnees knew they were coming. Tecumseh led a small party of scouts that monitored St. Clair's advance and reported his position to the villages along the Auglaize. Other warriors rode to Indian villages in Ohio, Indiana, and Michigan, soliciting assistance against the approaching Americans. By late October over 1,000 warriors, well supplied by British traders, had assembled on the Maumee River. Impatient with St. Clair's progress, on October 28, 1791, the Indians broke camp and moved south to meet the Americans. The Indians' morale was excellent. They had easily defeated Harmar. Now other American scalps would hang in their lodges.

The information the Indians received from Tecumseh was encouraging. St. Clair's march had been plagued by incessant rainfall, and as the army crossed southwest Ohio almost 900 militiamen had deserted. The soldiers seemed dispirited and suffered from low morale. On the evening of November 3 the scouts reported that the American column had camped on the headwaters of the Wabash, in extreme western Ohio.

Although St. Clair dispatched reconnaissance patrols, he learned nothing about Indian movements. After the Americans bedded down for the night, the large war party from the Maumee surrounded their encampment.

The Indian attack came shortly after dawn. As the soldiers were preparing breakfast, the warriors fired from the surrounding underbrush. The militia panicked and fled pellmell back into the ranks of the regulars, creating confusion among the only segments of St. Clair's army that had any semblance of discipline. The regulars fought valiantly, but were cut down by an enemy they couldn't see. By mid-morning hundreds of American soldiers lay dead, and St. Clair ordered a retreat. Breaking through the Indian lines on the southern perimeter of the camp, the troops fled in disarray through the forest. The United States suffered 647 dead and hundreds wounded. The Indians sustained about 150 casualties.

Although Tecumseh had reported the location of St. Clair's camp, he evidently took no part in the fighting. Contemporary sources indicate that he continued to lead a party of scouts, who established themselves some distance back along the line of St. Clair's march to prevent the war party from being surprised by any reinforcements. When the American retreat became general and fleeing soldiers began to appear in large numbers, Tecumseh and the scouts withdrew to avoid discovery. They then returned to the recent battlefield, where the jubilant warriors divided huge stores of captured weapons and equipment.

In the days that followed St. Clair's defeat, the ceremonial fires burned brightly in the Shawnee villages. Warriors danced their victory dances and recounted their exploits to other tribal members who shared in the spoils of the recent fighting. The extent of Tecumseh's participation in these celebrations remains unknown, but it must have been limited since he did not participate in the battle. Moreover, by December 1791, just one month after the victory, he had already departed from the villages to lead a hunting party along the Great Miami River in what is now western Ohio. There his party was surprised by a much larger number of Kentuckians, also hunting in the region. Led by Robert

McClelland, the Kentuckians were attracted by the smoke from the Shawnee campfire and came upon the Indians early in the morning, shortly after the Shawnees had climbed from their blankets. Afraid to approach the camp too closely, the white hunters fired on the Indians from a distance, but were repulsed when Tecumseh and his party advanced upon them. Although the Kentuckians fled, the Shawnees managed to kill two of them. Two warriors also were wounded.

Following the skirmish the Shawnees returned to their villages, where they spent a comfortable winter, well supplied with the clothing and provisions captured from St. Clair. Flushed with their victories, the Shawnees and their neighbors remained confident they could defend their homeland. During the spring of 1792 they rebuffed American peace overtures, and in late March, when the grass was high enough to feed their horses, Shawnee warriors again rode south, raiding the settlements in southern Ohio. On one of these forays Tecumseh and a large war party were attacked by a group of Kentuckians led by the famed frontiersman Simon Kenton. The skirmish took place on the Great Miami River, near modern Hamilton, Ohio, and Tecumseh and the Shawnees successfully defended themselves, driving off the Americans. During the following year the two adversaries fought again when another party led by Tecumseh was attacked by Kenton and a large force of Kentuckians near the junction of Paint Creek and the Scioto River. In the second encounter the Americans greatly outnumbered the Shawnees and surprised them while they were sleeping. Taking advantage of the darkness, Tecumseh rallied his men, broke through the American lines, and seized the Americans' horses. Deprived of their mounts, Kenton and the other Kentuckians were forced to watch in frustration as the Indians rode away through the forest.

While the Shawnees and Kentuckians were skirmishing in Ohio, the federal government again attempted to negotiate a permanent peace. In July 1793 federal officials met with delegates from the Shawnees and other tribes at Niagara, where three commissioners, Benjamin Lincoln, Timothy Pickering, and Beverly Randolph, offered a series of concessions to the tribes. If the Indians would give up their claims to the region east of the Muskingum, the United States would acknowledge Indian hegemony over the rest of Ohio, excluding those regions already purchased by private citizens and military posts supposedly surrendered by the British at the Treaty of Paris. The government agreed to evacuate most of its other posts north of the Ohio River and to pay the tribesmen $50,000 in goods and an annuity of $10,000. The Indians, in turn, would remain at peace and accept their new white neighbors.

After conferring throughout the summer, the Indians rejected the proposals. Although the Iroquois urged the western tribes to accept the compromise, the more militant Shawnees persuaded their neighbors to demand the return of the region east of the Muskingum. Still elated by their victory over St. Clair, the Shawnees were certain they could repulse other American expeditions. As for the offers of American goods and annuities, the tribesmen suggested that the money be given to those settlers who were illegally living north of the Ohio. As the Indians stated:

> We are persuaded that they would most readily accept it, in lieu of the Lands you sold them. If you add also the great sums you must expend in raising and paying armies, with a view to force us to yield you our country you will certainly have more than sufficient for the purposes of repaying these settlers for all their labor and improvements.

The Shawnees' intransigence was strengthened by the British. Alexander McKee, Matthew Elliott, and other British Indian agents remained active among the tribe, and many of these trader-diplomats were decidedly anti-American. Evidence suggests that although officials in London might have favored the compromise, the local agents used their influence against it. Since many of these individuals were married to Shawnee women and had lived for years among the tribe, their influence was extensive. Yet other events also added fuel to the Shawnee resolution. In April 1794 Royal Engineers began the construction of Fort Miami, on the lower Maumee, near modern Toledo. To the Shawnees the construction of this new British post in a region adjacent to their villages was tantamount to the Crown's approval of their stance. Let the Long Knives come!

The Shawnees' British Father would provide them with all his assistance and the Americans again would be defeated.

The Americans made plans of their own. Convinced of the necessity for another military expedition, federal officials took steps to insure its success. In 1792, after much deliberation, they appointed Major General Anthony Wayne as their new military commander in the west. A strict disciplinarian, Wayne spent two years rebuilding American forces, and in 1793 he constructed two new posts to be used as supply depots in any future campaign against the Indians. Fort Greenville was erected about twenty miles west of modern Piqua, Ohio, and Fort Recovery, a small post, was built on the site of St. Clair's defeat, in extreme western Ohio. After the American peace initiative failed, Wayne made preparations for another expedition. In the spring of 1794 he strengthened Fort Recovery, and after stockpiling munitions at Greenville, in late June he brought about 3,500 men to the post. The stage was set for a new confrontation.

Tecumseh's role in the peace negotiations was minimal. Still a relatively young warrior, he was not included among the Shawnee delegates who met with the American officials at Niagara. Undoubtedly he supported the Shawnees' hardline stance, but he had yet to achieve the status that enabled older warriors to represent their tribe in council with the Americans. But as Wayne's army moved north toward Fort Greenville, Tecumseh and other young warriors came to the forefront. Informed of the American advance, the Shawnees sent messengers to the other tribes and by mid-June almost 1,000 warriors had assembled at the Indian towns along the Maumee. Impatient with Wayne's slow progress, on June 20 Tecumseh joined with most of the other warriors and started south, intending to attack the American column as it neared Fort Recovery.

The Indians arrived at Fort Recovery on June 29, but found that Wayne's army still remained at Greenville. While the war chiefs were discussing whether to attack the post, scouts brought information that a supply train of almost 300 horses was scheduled to leave the fort to return to Wayne's army on the following morning. Envisioning an opportunity to capture

THE OLD NORTHWEST

miles
0   50   100

LAKE ERIE

LAKE MICHIGAN

Pittsburgh

Presque Isle

Point Pleasant

Amherstburg

Kanawha R.

Muskingum R.

Big Sandy R.

Sandusky R.

Detroit

Scioto R.

Fallen Timbers

Maumee R.

Auglaize R.

Chillicothe

Mad R.

Cincinnati

Maysville

Wapakoneta

Fort Recovery

Greenville

Greenville Treaty Line

Great Miami R.

Ohio R.

Licking R.

St. Joseph R.

Fort Wayne

Wabash R.

Mississinewa R.

Greenville Treaty Line

Tippecanoe R.

White R.

Prophetstown
(Battle of Tippecanoe)

Fort Harrison

Vincennes
(Fort Knox)

the animals, the Indians decided to remain concealed and to attack the supply train after it left the safety of the pallisade. Shortly after seven o'clock on the following morning, the gates of the fort opened and the empty pack horses, escorted by about 30 soldiers, moved across the clearing toward the forest. There they were met by a volley of musket fire that killed half of the Americans and sent the others fleeing back toward the stockade. The Shawnees and Delawares then moved in to seize the horses while Potawatomi, Ottawa, and Chippewa warriors, exhilarated by their success, rashly attempted to storm the fortress.

Unfortunately, attacking a fortified position well defended by disciplined troops differed markedly from ambushing an unsuspecting supply column, and the Indians were driven back with heavy losses. Embittered by their casualties, the three northern tribes complained that the Shawnees and Delawares had failed to support their assault but had retained most of the horses. Although all the warriors kept up a desultory fire at the stockade, throughout the day the bickering continued, and in the evening the warriors abandoned the siege and withdrew toward the Maumee. Still disgruntled, many Potawatomi, Ottawa, and Chippewa warriors refused to associate with the Shawnees and Delawares, and when the war party reached the Maumee the northern Indians abandoned their allies and returned to their villages.

Although Tecumseh's role in the attack upon Fort Recovery remains unknown, the evidence suggests that he joined with other Shawnee warriors in the attempt to gain control of the horses. Like most other Shawnees and Delawares, he must have resented the northern tribes' accusations of cowardice. Since the assault upon the fort had not been planned, the Shawnees and Delawares were not in position to support the attack by the other Indians. Moreover, most of these warriors had their hands full attempting to catch and restrain the panic-stricken pack animals. Yet the loss of the northern warriors was a significant blow to the Indian army assembled on the Maumee, for at least 300 Potawatomi, Ottawa, and Chippewa warriors left the Shawnee villages and returned to Michigan.

Advised of the Indian defections, Wayne marched north toward the Indian villages. On August 8 he reached the Shawnee towns on the Auglaize and found them deserted. After burning the villages and destroying nearby cornfields, the Americans moved to the juncture of the Auglaize and Maumee, where Wayne constructed a new post, Fort Defiance. He then dispatched a messenger to the tribesmen, asking them to meet with him and negotiate a peace.

As Wayne marched north, Tecumseh and the other Shawnees had abandoned their villages and retreated down the Maumee toward the new British post, Fort Miami. After sending their women and children north into Michigan, the war chiefs decided to make their stand near Roche de Bout, where a recent storm had felled a grove of trees along the north side of the river. Although the Indian army numbered almost 1,300 warriors, it was still considerably smaller than Wayne's forces, and runners were sent to the recalcitrant Potawatomis, Ottawas, and Chippewas, asking them to rejoin their allies. Hoping to slow Wayne's advance, on August 17 the tribesmen sent an evasive answer to his message, asking him to wait for ten days, after which they would make a formal reply to his proposal. But on August 15 the Americans had left Fort Defiance and proceeded on toward the Indian position. Believing a battle was imminent, Tecumseh and the other Indians took up their positions among the fallen trees. Yet Wayne's army marched to within ten miles of the Indian lines, then stopped to construct a small supply post and rest for two days before again moving forward. Meanwhile, on the evening of August 19, a severe thunderstorm swept through the region, pouring rain upon the Indians and causing many to leave their positions and seek shelter in the Indian camp adjoining Fort Miami, a few miles downstream. When Wayne's forces reached Fallen Timbers—as the place came to be known—early on the morning of August 20, fewer then 400 Indians and a few British traders were all that remained.

Tecumseh was among the defenders. Although he had not been asked to participate in planning the Indian defense, his prowess as an emerging young war chief gave him sufficient stature to attract a party of young Shawnee warriors who joined him in taking positions among the maze of fallen trees and branches. When Wayne's army moved forward on the morning of August 20, Tecumseh and his followers were in the forefront of the Indian position. Accompanying Tecumseh on this occasion were two of his brothers, Sauwauseekau and Lalawethika, one of the surviving triplets, now a ne'er-do-well young warrior, nineteen years of age. Anticipating the American advance, the Shawnees moved forward from the breastwork and concealed themselves in some underbrush in front of the Indian lines. There they surprised a party of mounted volunteers in the vanguard of Wayne's army, ambushing the horsemen and throwing them into a panic.

But the new American army was far different from the poorly disciplined troops that had followed Harmar and St. Clair, and instead of fleeing the Americans regrouped and continued forward. Falling back, the Shawnees took refuge behind the fallen trees and fired at the advancing enemy, but the Long Knives were too many for them. Wayne's dragoons swept around the Indian flanks, threatening their retreat, while the infantry fixed their bayonets and stormed over the barricades. Although hard pressed, Tecumseh and his party maintained their position until Tecumseh's musket became jammed. Finally obtaining another weapon, Tecumseh rallied his party and they took refuge in a thicket, again firing upon the advancing Americans. But the battle was nearly over. Most of the warriors had fled toward Fort Miami, and to make their escape Tecumseh and the survivors of his party attacked an American artillery squad, cut the horses loose, and rode to safety.

The Battle of Fallen Timbers was a major defeat for the Indians. Not only did they suffer significant casualties, but their confidence in British assistance was shaken. As the retreating warriors reached Fort Miami, Major William Campbell, the commander of the post, refused to give them refuge. Bewildered, the fleeing warriors continued on down the Maumee where they dispersed into the forests. The battle also had an impact upon Tecumseh's personal life. Although he had fought valiantly and his influence as a war chief subsequently increased, he lost another member of his family. Lalawethika had fled to safety but Sauwauseekau, several years older than Tecumseh, had fallen. Now his father and two brothers had been killed by the Long Knives. And the British, who had promised so much, had also broken their promises. Embittered, Tecumseh withdrew from the Maumee and refused to meet with British Indian agents. He spent the winter of 1794–1795 hunting with a small party of family and friends in northern Ohio.

Other Indians scrambled to make peace with the Americans. Although they still accepted food and clothing from the British, most of the tribesmen realized that the Long Knives now held the upper hand, and in the fall of 1794, when Wayne sent messages to the tribes asking them to accept an end to the fighting, they gladly did so. After preliminary meetings with American officials, in July 1795 the Shawnees and their allies met with Wayne and other dignitaries at Greenville in western Ohio. The negotiations continued for over two weeks, and on August 3, 1795, the Indians made their signs on the Treaty of Greenville. In addition to agreeing to remain at peace and to relinquish all prisoners, the tribesmen gave up their claims to lands in southern, central, and eastern Ohio. In return, the United States furnished the assembled Indians with trade goods valued at $20,000 and agreed to pay the various tribes annuities ranging from $500 to $10,000. The government also assured the tribesmen that they could hunt in the ceded regions until those areas were actually settled by farmers.

Tecumseh took no part in the treaty proceedings. The Shawnees were represented by older chiefs such as Black Hoof, Red Pole, and Blue Jacket. In return for their acquiescence, the Shawnees received a share of the treaty goods and an annuity of $1,000. But they gave up their claims to most of their homeland. Now Shawnee lands were restricted to the northwest quadrant of Ohio, and they hunted over their old village sites along the Scioto and Muskingum only at the pleasure of the Americans. Of course the Treaty of Greenville guaranteed that the remaining Shawnee territory was inviolable, but thinking men on

Known as the Le Dru-Lossing portrait of Tecumseh, this composite portrait is from Benson J. Lossing's *The Pictorial Field Book of the War of 1812*. (Private Collection, Peter Newark American Pictures/The Bridgeman Art Library International)

both sides of the treaty line knew that the boundary would only be temporary. The new American nation was devoted to expansion. The Shawnees were in the way.

* * *

Although not a dominant figure in tribal politics, Tecumseh had emerged by 1795 as an influential young war chief with a growing following among many of the younger, more anti-American warriors. His refusal to participate in the negotiations surrounding the Treaty of Greenville indicates that he remained politically naive about the role that the federal government would henceforward play in Shawnee politics, but his intransigence only strengthened his position among his small band of followers. Black Hoof, Red Pole, and other older chiefs might now walk the white man's road, building their influence through access to government annuities, but Tecumseh still followed the warrior's path, a traditional Shawnee fighting man tied to traditional Shawnee ways.

By all accounts the 27-year-old war chief epitomized most of the qualities long venerated by tribal society. At five feet and ten inches, he stood slightly taller than the average Shawnee warrior, and contemporary accounts all indicate that he was a muscular man of great physical vigor. A skilled hunter, Tecumseh supplied his family with innumerable deer, often sharing his kill with those members of the tribe whose cooking pots were empty. Even within the framework of a communal society, his concern for less fortunate tribesmen was legendary. Contemporary Shawnees described him as "kind and attentive to the aged and infirm, looking personally to their comfort, repairing their wigwams when winter approached, giving them skins for moccasins and clothing, and sharing with them the choicest game which the woods and seasons afforded." He was an open, honest man, and an excellent orator, although his speeches tended to address issues directly and avoid the extended metaphors often utilized by his contemporaries. Although whites often found him quiet or reserved, Shawnees of his generation commented that he had a good sense of humor, but that it was more often shared among his family and close friends than among strangers. Evidence indicates that as a young man he occasionally drank the white man's whiskey, but as he matured he became abstemious.

From the Shawnee perspective, perhaps his most atypical characteristics were his hesitancy to make war upon women and children and his refusal to condemn captured prisoners to death. For decades Shawnee warriors, as well as fighting men from other tribes, had followed both practices, and although some captives were adopted into the tribe, others were executed. By the late eighteenth century most frontier Americans also had adopted these modes of warfare, and Tecumseh's forbearance from such habits was an admirable aberration in a region where indiscriminate bloodshed had become the rule rather than the exception.

There is only limited information regarding Tecumseh's personal life during this period. He remained closely tied to Tecumpease and the other surviving members of his family and did not marry until 1796, one year after the Treaty of Greenville. The consummate warrior, Tecumseh evidently was unwilling to devote much time to the usual family obligations, and his relationship with his wives was not close. Contemporary accounts indicate that he was married twice. The first union lasted but a short time and ended when a disagreement caused the partners to separate. The name of Tecumseh's first wife remains unknown. His second marriage, to Mamate, a Shawnee woman older than himself, seems to have been a partnership of convenience, and Tecumseh probably entered into this relationship "more in compliance with the wishes of others than in obedience to the unbiased impulse of his feelings or the dictates of his judgement." Although Mamate "possessed few personal or mental qualities calculated to excite admiration," the marriage produced one child, a son named Pachetha, who was born sometime around 1800. Mamate died shortly after her son's birth, and not surprisingly, Tecumseh asked his sister, Tecumpease, to look after the boy. Tecumpease took Pachetha into her wigwam and served as a surrogate mother to the child. The relationship between the boy and his aunt was very close, for after Tecumseh's death Tecumpease attempted to champion Pachetha as his father's successor among British authorities in Canada. Tecumseh's relationship with his son seems to have been rather limited.

3

A Culture Under Siege

All cultures undergo continual change, and the Shawnee society into which Tecumseh was born in the late eighteenth century was no exception. Although they retained much of their traditional lifestyle, the Shawnees had adapted to changes engendered by the arrival of the Europeans. These changes permeated most areas of Shawnee life.

Prior to the European invasion, and well into the eighteenth century, the Shawnees had been organized into five major groups or divisions. Although these groups cooperated in tribal affairs, each was politically semi-autonomous and originally occupied a separate village often named after the division residing there. Each group also had particular responsibilities for certain aspects of Shawnee life. The Chalagawtha (Chillicothe) and Thawegila divisions supplied political leaders for the tribe, sometimes competing with each other for such positions. The Piquas were responsible for maintaining tribal rituals and had a special affinity for religious affairs. In contrast, the Kispokothas most often supplied war chiefs and were relied upon by the Shawnees to advise the tribe in matters concerning warfare. The Maykujays were specialists in medicine and health, and took great pride in their ability to provide cures for their ailing kinsmen.

Before the American Revolution, the five divisions had each maintained its own identity. For instance, evidence suggests that the Shawnees who fled to the Illinois River in 1683 were members of the Maykujay division, while those Shawnees who remained among the Creeks until the mid-eighteenth century were primarily Thawegilas. By the 1760s, when almost all the Shawnees were living in the Scioto Valley in Ohio, each of the divisions except for the Thawegilas seems to have resided in its own particular town. But following Dunmore's War, the distinct physical separation and explicit responsibilities of the divisions began to blur. In 1774 many of the Thawegila people returned to the Creeks, but a few remained in Ohio. During the American Revolution, when the large migration of Shawnees fled Ohio for Spanish Louisiana, most of these travelers were from the Kispokotha and Piqua groups, but some members from the other divisions accompanied the flight, and significant numbers of Piquas and Kispokothas (including Tecumseh) remained behind. Meanwhile, in response to the Kentuckians' invasions, those Shawnees who stayed in Ohio established new villages along the Auglaize River. Yet these villages contained members of all the divisions, and the old geographical separation of the groups declined.

The new amalgamation of the divisions in Ohio had a significant impact upon the tribe. Since the Ohio villages held a preponderance of Maykujay and Chalagawtha peoples, these divisions exercised considerable influence. Although sufficient Piquas and Kispokothas remained to provide for their particular tribal responsibilities (religion and war), their numbers were so diminished that they held considerably less power. Moreover, with the Maykujays and Chalagawthas in the ascendancy, evidence suggests that they were less willing to accept the advice of the other two divisions, even in those realms where the Piquas and Kispokothas traditionally exercised authority, and after a relatively short period of time the Maykujays and Chalagawthas began to usurp the other divisions' functions. This, of course, caused dissension among those Piquas and Kispokothas remaining in Ohio, and created a new political factionalization within the tribe.

The Shawnees' political organization also was undergoing change. Traditionally, the Shawnees had maintained a bifurcated political leadership of both peace chiefs and war chiefs. In theory, either the Chalagawthas or the Thawegilas supplied a hereditary peace chief with limited hegemony over the entire tribe, but in actuality, since the various divisions maintained isolated villages, these "tribal" chiefs exercised little authority. In contrast, each of the divisions, and in later times each particular village, also maintained a peace chief or village chief who served as the substantive leader of the local population. These chiefs represented their people in relations with external groups, negotiated with government officials, and attempted to mediate disputes within the village communities. Such positions also were "hereditary," but if the descendants of the most recent chief did not possess the necessary qualities of leadership, the office could pass to another family. Most often, peace chiefs were middle-aged or older men of broad experience whose good judgment was generally accepted among the village community.

War chiefs were younger men. Traditionally a tribal war chief had been appointed from the Kispokotha division, usually from the Panther clan, but in reality most of the separate divisions and villages possessed individuals who functioned in this position. War chiefs most often were warriors in the prime of life whose personal success against tribal enemies inspired the confidence of other warriors. Contemporary evidence indicates that a man could become a war chief only after leading other warriors on a series of raids in which his followers incurred minimal casualties while taking sufficient scalps from their enemies. Although he was a relatively young man, Tecumseh's experiences in the South and later against St. Clair and at Fallen Timbers gave him sufficient status to claim such a rank.

Since the Shawnees were continually at war during the last half of the eighteenth century, the position of war chief seemed to increase in importance. In this period the Shawnees' most important external relationship was with the Americans, and because this relationship was dominated by military actions, those leaders prominent in such activities moved to the forefront as tribal spokesmen. Formerly, the older peace chiefs controlled the tribe's negotiations with outsiders, but during these times of intensive warfare the war chiefs' role was enhanced to such an extent that many exercised a pervasive influence in tribal councils. Moreover, ʟne war chiefs tended to dominate tribal politics during this period, their image as a role model for younger Shawnees also was enhanced. Such a circumstance particularly undercut the authority that the older peace chiefs could wield among the younger warriors, the most volatile members of the tribe.

Other groups also contributed to the political structure of the tribe. Each village had a council made up of older warriors who provided insights and information regarding tribal activities. The village councils were comprised of men whose experience and common sense had earned them the respect of the community. Often these patriarchs also served as heads of their specific clans. Although the councils had no specific authority, their accumulated wisdom was taken seriously and their counsel was solicited by both peace and war chiefs. Supposedly a "tribal" council of elders also functioned, but like a "tribal" peace or war chief such a phenomenon could be effective only during the limited period when all the Shawnees lived in close proximity.

Women played a significant role in tribal affairs. In addition to the informal, yet pervasive influence that they exercised within the family structure, they controlled certain tribal activities and maintained some prerogatives over warfare. Each village possessed an informal group of leading women (often the close relatives of influential warriors) who governed certain tribal rituals and set the dates for many of the activities in which women were involved, such as corn planting and harvesting. "Peace chiefs" among the village women also had the right to appear before war chiefs and to plead with the warriors not to go on the warpath. Evidence suggests that in many instances these pleas were successful. Women also had the privilege to intercede on behalf of captives and to save prisoners from execution. Many of these captives were then adopted into the tribe.

Although the Shawnees' political structure provided formal roles for both men and women, many of the mechanisms that maintained continuity within Shawnee society were informal in nature. Most important was peer pressure. Within the framework of a close-knit, communal society, acceptance or rejection by one's peers can be of paramount importance. Among the Shawnees, those tribesmen who deviated markedly from the standard norms of behavior were subjected to teasing, gossip, or even scorn. Most often such tactics were successful in reducing or even eliminating deviant behavior, but when more obstinate individuals refused to comply, they were brought before the village council, which formally instructed them to conform with village norms. If they continued to thwart the council's directives, they could be driven from the village. Among the Shawnees and other tribal people for whom kinship and family ties were so important, such ostracism was viewed as an extreme penalty, tantamount almost to death.

Ordinarily, such drastic measures were rare. Within the tribal definition of such a term, the Shawnees were a generally "moral" people who sought to follow the Master of Life's teachings as they applied to everyday life. Evidence suggests that they were an open, honest people who attempted to live in harmony with fellow tribe members. Most often disputes between individuals were ameliorated by families or kinship groups, and conflicts were controlled or kept to a minimum. In extreme cases, when disputes led to murder, the crime was viewed as being committed by one family against another, and the appropriate retribution was determined by the kinship group of the victim. Expressing sorrow for the crime, the family of the criminal usually sought to "cover" the victim's death with presents offered to the relatives of the deceased. If the victim's family accepted the goods, then the matter was ended, but if the presents were rejected the dead man's relatives could seek a similar vengeance against the perpetrator of the crime, or in some instances against one of his kinsmen. The vendetta was then satisfied. Although peace chiefs or village councils had no authority to punish those accused of murder, they commonly intervened to facilitate the payment of goods to "cover" the dead and in this way assisted in the settlement of such affairs.

Family ties and kinship groups were important in many other facets of Shawnee life. By 1795 the Shawnees were organized into twelve patrilineal clans whose members were distributed among the various Shawnee villages. The distribution patterns remain unclear, but the proportion of each clan seems to have varied considerably from town to town; many of the villages apparently held large numbers of one group and few members of others. The clans took their names from specific animals (Raccoon, Panther, Deer, Turtle, Bear, and so forth) whose particular characteristics clan members were supposed to possess. Clan members, in turn, were given names which reflected their clan affiliation, and members of one clan would often make good-natured jokes about the less desirable properties of another clan's eponym. (Members of the Turtle clan were chided for being slow, those of the Deer clan for being timid.) Each clan also was responsible for certain ritual functions in the multitude of dances and ceremonies that marked the Shawnee year.

The clan system regulated the many relationships within the framework of the extended Shawnee families. Anthropologists refer to the Shawnee kinship system as the "standard Omaha type," and explain that many of the relationships which modern Americans extend no further than the nuclear family were widened by the Shawnees to include more distant family members of several generations. Although the system is too complicated to delineate in this space, a man referred to his father's brother also as "father," while the term "mother" was extended to all his mother's sisters. All children of his father's brother or his mother's sister were called "brother" or "sister," and the terms "son" and "daughter" were applied not only to a man's own children but to certain children of more distant relatives as well. In turn, through a complicated system that emphasized clan affiliation more than any specific generation, the terms "mother," "brother," and "sister" were applied to relatives one or two generations younger than oneself. The particular nomenclature for each Shawnee relative is less important than an understanding that among the Shawnees, as among many other Native Americans, family and kinship ties were important and extensive. One was less an individual than a member of a larger kinship group that provided certain rights and obligations to all its members. In many ways the intertwining family relationships were the threads that kept the fabric of Shawnee society whole.

Until the late eighteenth century, the Shawnees had followed a life cycle that had remained unchanged for generations. Shawnee children were born in a small hut, some distance from the family's regular lodge, where the Shawnee woman was attended by older female members of her family. About ten days after birth the baby was given its name in a formal ceremony conducted by an elderly warrior whose clan differed from that of the child. The child was wrapped in soft skins and diapered with moss or other absorbent materials. After one month, the baby was put in a cradle board where it remained most of the day. The cradle board provided a convenient carrying device for the child's mother and could be hung from tree limbs or lodge poles, enabling the child to be rocked by the wind or other children. The Shawnees also believed that the cradle board helped the infant to develop good posture, and most children were kept in the device until they were old enough to sit on their own.

Since the Shawnees had no system of formal education, each family was responsible for providing its children with the skills and information needed for life. Shawnee fathers taught their sons the ways of a warrior, while Shawnee mothers instructed their daughters how to plant corn and prepare food and clothing. Much of the children's play was modeled after the roles enacted by their parents, and the youngsters were encouraged to excel at those skills they would later use as adults. Although discipline was not harsh by eighteenth-century European standards, it was exacting, and children were expected to follow their parents' directives. Corporal punishment was the exception rather than the rule, but children were subjected to scolding and stern words designed to embarrass them and make them conform to more suitable standards of behavior. Indeed, much of the children's instruction was of a moral nature, and young Shawnees were expected to conduct themselves in a manner that would bring honor to their families.

Shortly before puberty (anthropologists disagree over the exact age), both boys and girls were encouraged to go into the woods and fast in pursuit of a vision. Like many other Native Americans, the Shawnees believed that young people who prepared themselves would be visited by a special guardian spirit that would take the form of an animal and appear in a vision. The spirit often instructed the young Shawnee how to improve his personal "medicine" and promised supernatural assistance in the years to come. Although the vision quest was a major rite of passage, not all Shawnee adolescents experienced the phenomenon, and failure to have a vision did not prevent the young person from entering the adult world. But an individual's inability to experience a vision did cast some doubts upon his personal medicine, and probably precluded his assuming any leadership role within the tribe.

Marriages were arranged by the partners' families, but required the consent of both parties. Shawnee women usually married between the ages of sixteen and eighteen, while men waited until they were older, probably eighteen to twenty-five. Most Shawnee marriages were monogamous, although by the late eighteenth century some men took more than one wife. Marriage ceremonies were quite simple. After the groom's family presented the bride's relatives with a small quantity of goods, the bride's family prepared food which was taken to the groom's parents' lodge, and both families and friends of the couple joined in the feast. After the guests left, the marriage was consummated.

Although divorce was relatively easy and either partner could dissolve the union, until the post-Revolutionary period such a separation was rare. Shawnee men were permitted to use corporal punishment on their wives, but such abuse traditionally was not common. Sexual relations between the couple were governed by Shawnee law and the punishment for adultery, especially for the wife, was quite severe.

Roles for adult Shawnees were prescribed according to both sex and age. Shawnee men in the prime of their lives were supposed to be hunters and warriors. Their families relied upon them to provide fresh meat for the cooking pots and to protect the tribe from its enemies. By the late eighteenth century Shawnee men also were expected to trap fur and gather hides, which could be traded to white merchants for the manufactured goods upon which much of the tribe relied. As men grew older, they relinquished their roles as warriors and took their places in the village council, where their accumulated wisdom might guide the tribe in meeting the problems of everyday life. Many older men continued to hunt and fish, but as the years passed they no longer joined the extended hunting trips of the younger warriors. Venerated for their knowledge, they sometimes served as peace chiefs and generally remained close to the village, where they often helped to instruct the children in the traditions of the tribe. When they became too infirm to hunt, they relied upon younger members of their family for food and shelter.

In contrast, women were responsible for preparing the family's food and clothing, and were expected to look after the younger children. In addition to "keeping house," Shawnee women also served as horticulturists, planting, hoeing, and harvesting the small fields of corn, pumpkins, and other vegetables that surrounded the Shawnee villages. Unquestionably, most women spent the majority of their days in what must have seemed an endless procession of drudgeries. Although their work probably was heaviest during the warm months when they were tending the crops, there was little respite from the many obligations that rested on their shoulders. The winter months were spent in repairing household utensils and in dressing hides and skins for clothing or for the fur trade. Women also were responsible for maintaining the family lodge and for gathering firewood. As they grew older, and no longer were capable of some of the heavier tasks, they helped to care for their grandchildren. In many ways this final stage of life may have indeed brought the "golden years" for a Shawnee woman. Although she still helped other family members with their work, she was relieved of most of the more unpleasant duties and devoted much of her time to the children. Shawnee tradition is rich in its description of the close relationships between children and their grandmothers, and the image of the kindly and wise grandmother has an almost hallowed place in Shawnee society.

When a Shawnee died, his body was painted and dressed in new clothing by friends, but never by members of his own clan. The body was then placed in a shallow grave lined with bark or planks, positioned so that the head of the corpse lay toward the west. Although no grave goods were placed with the body, friends of the dead man or woman gathered at the graveside and sprinkled tobacco on the corpse, asking the spirit of the dead person not to linger on earth but to proceed on toward the spirit world. After the body was covered with earth the friends and family assembled for a feast, and then most family members began a twelve-day mourning period in which they refrained from such usual activities as hunting and tending crops. Wives or husbands of departed Shawnees were obligated to maintain a one-year period of mourning during which they could not wash or change their clothing. At the end of the mourning period relatives of the dead Shawnee's spouse then prepared a feast as well as new clothing for the mourner, and he or she resumed a normal life.

That life followed the rhythm of the seasons. During the spring and summer the Shawnees assembled together in their villages while the women tended their fields of corn and other vegetables. The fields were prepared in March and corn was planted one month later. Although the women of the village cooperated in the planting process, individual households owned their own fields and harvested their own crops. Corn planting was supervised by the women and accompanied by important ceremonies such as the spring Bread and Green Corn dances. After a field was cleared, the women planted the corn in small holes made with digging sticks. Weeds were removed with short-handled hoes consisting of stone or bone blades attached to hickory or ash handles. After the corn was about knee-high, beans, squashes, and pumpkins were planted amidst the rows, so the vines could attach themselves to the cornstalks. The crops were cultivated through the summer and usually harvested in the fall. The vegetables were either consumed immediately or boiled and dried for use later in the season.

Late in the fall, many Shawnee families left the major villages and scattered through the forest, establishing smaller winter camps devoted to hunting and trapping. During the fall and winter the economic activities of the men were more important than those of the women. Under ordinary circumstances, much of the fall was spent in deer hunting, with the warriors leaving their camps on short hunting trips through the surrounding country. After the hunters returned, the women would skin and dress the carcasses, slicing the venison into long, thin strips which were dried for use throughout the winter. Other parts of the deer were boiled and made into soup, or prepared with various corn dishes. Shawnee hunters also killed a variety of other animals, including bison, bears, and turkeys, but venison remained the preferred game and dominated the Shawnee menu when it was available.

In late December, after sufficient meat was stored for the winter, most Shawnee men concentrated upon trapping. Prior to the European invasion the Shawnees had taken only enough pelts to furnish skins for their immediate needs, but with the Europeans' great demand for fur, trapping soon rivaled hunting as a primary economic enterprise. In the late seventeenth and early eighteenth centuries, Shawnee trappers had concentrated their efforts upon the Ohio Valley's dwindling beaver population, but by mid-century most of the beavers were gone and the Indians turned to other animals. In the post-Revolutionary period they took numerous muskrats, raccoons, otters, wolves, and smaller animals. They also exchanged large quantities of deerskins and some bearskins with British and American merchants for guns, ammunition, and other trade goods.

In the latter decades of the eighteenth century these trade goods played an ever-increasing role in the Shawnees' life. Once they had been a self-sufficient people, manufacturing their clothing and utensils from the products they found in the forests. Before the white men arrived Shawnee craftsmen fashioned wooden bowls, spoons, and ladles. Sharpened bone was used for needles, awls, and fishhooks, while animal horn or turtle shell was made into other utensils. Shawnee arrowsmiths pressure-flaked flint cores into cutting tools and razor-sharp arrowheads, while all members of the tribe fashioned less sophisticated stone tools, such as hoes and scrapers. Prior to the arrival of the Europeans, Shawnee women boiled their corn in grit-tempered, cord-marked pottery. They also wove tightly constructed hickory and elm baskets, which were used to transport and store food and other belongings.

Women also made their family's clothing. Originally the Shawnee costume had been sewn entirely from buckskin and other animal hides. Shawnee men wore buckskin leggings, fringed along the sides and attached to a belt around the waist. The belt also held a breechcloth, which extended over the belt and hung down about a foot in both front and rear. In the summer Shawnee men often went bare-chested, but in the colder months they wore a long-sleeved buckskin shirt which they pulled over their heads. Women wore leggings similar to those of the men and a knee-length, sleeveless buckskin dress. Both sexes used buffalo robes or bearskins in winter and wore moccasins with a single seam on top and large ankle flaps. Shawnee infants wore a simple, soft buckskin dress, but after they were toilet-trained they dressed in clothing similar to their elders'.

But when the fur trade expanded, the Shawnees' old self-sufficiency disintegrated as they became increasingly dependent upon the white man's trade goods. Items once deemed luxuries became necessities, and when the Shawnees and other Indians were denied these products they suffered. The most obvious case was the introduction of firearms. For centuries Shawnee hunters had filled their larders using the bows and arrows of their fathers, but by the Revolutionary period they had become so dependent upon trade muskets that, when their ammunition was depleted, they no longer could hunt effectively. Metal kettles, knives, and other utensils soon replaced those of aboriginal manufacture, and by the late eighteenth century most Shawnee women used cloth obtained from traders for much of their clothing. Cloth shirts soon replaced leather shirts, and blankets were readily substituted for the more traditional winter clothing. The Shawnees still wore moccasins, but they decorated them with brocade and glass beads obtained from traders, and they adorned themselves with paint, silver ornaments, and other items of European origin. Shawnee warriors continued to decorate their hair with feathers, but by 1800 they preferred to trade for ostrich plumes which they inserted into turbans of trade cloth wound around their heads. The Shawnees remained a hunting and gathering people who planted their small fields of corn, but they now needed the white man's trade goods to continue their traditional lifestyle.

Housing changed much less than many other material aspects of Shawnee life. Traditionally the Shawnees utilized two types of dwellings: a summer house and a winter house. Summer houses were rectangular in shape, often about fifteen feet by thirty feet. They featured a pole construction and a gabled roof, and were covered by sheets of elm bark which overlapped to keep the rain from entering. They were sometimes divided into two rooms, with the door to the outside in one end of the building. Constructed less tightly than the winter houses, they often boasted an attached arbor which provided shade for family members as they sat in front of the house, near the door. Winter houses were much smaller and more tightly constructed. They resembled the domed, bark-covered wigwams of other tribes in the region, and they featured a hearth in the center of the single room around which the family spent the cold months. The floors of the winter houses were usually covered with hides or skins to provide an extra measure of warmth, and a smoke hole in the top of the structure allowed smoke to escape. By the late eighteenth century some of the Shawnees abandoned their traditional winter houses in favor of log huts resembling the familiar log cabins of the American frontier, but all tribesmen still used the more spacious and better-ventilated summer houses during the warm months.

Within a Shawnee village, the houses were clustered around a central council house much larger than the lodges of individual families. The council house was usually a well-built log structure, sometimes as large as thirty by eighty feet. With the roof supported by the log walls and heavy internal supports, the council house served not only as an assembly hall for village meetings, but also as a fortification if the village was attacked. Seats were constructed around the perimeter, and many of the pillars and support beams were heavily carved to represent animals or religious figures.

Modern scholars disagree over the dominant figure in traditional Shawnee religion. Today the Shawnees believe that their lives are most closely controlled by a female deity, usually called "Our Grandmother" or the "Creator," and many anthropologists argue that she always has been the most important figure in the Shawnee pantheon. Other students of Shawnee culture assert that the ascendancy of Our Grandmother occurred after the 1830s, and that in the earlier period the tribe prayed to a male figure called the "Finisher" or the "Master of Life" as the primary power in the universe. Historical evidence strongly supports the second position. Almost all Shawnee speeches or commentaries upon religion that have been preserved from the earlier period refer to the supreme being as a male and mention Our Grandmother only in passing, as his subordinate. Indeed, the most complete discussion of Shawnee culture in the early nineteenth century, a series of interviews conducted in 1824 by Lewis Cass and C. C. Trowbridge with Tenskwatawa (Lalawethika), Tecumseh's brother, illustrates that the eastern Shawnees still assumed that a male "Great Spirit" reigned over the universe.

The Shawnees believed that when the Master of Life made the world, he made the Indians and furnished them with all the animals and plants they needed for their existence. In addition, he supplied the Shawnees with their sacred laws, which instructed them how to live and informed them of their relationship with various animals. If the Indians followed his precepts and lived in accordance with his wishes, they would prosper and their world would be orderly. The Shawnees therefore knew they should live as the Master of Life intended. They should dance the sacred dances and perform the age-old ceremonies and be respectful to the Master of Life and the lesser spirits that filled the universe. When they died, they would then enter "a rich, fertile country, abounding in game, fish, pleasant hunting grounds and fine corn fields."

But there were other, more malevolent forces in the universe. Motshee Monitoo, or the Evil Spirit, also held sway over men's lives, and although he was not as powerful as the Master of Life, he was capable of great mischief. Shawnee religion, like that of many other tribes of the Old Northwest, often incarnated the Evil Spirit as a Great Horned Serpent who lived in water and who was assisted by lesser spirits and witches. The Shawnees believed that in the distant past, when some of their people were emigrating to their homeland, they encountered this Great Serpent in a body of water, and by using all their medicine they were able to kill it and cut its body into pieces. The pieces held a very powerful magic that could be used for good or evil, and although these events had happened centuries ago, the flesh was "still preserved . . . , as fresh as if it had just been killed." Most of the pieces had been lost, but some were still used by witches to spread malevolence and disorder through the tribe. Meanwhile, the Evil Spirit had reconstituted itself and continued its reign as the Great Serpent of the Waters, ever intent upon plaguing the Indians.

* * *

By 1800 the Shawnee way of life represented a combination of aboriginal and European cultures. The Shawnees still followed a lifestyle based on hunting and gathering and horticulture, but they were much more dependent than before upon the outside world. Shawnee hunters still pursued deer through the forests, but they now killed the animals with white men's weapons, and prepared the meat with white men's utensils. Their clothing still reflected their ancient traditions, but much of it was made of the white man's cloth instead of the skins utilized by their fathers. The European technology was a mixed blessing. It provided the Shawnees and other Indians with more durable and efficient tools. Yet it made them more susceptible to innumerable influences over which they had little control. As they became more dependent upon European trade goods, they became more tightly entangled in the interlocking strands of the fur trade. When the trade was going well, they prospered. But when the price of fur fell, or the trade goods were late in arriving, or when the population of fur-bearing animals decreased, they suffered. Once a self-sufficient people of the forest, the Shawnees and their neighbors now were tied to an economic system that stretched over the Appalachians and even across the Atlantic. Decisions rendered by strange men in Washington or London now had a profound impact upon their lives, but these men were removed from much of the influence exerted by the Shawnees.

The Shawnees also lost much of their political independence. Once they had been a tribe among tribes, a peer among equals. Of course they periodically had to adapt to the pressures of other Indians, particularly the Iroquois, but this could be done through minor accommodations, or through flight until any temporary threat diminished. And the accommodations did not require significant changes for the Shawnees. But after the middle of the eighteenth century their sovereignty diminished. First they were drawn into the entangling alliances of the colonial and Revolutionary wars. Then they were defeated by Anthony Wayne and forced to sign the Treaty of Greenville. Afterwards they were subjected to an increased volume of white men's regulations—laws that infringed upon their traditional lifestyle. No longer were they a sovereign people who controlled their own political destiny. Now they were vassals, unwillingly tied to the Long Knives.

Tragically, for the Shawnees and their Indian neighbors, the winds of change had only started to blow. At issue were the Indians' remaining lands. Although the Treaty of Greenville had drawn a legal boundary between Indian and white territories, the line of demarcation meant little to American frontiersmen. Following the treaty, white settlers poured into southern Ohio. Although much good land remained unsettled, many frontiersmen looked longingly at Indian lands north of the boundary, and by 1800 significant numbers of squatters were erecting cabins north of the Greenville line. Meanwhile, other settlers intruded upon Miami, Delaware, and Kickapoo lands in southern Indiana and Illinois. Indeed, the Ohio River, which had once formed a de facto border between Indian and white regions throughout its lower valley, now served as a great avenue of penetration for those settlers who wished to move west and carve out new homes in the wilderness. Many of these newcomers were natives of Virginia and Kentucky and had few qualms about usurping Indian lands. After all, hadn't they suffered enough at the hands of the tribesmen? Didn't all white men know that the Indians really never used the lands? Soon all the West would be "civilized." Boundary lines were only temporary expediencies. If enough "sons of the new republic" settled in a region, it would have to become "white man's country." Although federal officials made a desultory attempt to halt such illegal immigration, there was little they could do. The tide of empire rolled westward and government agents had neither the will nor the resources to stop it.

Land was not the only thing the new immigrants took illegally. Even many of those who settled within the white areas crossed over into Indian territory to hunt game and run trap lines. White hunters soon decimated the deer herds, and in 1802 a delegation of Shawnees and Delawares complained to their agents that their people were going hungry. At Vincennes, Governor William Henry Harrison of the Indiana Territory acknowledged the problem.

> The people of Kentucky living on the Ohio from the mouth of the Kentucky river down to the Mississippi make a constant practice of crossing over onto the Indian lands opposite to them every fall to kill deer, bear, and buffaloe—the latter from being in great abundance a few years ago is now scarcely to be met with. One white hunter will destroy more game than five of the common Indians—the latter generally contenting himself with a sufficiency for present subsistence—while the other eager after game hunt for the skin of the animal alone.

Miami and Kickapoo villagers in the Wabash Valley registered similar complaints, and even the tribes of northern Indiana and Michigan reported to traders that game was diminishing. Of course few American hunters penetrated that far north, but the tribes of those regions still blamed the Long Knives for the scarcity.

The fur trade followed a similar pattern. Although the quantity of pelts traded had remained fairly constant in the post-Revolutionary period, after 1797 the number of fur-bearing animals dwindled and many warriors could not obtain enough skins to provide the new necessities for their families. The Shawnees were particularly adept at trapping mink and raccoons, but even these smaller fur-bearers declined in number. At first the decline was not so serious that it threatened the Indians with starvation, but it did force Indian trappers to scatter over wider geographic regions and to remain longer in their winter camps. The extended winter camps were disruptive to the familial and social cohesion of many tribes, since the widely scattered trapping activities prevented some kinship groups from functioning in their traditional manner and caused the postponement or alteration of seasonal ceremonies. Moreover, as the supply of fur diminished, more and more Shawnees, as well as other Indians, were forced to purchase goods on credit, placing themselves and their families deeply in debt to frontier merchants.

Unfortunately, many of the tribe's shrinking resources were squandered on alcohol. Whiskey had long been an important commodity in the Indian trade, but in the years after the American Revolution the flow of alcohol up the Miami and Wabash rivers reached flood-tide proportions. Frontier whiskey was cheap and plentiful, and much in demand in many of the Indian villages. Although the whiskey trade was illegal, federal officials could do little to stop it. At Vincennes, Governor William Henry Harrison reported that many young warriors were being plied with liquor, then "made drunk and cheated of their peltries." Whiskey traders near Fort Wayne, at the headwaters of the Maumee, were so brazen that they set up shop within sight of the post and dispensed liquor by the gallon, while in Ohio responsible Shawnee chiefs pleaded with Indian agents to use troops to prevent the peddlers from coming to the Indian villages.

But their pleas went unanswered. Whiskey merchants continued to permeate western Ohio and the Shawnees suffered accordingly. Moravian missionaries complained that the Shawnees were drinking whiskey by the barrelful and indulging in drunken brawls that often involved entire villages. Although the missionaries' reports were probably exaggerated, the drinking took a horrible toll within the tribal communities. After 1800 many Shawnee warriors had difficulty providing for their families and could ill afford to barter their pelts for whiskey. Moreover, evidence suggests that the alcoholism was not limited to warriors, but that many Shawnee women also drank to excess, compounding the strain upon the tribe's family systems. And even those Shawnees who refused to partake of the fiery liquid were affected, for as the drinking spread throughout the camps, drunken warriors played havoc with the lives and property of innocent bystanders. Although some Shawnees threatened to withdraw from the ongoing bacchanalia, they remained a communal people and such isolation was viewed as a last resort. And where could they go? The whiskey was everywhere.

Debilitated by the alcohol, many Shawnees fell victim to disease. White men's ailments had always plagued the Shawnees, for they, like other Indians, had no natural immunities to the many Old World diseases introduced into North America by the Europeans. Throughout the eighteenth century numerous maladies swept west along the Ohio Valley, passing from tribe to tribe, felling Indians of all ages. Measles, whooping cough, influenza, and other diseases all took a heavy toll but the great killer was smallpox, and in the years following the French and Indian War it had decimated whole villages in Ohio and Michigan. After several generations of exposure, many Shawnees developed some immunity to "this most dread of diseases," but new strains of influenza and other respiratory ailments continued to sweep across their homeland, and tribal shamans had no medicine for either cure or prevention. Dispirited, the Indians watched new "coughing sicknesses" carry away their children, and they complained to missionaries that they suffered from "many diseases that our forefathers were ignorant of, before they saw you."

They also complained to federal officials about a myriad of other problems. Most grievances centered upon the

Indians' failure to receive adequate justice from the American legal system. The white hunters who intruded onto Shawnee lands often took other goods in addition to deer and fur-bearing animals. Unattended or isolated hunting camps were fair game for intruders who would seize any items that could be sold back in the settlements. Shawnee horses, loosely tethered in the forests, were especially vulnerable to such outlaws, for once the animals were driven south into Kentucky they could never be recovered. And the pillagers took other things much dearer to the Shawnees' hearts. Shawnee children, especially youngsters between the ages of two and six, were sometimes swept up by the hunters and carried back across the Ohio where they were adopted by white settlers or apprenticed to tradesmen. For a people among whom family ties were so strong, the loss of their children was particularly heart-rending.

Of course the Shawnees resisted such forays. Although they remained technically at peace, when white intruders raided their camps they defended themselves. Sometimes fire fights occurred, and lives were lost on both sides. Much of the problem, as Harrison admitted, resulted from the fact that most frontiersmen "consider the murdering of the Indians in the highest degree meritorious." Any Shawnee who came within the settlements to trade risked his life, and many border ruffians took particular pleasure in insulting or threatening Indians.

Crimes against the Indians often went unpunished. Between 1800 and 1803 several Shawnees, on peaceful trading missions to settlements near Cincinnati, were murdered in cold blood, but federal officials were unable to convict the perpetrators. Although numerous eyewitnesses testified against those accused of the crimes, juries of the culprits' peers found them "not guilty." Harrison complained that he was helpless to eliminate such injustice and commented that the Shawnees and other Indians were bearing "these Injuries . . . with astonishing patience." Undoubtedly, Shawnee lawbreakers occasionally stole American horses or other property, but in these instances Harrison and other agents had recourse for repayment. If claims against the tribe were deemed legitimate, the cost of the stolen merchandise was deducted from the Shawnees' annuities.

Convinced that their traditional way of life no longer could cope with the changes swirling around them, some Shawnees decided to walk the white man's road. Led by Black Hoof, an old village chief prominent since the French and Indian War, most of the Maykujays remaining in Ohio established permanent villages on the Auglaize and upper Miami rivers. From there they solicited federal officials to provide them with farm implements and Indian agents qualified to teach them agriculture. During the winter of 1802–1803, Black Hoof led a delegation of Maykujay Shawnees to Washington, where they met with Secretary of War Henry Dearborn. Repeating his pleas for assistance, Black Hoof informed the secretary that his people wished to establish farms modeled after their white neighbors'. According to the chief, the Maykujays wanted log cabins, rail fences, and domestic livestock. He also asked Dearborn for a deed or some other legal instrument to assure the Shawnees that they could remain on their lands in western Ohio.

Black Hoof's requests met with a mixed reception. Aware that Ohio would soon become the seventeenth state in the union, Dearborn was reluctant to award the Indians any legal document which would enhance their claims to the region. Instead, he assured Black Hoof that the government would protect their right to remain in the Auglaize Valley, and he promised to send them farming implements, livestock, and "other articles equally beneficial."

The Shawnees' request for farm implements especially pleased the secretary. Since the Treaty of Greenville, officials in the War Department had consistently urged the tribesmen to adopt many aspects of American culture. Thinking that the Indians might become small yeoman farmers, both federal agents and certain religious groups actively pushed a policy of acculturation upon the tribesmen. Moravian evangelists had been active among the Delawares for several decades, and Quaker missionaries also were eager to spread "the Word of God" and "Christian institutions" among the

Black Hoof, or Catahecassa. An active opponent of Tecumseh, Black
Hoof led the Shawnees at Wapakoneta, Ohio. This portrait is from
the McKenney-Hall portfolio. (Courtesy of the Amon Carter
Museum, Fort Worth, Texas.)

tribes of the West. Following Black Hoof's visit (and the vis-
its of other western chiefs), both the government and the
Quakers channeled their efforts into the establishment of a
mission and model farm among the tribes near Fort Wayne.

At first the mission had little impact upon the Shawnees.
From 1804 to 1807 several Quaker missionaries and government agents labored among the Miamis and Potawatomis
with little permanent success. Meanwhile, Black Hoof and
his people sent repeated pleas to Washington, asking the
government, which already had furnished some implements,
to provide agents qualified to instruct the Shawnees in agriculture. In 1807 these efforts were rewarded. During July

William Kirk, a Quaker missionary with previous experience at Fort Wayne, established a new mission at Wapakoneta, Black Hoof's village on the Auglaize River.

The mission was immediately successful. Following Kirk's directions the Shawnees cleared over thirty acres, using rails hewn from the fallen trees to fence their fields against horses and other animals. Although the season was advanced, they planted corn, and by garnering their harvest the five hundred members of the village had sufficient grain to last them through the winter. In the following spring they cleared another four hundred acres and diversified their agriculture, planting potatoes, cabbage, and other vegetables. They also set out apple seedlings and purchased breeder stock of hogs and cattle. Expanding the mission, Kirk hired a blacksmith, began construction of a sawmill, and made plans to erect a gristmill so that the Shawnees could process their grain. Many of the Shawnees built new houses modeled after the log cabins used by white settlers in the region, and they exchanged their traditional clothing for garments resembling those worn by the Americans. According to Kirk, their behavior was both "civilized" and "sober," and he was so encouraged with his success at Wapakoneta that he planned to expand the mission to nearby Wyandots and Ottawas.

But Kirk's successes soon came to an end. The missionary was so busy instructing the Shawnees that he failed to file all the necessary reports with officials in Washington, and in December 1808 the government terminated his position. Charging that he had not adequately accounted for federal funds, the War Department ordered Kirk away from Wapakoneta. Both the Shawnees and the white settlers in the region petitioned in Kirk's behalf, but their pleas were fruitless and the mission ended. Although Black Hoof's people attempted to continue their agriculture, without the missionary's expertise and encouragement their fields fell into ruin.

While Black Hoof's followers stumbled along the white man's road, the more traditional Shawnees eked out an existence similar to their forefathers'. Scattered in small camps across northwestern Ohio and eastern Indiana, these people still hunted the rapidly dwindling deer herds and ran their empty trap lines. Unlike the Shawnees at Wapakoneta, many of these tribesmen retained strong ties with the British. Although the federal government provided "Indian factories" or government-sponsored trading posts, most of the traditionalists traded with British traders who still traveled throughout the Maumee Valley. Many of these traders, including Matthew Elliott and Alexander McKee, had taken Shawnee wives and exercised considerable influence in tribal councils. They persuaded the Shawnees to make periodic pilgrimages to visit British officials at Amherstburg, in Canada, and they sympathized with the Shawnees' complaints against the Long Knives. Although these traders, who also served as British Indian agents, did not urge the Shawnees to actively oppose the United States, they worked to strengthen the Indians' conviction that much of their trouble was caused by the Americans.

* * *

By 1800 it was obvious that the traditional Shawnee socioeconomic system no longer could adjust to the many changes sweeping through the Ohio Valley. Their hunting-gathering-horticultural society that had adapted successfully to European technology and to the fur trade was unequipped to meet the challenges that the onrushing American culture forced upon it. Shawnee society had venerated hunters and warriors, but now there was little opportunity for either. In contrast, both government agents and missionaries urged Shawnee men to lay aside their ancient ways and to become small yeoman farmers. But to traditional Shawnees such an occupation was both foreign and demeaning. Farming was women's work. If white settlers wished to scratch in the dirt like old women, let them, but Shawnee warriors had too much dignity for such menial chores. Better to sit in one's wigwam and sometimes go hungry than to follow the plow and the oxen.

Yet idle warriors dependent upon annuities also lost their dignity, and as their frustration increased, they often turned their resentment upon those closest to them. Shawnee society, once interlaced with well-defined bonds of respect and obligation, came apart as the villages deteriorated into scenes of violence. Inflamed by alcohol, once-peaceful families quarreled among themselves or fought with neighbors. Communal patterns of sharing and assistance declined. Sexual promiscuity increased. The old ways no longer seemed adequate, but the Shawnees had nothing to take their place.

Uncertain of their future, the Shawnees pondered the past. Tribal storytellers told of a proud people especially favored by the Master of Life. Older Shawnees remembered a golden age, when cooking pots were full and warriors walked with their heads held high. Once the world had been orderly, and they had lived in harmony with it. But now disorder reigned, and the Shawnees seemed lesser men than their fathers. Unwilling to admit that the old ways no longer were viable, many Shawnees turned inward, seeking the source of their troubles in themselves. Perhaps the Master of Life had forsaken them because they had forgotten his ways. Perhaps their lives were full of chaos because they no longer followed the sacred Shawnee laws. Perhaps disorder prevailed because the Great Serpent and his servants, the witches, had gained the upper hand in Shawnee society.

By 1800 many Shawnees, and Indians of other tribes, believed that witches were active, spreading their malevolent poison through the Indian communities. Not surprisingly, many Indians associated such evil medicine with the Americans. Tribal traditions had always linked the Great Serpent with water, and many Shawnees believed the ocean abounded with his creatures. Shawnee mythology warned that a race of light-skinned usurpers might emerge from the waters to spread disorder through the world. Since the Americans first arrived on the eastern seashore, many Shawnees believed that these were the Serpent's children, intent on playing havoc with the Indians' universe. Some Indians suggested that those tribesmen who had adopted American ways already had embraced the Serpent. Perhaps their affinity for the Americans gave these witches a particularly potent medicine. Maybe the Serpent's power already was so great that the Shawnees' days were limited.

Other Shawnees clung to the hope of a new beginning. Meeting with federal officials in Indiana, they recounted how their forefathers had stood by the Atlantic, watching a ship as it approached the shore.

> At first they took it for a great bird, but they soon found it to be a monstrous canoe filled with the very people who had got the knowledge which belonged to the Shawnees. After these white people had landed, they were not content with having the knowledge which belonged to the Shawnees, but they usurped their land also. They pretended, indeed, to have purchased these lands but the very goods they gave for them were more the property of the Indians than of the white people, because the knowledge which enabled them to manufacture these goods actually belonged to the Shawnees. But these things will soon end. The Master of Life is about to restore to the Shawnees their knowledge and their rights and he will trample the Long Knives under his feet.

Perhaps all was not lost. Perhaps the Master of Life would soon provide a day of reckoning.

CHAPTER

4

Red Messiah

The years had not been kind to Lalawethika. Unlike Tecumseh's boyhood, exemplary by Shawnee standards, Lalawethika's early years were steeped in difficulty. Born after their father's death, Lalawethika and Kumskaukau, the other surviving triplet, were abandoned by their mother in 1779, when she fled from Ohio following Bowman's raid. Like Tecumseh, the two younger brothers were taken into Tecumpease's wigwam, but the close relationship that developed between Tecumseh and his older sister never materialized for Lalawethika. He was not a handsome child, and a tendency toward corpulency prevented him from excelling at many of the childhood games played by the other Shawnee boys. Frustrated, the young Shawnee overcompensated for his failures, developing a truculent, bragging personality that earned him his nickname Lalawethika (The Rattle or Noisemaker), but won him few friends.

Chiksika also avoided him. Although the older brother invited Tecumseh on hunting trips, he disliked Lalawethika and refused to take him along. Consequently, Lalawethika was poorly trained in those skills needed by hunters and warriors, and although he occasionally killed game in the forest, he disliked hunting and preferred to remain in the village. While still a child (and perhaps because of his awkwardness with weapons) Lalawethika had managed to blind his right eye with an arrow, and the disfigurement only added to his disheveled appearance. As an adolescent he developed a fondness for the white man's whiskey, and never one to deny himself any indulgence, Lalawethika soon began to drink to excess. His alcoholism only increased his loud braggadocio, which in turn further alienated his limited circle of friends and family.

Never a warrior, Lalawethika did not participate in the raids against Kentucky, and when Harmar and St. Clair invaded the Shawnee homeland, he retreated with the women and children. He did take part in the Battle of Fallen Timbers, where he joined the war party led by Tecumseh, but there is no evidence to suggest that he distinguished himself. Following the Treaty of Greenville he married a Shawnee woman, but he was not a good provider, and the kettle in their wigwam often went empty. Unlike Chiksika, Tecumseh evidently felt some responsibility toward his younger brother and attempted to provide for his wife and family. In the years after 1795 Lalawethika joined a small band of younger Shawnee warriors led by Tecumseh, and although few of the Shawnees relished his company, they tolerated the ne'er-do-well out of respect for Tecumseh.

The small village of Shawnees led by Tecumseh moved several times in the decade following the Treaty of Greenville. Refusing to participate in the treaty, Tecumseh took his followers to Deer Creek, a tributary of the Mad River, where they passed the winter of 1795–1796. In the following spring they moved to the Great Miami, where they spent the summer growing corn, but in the fall Tecumseh led them west into Indiana, where game was more plentiful. There they established a new village on the Whitewater River. Since the river valley was fertile and the Whitewater abounded in fish, the Shawnees remained in eastern Indiana until 1798, when they moved again, relocating on the White River in east-central Indiana, near the site of modern Anderson. Although several villages of Delawares were located nearby, deer were more plentiful than at the earlier sites and Tecumseh kept his followers in the region for several years.

The sojourn in Indiana did not go well for Lalawethika. Tecumseh's followers were conservative and refused to follow Black Hoof's advice, but like many other Indians they found their economic base dwindling and sometimes were hard pressed to support their families. Lalawethika fared worse than most. Now a fully grown man in his mid-twenties, he still failed miserably at hunting, and although friends and relatives provided his family with meat, he became the laughing-stock of the village. Reacting to the taunts, Lalawethika at first sank more deeply into alcoholism, then attempted to associate with Penagashea (Changing Feathers), an old shaman living in Tecumseh's village. Penagashea initially disliked the young alcoholic but Lalawethika was persistent and the old medicine man eventually taught him about herbs, healing, and incantations. In 1804 Penagashea died, and Lalawethika tried to take the old man's place. But the other Indians still distrusted him, and in 1805 an epidemic added to his problems. Sweeping through the village in February, the malady seemed immune to his medicine and several of the Shawnees died from the illness. Whatever limited status Lalawethika had begun to achieve as a man of healing immediately plummeted. Dejected, Lalawethika withdrew into his wigwam and brooded over his misfortune.

But Lalawethika's brooding was of short duration. The Master of Life, who had so frowned upon Lalawethika before, now took a special interest in the Shawnee. On a chilly evening in April 1805, while lighting his pipe in his wigwam, Lalawethika collapsed into a trance so deep that his wife and neighbors believed him to be dead. Yet after several hours, while his wife began to make the preparations for his funeral, Lalawethika first stirred, then regained consciousness. Obviously shaken, he startled the tribesmen who crowded his wigwam with a tale of death, resurrection, and deliverance.

According to Lalawethika, he had indeed died and his soul had been carried to the spirit world by two young men sent by the Master of Life. They had transported him to a mountain top overlooking heaven, and had allowed him to gaze upon a celestial paradise with abundant game and fertile cornfields. There the souls of virtuous Shawnees and other Indians would take their ease, living the life of plenty they no longer possessed in their homeland. But the souls of sinful Indians would journey to another place where eternal fires burned inside a large wigwam. There the transgressors would be subjected to fiery tortures in punishment for their wickedness. The most sinful would be reduced to ashes, while unrepentant drunkards would be forced to swallow molten lead until flames poured out their nostrils. All sinners would be compelled to repeat the torments until they had atoned for their evil, and then they would be permitted to enter paradise. Yet they could never share in all the pleasures enjoyed by the souls of their more virtuous kinsmen. Finally, Lalawethika assured his audience that he was a changed man. No longer would he drink the white man's whiskey. The Master of Life had chosen him to lead the Indians back down the road toward salvation. From this day forward he should be known as Tenskwatawa, the "Open Door," a name symbolic of his new role as the religious leader of his people.

During the following summer Tenskwatawa experienced additional visions, and in August 1805 he led a growing band of disciples to Greenville in western Ohio, where they established a new village. Three months later, in November, the new holy man met with delegations of Shawnees, Senecas, Wyandots, and Ottawas at Wapakoneta, Black Hoof's village on the Auglaize River, to elaborate upon his new religion. Much of Tenskwatawa's teachings focused upon the decline of traditional values and mores in Indian society. He particularly condemned the violence that had recently permeated much of Indian life. Tenskwatawa exhorted his followers to treat their kinsmen with kindness, and especially to show respect for tribal elders, whose traditional ways the Master of Life favored. He also urged his disciples to provide food and shelter to widows, children, and all who could not care for themselves. All tribesmen should stop their quarreling and regard each other as brothers. If disagreements arose, they should be settled amicably.

Tenskwatawa was particularly adamant about alcohol. Since he once had been an alcoholic, he considered the rotgut whiskey that flooded the Indian villages as "the white man's poison" and admonished his followers to reject it. According to the Prophet—as he also came to be known—the consumption of alcohol led to a multitude of sins and was the most important factor in the Indians' recent decline.

One such sin was sexual promiscuity, a malady that had infected the tribesmen. He warned his followers to be faithful to their spouses, and especially forbade Indian men to prostitute their wives or daughters. The Master of Life expected Indian women to marry only Indian men, and those women living with white men should return to their own people. Any children resulting from a mixed union should be forbidden in the Indian villages. And Shawnee men should take only one wife. Although polygamy had existed in the past, it displeased the Master of Life and should continue no longer.

Tenskwatawa also railed against the accumulation of property. He warned that the Shawnees and other tribesmen had adopted too many of the white man's values, and no longer shared the Master of Life's gifts with their kinsmen. Traditionally the Shawnees had been a communal society, but now some tribesmen hoarded food or gunpowder while others went hungry. The Master of Life considered such selfishness to be particularly wicked, since it spread dissension throughout the Indian camps and contributed to the violence that had so decimated his people. Accumulated wealth was only valuable when it was given away. The Shawnees must return to the ways of their fathers.

The Prophet's denunciation of the Americans' devotion to private property was indicative of his general distrust of American ideas and technology. He urged his disciples to return to the food, clothing, and implements used by their ancestors. The tribesmen should rely upon wild game and fish for their meat, and they should cultivate such native crops as corn, beans, and pumpkins. Salt should be obtained only from salt springs, such as those found along the Licking River in Kentucky, and food could be sweetened only with maple sugar taken from the forest. Under no circumstances should the Indians consume such domesticated animals as cattle, hogs, or sheep, and they were forbidden to eat bread, which Tenskwatawa condemned as fit only for white men.

The Prophet advised his followers to put aside their American clothing and to dress as their forefathers. Warriors should again shave their heads and wear the scalp locks worn by their ancestors. In a similar manner, the tribesmen were instructed to return to stone and wooden implements and to discard the metal utensils they had obtained from traders. Guns could be used for self-defense, but meat should be killed with stone-tipped spears and arrows. Metal kettles were forbidden, and women were encouraged to manufacture the ceramic and wooden vessels used by their grandmothers.

Tenskwatawa's condemnation of American technology resulted from his revelation that the Long Knives had not been created by the Master of Life, but by "another spirit" who directed their lives for his own purposes. According to the Prophet, the Master of Life had informed him, "The Americans I did not make. They are not my children, but the children of the Evil Spirit." Since the Evil Spirit or Great Serpent lived in the water, it was only natural that the Americans first appeared on the eastern seashore, arriving from the Great Serpent's home. Since that time they had spread their numbers across the land, but the Master of Life assured his people, "They are unjust. They have taken away your lands, which were not made for them." Therefore the Shawnees and other Indians were ordered to minimize their contacts with the Long Knives. They might speak to the invaders, but they should avoid touching them. No more corn could be sold to the Americans, and although the fur trade might temporarily continue, as the Indians regained their self-sufficiency they should cut their ties with the traders. Eventually all intercourse between the two peoples would cease, and if the Indians needed guns or powder they would obtain them from the French or British (also white, but created by the Master of Life). The Master of Life promised that when the tribesmen had done everything that he asked, "I will overturn the land, so that all the white people will be covered and you alone shall inhabit the land."

Although the Prophet directed many of his teachings against the Americans, he also denounced Indian witches, those tribesmen also in league with the Great Serpent. According to Tenskwatawa, the witches spread their evil medicine in two separate ways. Sometimes they attempted to seduce their kinsmen into following the Great Serpent by emulating his children. Therefore those Shawnees who had adopted many of the white man's ways were immediately suspect. If they prospered, it was part of the Great Serpent's plan to tempt other Shawnees away from the more righteous, traditional lifestyle the Master of Life favored. If the acculturated Indians failed, this reflected the displeasure of the Master of Life with those of his children who had abandoned his teachings. In either case, all Indians who followed the white man's road were the objects of Tenskwatawa's suspicion.

Other witches used more traditional methods to spread their poison. The Prophet warned that many of these sorcerers possessed part of the Great Serpent's body, a powerful medicine enabling them to disrupt Shawnee life. Through their spells and incantations, these shamans gained control over their kinsmen, causing illness and death. Like other Shawnees, Tenskwatawa believed that sorcerers could change themselves into animals or become invisible. As servants of the Evil Spirit, they were agents of discord, and if they opposed the Prophet and his new religion, it was obvious that they also opposed the Master of Life.

In this way the acculturated followers of Black Hoof, who disliked the Prophet's rejection of American values, were grouped with traditional shamans who might oppose his new religion because it challenged their influence. All were servants of the Serpent. Regardless of his religious experiences, Tenskwatawa understood tribal politics. He was effectively neutralizing the two groups that might offer him the most opposition.

According to the Prophet, his new faith was necessary because some of the traditional Indian ceremonies had lost their effectiveness. He also instructed his followers to discard their medicine bundles. Such items of personal medicine would no longer be needed since all true children of the Master of Life would share in the spiritual power transmitted through the new religion. To replace the old ceremonies, Tenskwatawa suggested new songs and dances which would

Tenskwatawa, the Open Door. Based upon an earlier painting completed by J. O. Lewis at Detroit in 1824, this portrait of the Shawnee Prophet was included in the McKenney-Hall portfolio. (Courtesy of the Amon Carter Museum, Fort Worth, Texas.)

restore the happy days of the past. In addition, he admonished his disciples to extinguish the fires in their wigwams and to kindle new ones, using only traditional Indian methods. Once started, these new fires must never be extinguished, but should burn continually, for "the life in your body and the flame in your lodge are the same." If the fire died, so would the wigwam's inhabitants.

Other rituals facilitated the spread of the faith. Eager to proselytize more distant tribesmen, Tenskwatawa provided some of his followers with ceremonies designed to convert Indians who could not journey to his village. After confessing their "sins," potential disciples were asked to "shake hands with the Prophet," a rite which borrowed heavily from the outward manifestations of the Catholic rosary. The converts were given strings of beans and told that the beans "were made of the flesh of the Prophet." They were instructed to draw them gently through their hands while promising to follow Tenskwatawa's teachings. Once converted, the neophytes were obligated to travel to more distant villages, further spreading the new faith. If a village refused to accept the Prophet's emissaries, the inhabitants should be warned that they were courting disaster. The Master of Life would "cut them off from the face of the earth."

In contrast, all those Indians who followed the Master of Life's (and Tenskwatawa's) teachings would find order and harmony restored to their world. Their forests would run with deer and their cornfields would be heavy. The golden age of the past would be born again, and true believers would "find your children or your friends that have long been dead restored to life." Somehow (and Tenskwatawa remained vague about this point), the Americans would be swept away. The land would be restored to the Indians.

* * *

In retrospect, Tenskwatawa's "new" doctrine of deliverance fits admirably into a general pattern of revitalization movements found among Native Americans and in other parts of the world. Obviously, the Shawnees and most other tribesmen in the Old Northwest were being overwhelmed by the changes rushing upon them. Both as individuals and as members of a larger tribal culture, the Shawnees could not cope with the stress engendered by these changes. Their traditional economy, which had readily adapted to the fur trade, floundered in the face of American agrarianism. Moreover, the Shawnee political system, characterized by decentralization and relying upon a slowly emerging general consensus, was no match for the more highly organized American governments that confronted it. Even the kinship system, the very warp of tribal life, came apart as the Shawnees were subjected to continual warfare and dislocation. It seemed to many Shawnees and other Indians that they were powerless to stem the tide of disasters. Only with supernatural assistance was there any chance for deliverance.

The Prophet, of course, supplied them with such a remedy. His teachings assured them that the Master of Life had not forgotten his children, and if they would follow Tenskwatawa they would, indeed, be revitalized. Of course most Shawnees had never experienced a vision in which they conversed directly with the supreme power in their universe, but they were willing to believe that Tenskwatawa, who seemed to offer a solution to their problems, had been accorded such a blessing. His promise of a new deliverance seemed their only hope in a world grown more and more hostile. Even his former life of dissipation did not detract from Tenskwatawa's message, for following his visions he appeared to be a different man and drank no more of the white man's whiskey. For many Shawnees, the remarkable change in the former alcoholic only strengthened their conviction that the Master of Life had chosen him as a prophet, and they readily accepted his expositions as divinely inspired.

Like other leaders of religious revitalization movements, Tenskwatawa promised to restore harmony and order in a world full of chaos. Since Shawnee culture at the beginning of the nineteenth century seemed incapable of meeting the problems that faced it, the Prophet proposed a new system, guaranteed to satisfy the Indians' needs. In addition, the new faith provided a strong and benevolent father figure (for the Prophet, the Master of Life; and for the Indians, Tenskwatawa) to watch over the disciples as they journeyed along the road to salvation. During periods of stress men have often sought strong leaders. The emergence of one among the Shawnees was neither unique nor surprising.

And many of Tenskwatawa's teachings really were not very new. The vast majority of his doctrines were based upon those practices that he believed the Shawnees had followed in the past, before they were corrupted by the Americans. Other dogmas emphasized new rituals designed to replace those ceremonies "vitiated by age" or tainted by the Long Knives. Yet even these new tenets were a syncretic blending of traditional Shawnee beliefs and ideas introduced by the

Americans. Although Tenskwatawa failed to recognize their origin, many of his concepts were borrowed from Christianity. Certainly the prohibition of alcohol and the vivid descriptions of hell could be traced to the fundamentalist ministers who swarmed across the Ohio and Kentucky frontiers. "Shaking hands with the Prophet" obviously reflected Roman Catholic influences, while his attempts to proselytize other tribes owe more to Christian evangelism than to any aspect of traditional Shawnee religion. Even his denunciation of American manufactured goods was hedged by the realization that his people depended upon such technology. They were forbidden to purchase merchandise from the Long Knives, but essential items might still be obtained from French or British traders. If the good ways from the golden age were revitalized, they also were blended with both clerical and secular influences from early-nineteenth-century America.

* * *

The decade following the Treaty of Greenville was a relatively quiet period for Tecumseh. After 1795 he led a small village of Shawnees who first settled in western Ohio, then moved to Indiana. Comprised of younger warriors and their families, Tecumseh's village attracted many of the Shawnee firebrands, men committed to traditional ways who resented the American encroachment into Ohio. Although government officials and older Shawnee village chiefs did not consider Tecumseh to be a leader of the first rank, they obviously respected him, and when confrontations emerged between whites and Indians they sometimes sought his counsel. In 1799 he joined with other Shawnee chiefs to meet with local officials on the Mad River, near modern Urbana. The council was designed to ameliorate some differences between the Shawnees and settlers in the region, and although the minutes of the conference no longer exist, white participants indicate that Tecumseh spoke "with force and eloquence."

Four years later, in April 1803, violence again erupted between Indians and settlers in the Scioto Valley. Only two people were killed (one white and one Indian), but frontiers-men near Chillicothe became alarmed and abandoned their outlying farms, fleeing toward the settlements. To stop the panic, a delegation of officials asked Tecumseh and several other Shawnees to meet with Governor Edward Tiffin and to assure American settlers that an Indian war was not immi-nent. The Shawnees agreed, and in May they journeyed to Chillicothe, where Tecumseh spoke for the delegation to an assemblage of merchants and frontiersmen. Once again, the speech was not recorded, but he assured the Americans that the Shawnees intended to live in peace and would not violate the Treaty of Greenville. Impressed with his sincerity, many of the frontiersmen who had fled to Chillicothe returned to their homesteads, and "business generally was resumed throughout the region."

Tecumseh's role in the initial phases of the religious revi-talization remains a mystery. Like many Shawnees, he must have been skeptical at first, but as Tenskwatawa experienced additional visions and as his influence spread among the tribes of western Ohio, Tecumseh also was converted. When the Prophet left the White River to found his new village at Greenville, Tecumseh accompanied him, and although the holy man remained the dominant force in the encampment, Tecumseh assisted his brother. Tenskwatawa might be favored by the Master of Life, but he had little practical experience in leading a village.

Undoubtedly, there was much to do. As word of the new faith spread to other tribes, Indians from distant villages journeyed to Greenville to meet with the Prophet and receive his teachings. Caught up in the religious frenzy, Tenskwatawa had little time to devote to the mundane prob-lems of everyday life, and Tecumseh and other experienced leaders in the village used their influence to keep the rapidly growing settlement running smoothly. In 1806 their responsi-bilities increased significantly. During much of the spring the Prophet was absent from Greenville. In March he traveled to the Delaware villages in Indiana, where he assisted the Delawares in identifying several of their kinsmen who had allegedly practiced witchcraft. Although Tenskwatawa did not order the executions, the Delawares eventually burned four of these poor souls at the stake, and Moravian missionaries among the tribe blamed the holy man. In May he visited the Wyandot villages along the Sandusky River where he condemned four old women as "sorcerers," but Tarhe (The Crane), an influential village chief friendly to the government, interceded for the women and their lives were spared.

Evidence suggests that Tecumseh opposed the killings. Although he believed that his brother had been chosen by the Master of Life, Tecumseh was repelled by the religious fanaticism apparent in many of the Prophet's followers. A practical man, the Shawnee war chief realized that the executions among the Delawares not only would alienate many of the Prophet's more moderate followers, but also would create alarm along the frontier and cause problems with the Americans.

Those problems emerged sooner than either Tecumseh or the Prophet anticipated. Reacting to reports of the witch hunts, Indiana Governor William Henry Harrison wrote to the Delawares in mid-April and ordered them to stop the burnings. He denounced Tenskwatawa as an imposter, and urged the Delawares to test the Prophet's credentials.

> Who is this pretended prophet who dares to speak in the name of the Great Creator? Examine him. Is he more wise or virtuous than you are yourselves, that he should be selected to convey to you the orders of your God? Demand of him some proofs at least of his being the messenger of the Deity. If God has employed him he has doubtless authorized him to perform some miracles, that he may be known and received as a prophet. If he is really a prophet, ask of him to cause the sun to stand still—the moon to alter its course—or the dead to rise from their graves. If he does these things, you may then believe that he has been sent by God.

Yet Harrison's challenge had ramifications beyond what either he or Tecumseh imagined. During the spring of 1806 several astronomers had visited the Ohio Valley in preparation for a total eclipse of the sun scheduled to occur on June 16. If Harrison was aware of the upcoming event, he must have forgotten about it when he wrote to the Delawares, for his message played into Tenskwatawa's hands. Somehow (through either divine or secular sources) the Prophet had learned of the eclipse, and when the Delawares brought Harrison's letter to Greenville, Tenskwatawa surprised even his most fanatical disciples by informing them that indeed he would cause "the sun to stand still," and instructed them to assemble at his village on June 16. When the eclipse occurred, even many Indians who had doubted the Prophet's medicine now believed he had been chosen by the Master of Life, and his reputation spread north through the Great Lakes and west to the Mississippi.

In Illinois, news of the Shawnee miracle worker struck a favorable response among the Kickapoos. Scattered in villages along the Vermilion and Sangamon rivers, the Kickapoos bitterly resented the white settlers approaching from the Ohio Valley. During the summer of 1806 Kickapoo warriors from the Sangamon rode to Greenville, where they listened attentively to Tenskwatawa; then they returned to their villages to spread the new faith among their kinsmen. At Vincennes, Harrison attempted to intercept the pilgrims, and when he failed he wrote to their chiefs warning them to keep the young men in their villages. But those chiefs friendly to the government reported that their influence was diminishing, and reports reached federal officials that the Kickapoo converts intended to carry the new faith to other tribes in the Illinois country.

The arrival of large parties of western Indians at the new village at Greenville alarmed officials in Ohio. Moreover, the murder of a white settler on the Mad River by unknown assailants sparked rumors of an Indian war. To forestall such a conflict, Governor Tiffin sent a delegation of agents to Greenville to meet again with Indian leaders. Led by two experienced Indian-fighters, Simon Kenton and Isaac Zane, the party arrived at the Indian village during August. Although the Prophet refused to attend the meeting, Tecumseh, Blue Jacket, and several other leaders of the village met in council with the frontiersmen and assured them that the tribesmen were not hostile. Speaking for the assembled Indians, Tecumseh disavowed any responsibility for the recent murder and suggested that it had been committed by some of Black Hoof's followers at Wapakoneta. The Indians at Greenville, he explained, had come together "with no other object than to worship the Great Spirit, and to live quietly with their women and children." For many years the Shawnees had been separated, but now they all would be united through their faith in Tenskwatawa. Although most of the delegation were convinced of Tecumseh's sincerity, Kenton still harbored misgivings, so the Shawnees sent a message back to Tiffin again avowing that they wished to live in peace.

American apprehension over the Indians at Greenville was shared by Black Hoof and the more acculturated Shawnees. Still under the tutelage of William Kirk, Black Hoof found that his subscription to American ways made him and his people vulnerable to the Prophet's charges of witchcraft. The execution of the four Delawares had not gone unnoticed at Wapakoneta, and Black Hoof was markedly relieved when Tarhe stopped the witch hunt among the Wyandots. In addition, Black Hoof and many of his people still remembered Tenskwatawa as Lalawethika, the drunken loudmouth, and they refused to accept his claims to be a messenger from the Master of Life. Black Hoof also opposed the village at Greenville for other reasons. In the quarter century since the American Revolution he had slowly emerged as the leading village chief in the Shawnee negotiations with the federal government, and he undoubtedly resented Tecumseh's role as a spokesman for the Indians at Greenville. The quarrel was further aggravated by the schism between the different Shawnee divisions. Black Hoof was a member of the Maykujays, who with the Chalagawthas dominated the remaining Shawnee villages in Ohio. In contrast, both Tecumseh and the Prophet were Kispokothas (most of whom had fled across the Mississippi), and Black Hoof believed they had no right to represent his people. Finally, by 1807 Black Hoof realized that the Shawnees were growing more dependent upon government annuities. Through Kirk's influence, most of those annuities were channeled through Wapakoneta, but if the rival village at Greenville made a claim for the goods, Black Hoof's share of the money and merchandise might be diminished.

At Greenville the Indians were sorely in need of such assistance. During March 1807 a delegation of Shakers visited the village and reported that the Indians were desperately short of provisions. The encampment had grown to sixty lodges and included a large council house, 150 by 35 feet in dimension. The council house served both as a center for the Prophet's religious ceremonies and as a shelter for the large numbers of tribesmen arriving in the village. Both Tecumseh and the Prophet received the delegation favorably, but food was so short that the Shakers were reluctant to share in the Indians' scanty provisions. Unlike other frontiersmen, the Shakers saw no threat in the camp, and when they left they provided the Indians with money to purchase corn and other provisions. During the following summer they continued to furnish the tribesmen with cornmeal, but were forced to halt their generosity after being threatened by other settlers in Ohio.

Meanwhile, federal Indian policy contributed to the new movement's success. As American immigration flooded into the region, federal officials attempted to purchase additional lands from the Indians in the Old Northwest. In 1805 the Wyandots, Ottawas, Chippewas, Delawares, Potawatomis, Miamis, Weas, and Piankashaws signed treaties relinquishing part of their lands to the United States; and in 1807 the Ottawas, Chippewas, Potawatomis, and Wyandots gave up additional territory. Most of these treaties were negotiated by elderly "government chiefs" long friendly to the United States. In turn, federal Indian agents allowed these chiefs to distribute the annuity payments, which reinforced the old chiefs' position of leadership within their tribes. But the treaties angered many of the more traditional tribesmen, who argued that the government chiefs were selling their birthright. Less willing to accommodate the Long Knives, discontented younger warriors vowed to retain their homelands. They also sought new leadership. When word reached them that a Shawnee holy man promised a return to the ways of their fathers, they listened attentively. During the spring of

1807 many of these younger warriors left their villages and traveled to Ohio.

They arrived at Greenville in large numbers. During the spring of 1807 parties of Ottawas, Chippewas, and Potawatomis from the eastern and northern shores of Lake Michigan crossed Indiana en route for the Prophet's village. Most prominent among these "Indians of the Lakes" was Le Maigouis (The Trout), an Ottawa warrior from L'Arbre Croché, a village near the tip of Michigan's lower peninsula. Following his visit to Greenville, Le Maigouis returned to his homeland to serve as a missionary for the new religion, carrying word of Tenskwatawa's doctrines to the Chippewa villages bordering the southern shores of Lake Superior. There the message of revitalization received such a favorable response that entire villages of Chippewas were swept up in a religious frenzy. Some spent the summer dancing the new dances prescribed by the Prophet, while others journeyed to more distant villages spreading word of the new deliverance to their kinsmen in the West. By late summer, however, Chippewas from throughout the western Great Lakes region were en route to Ohio.

They were joined by Indians from Wisconsin and Illinois. Menominee tribesmen also received news of the new religion, and although such older chiefs as Tomah opposed their leaving, young warriors from the Green Bay region set off for Greenville. Some of them were joined by parties of Winnebagos from southern Wisconsin and by Sacs and Foxes from northern Illinois. Most of these warriors traveled by horseback, and they arrived in Ohio throughout the late summer and fall. Upon reaching their destination they found the Prophet's village crowded with pilgrims, for in addition to the western tribes small parties of Miamis, Weas, and Delawares were present. And to add to the population, many of the more militant Wyandots, led by the war chief Roundhead, had broken away from Tarhe's influence and had settled permanently at Greenville.

Although Tecumseh welcomed the new arrivals, they presented the Shawnee war chief with a multitude of problems. First and foremost was logistics. Although the Prophet continued to spend his time in religious ceremonies, Tecumseh and other leaders in the village felt obligated to feed the new disciples, and food was in short supply. Crops of corn, squash, and pumpkins had been planted in fields adjacent to the village, but the harvest was inadequate for the large numbers of strangers. Of course the Shakers had provided some foodstuffs, but their generosity was insufficient for the Indians' needs, and most of the newcomers arrived with empty foodbags, hungry after many days on the trail. To remedy the situation Tecumseh first applied to Indian agents in Ohio for part of the Shawnee annuity, but when this was refused, a delegation of warriors was sent to Detroit, where they pled their case before General William Hull. Led by the wily Blue Jacket, the delegation met with some success. Blue Jacket convinced Hull that the Indians at Greenville remained friendly to the United States, and the general provided them with half of his Shawnee annuities. Still, Tecumseh and other village leaders had barely enough provisions to feed the Indians in their village.

The refusal of Indian agents in Ohio to provide the residents of Greenville with any part of the Shawnee annuities available in that state reflected the government's growing alarm over the influx of Indians. At Fort Wayne, Indiana, Indian agent William Wells was particularly concerned over the large parties of foreign tribesmen passing through his post. He repeatedly warned his superiors that the Indians at Greenville were a threat to the United States. Since the village at Greenville was south and east of the Greenville Treaty line, he considered the Indians to be trespassing upon lands belonging to the government, and he urged federal officials to disband the village and force the Indians to return to their homes.

When both William Henry Harrison and Secretary of War Henry Dearborn seemed to ignore his pleas, Wells decided to act on his own. In April 1807 he sent Anthony Shane, a mixed-blood Shawnee, to instruct Tecumseh, the Prophet, and two other Indians to come to Fort Wayne where they would receive a message from President Jefferson. When Shane reached the Shawnee village he received a negative response. The Prophet refused to meet with him, and when Shane delivered the request to Tecumseh, the Shawnee war chief interrupted him to reply that none of the Indians would go to Fort Wayne. According to Tecumseh, their lodge fires had been kindled on the place appointed by the Master of Life, and if Wells had anything to say to the Indians he should come to Greenville. Tecumseh promised to guarantee Wells's safety while in the village and even offered to invite other officials for the conference, but the council would have to take place in Ohio. Tecumseh then suggested that Wells appear for the appointed conference in six days, on April 23, 1807.

The request was unrealistic. William Wells had spent the past six months denouncing the Indians at Greenville and warning all who would listen that the Prophet and his followers loomed as a threat to American security. If the Indian agent had complied with Tecumseh's bidding, he would have lost considerable face. Wells therefore refused to compromise his position by going to the Indians. Instead, he again dispatched Anthony Shane with a letter summarizing the government's demand that the tribesmen disperse from Greenville and return to their villages.

Shane arrived at Greenville on April 23 to find a large number of Indians assembled for the conference. Expecting to meet with William Wells, the tribesmen were angered that the Indian agent refused to attend, but they listened in silence as Shane read Wells's message. Part of the letter was particularly offensive to Tecumseh. Wells opened his remarks with a hypocritical statement:

> Brothers, the Great Chief of the Seventeen Fires loves his red children and will not suffer his white children to interrupt his red ones, by going into the country belonging to his red children and making settlements on their lands, or by disturbing any thing that belongs to his red children.

Since the government was so concerned with the Indians' welfare, the tribesmen should be grateful to their Great Father and "move from that place and off the land of the United States immediately." Then "the dark clouds that appear to be hanging over you" will pass, said the messenger, and the Indians could return to "the path that will lead you to happiness."

Tecumseh disliked Wells, who had been captured as a small child and raised by the Miamis, only to return to the Americans and serve as a scout for Anthony Wayne. Wells had eventually gone back to Fort Wayne and married a daughter of the Miami chief Little Turtle; in 1798 he had been appointed Indian agent at the post. Like his father-in-law, Wells urged a program of acculturation upon the tribesmen, but Tecumseh and many other Indians knew that Wells had also used his position as Indian agent to amass a personal fortune. For Tecumseh, both Wells and Little Turtle epitomized Indian leadership at its worst: former foes of the Long Knives who had been broken and now served the government.

The Shawnee chief answered Wells's message at some length. In "an impassioned and glowing harrangue," he detailed the many encroachments of white settlers upon Indian lands and property. Such lands, he asserted, had been given to the Indians by the Master of Life and no one had the right to take them away. According to Tecumseh, the Master of Life "has appointed this place for us to light our fires, and here we will remain. The Master of Life knows no boundaries, nor will his red people acknowledge any." He concluded his speech by informing Shane that if the president of the United States had anything else to say to him, "he must send a man of note." Tecumseh "would hold no more intercourse with Captain Wells."

Following Tecumseh's speech, the Prophet also denounced the agent, and Shane returned to Fort Wayne empty-handed. The failure of Shane's mission did little to ease tensions between Indians and whites in western Ohio, and during the spring of 1807, when several settlers in the region were killed by unknown attackers, white farmers began to abandon their farms. Reacting to the panic, Governor Tiffin called out the militia and sent messengers to both Greenville and Wapakoneta demanding that the Shawnees and other Indians assemble at Springfield, a village on the Mad River, to ascertain who was responsible for the deaths.

The council, which took place in late June 1807, illustrated the animosity between the two Shawnee camps. Aware that Black Hoof's and the Prophet's followers had quarreled, officials conducting the conference asked both sides to stack their firearms, but many of the Indians carried personal weapons such as knives or tomahawks. Tecumseh contributed to the tension, since he refused to give up a pipe-tomahawk which he claimed he intended to smoke during the meeting. As "principal speaker" Tecumseh talked at some length, again assuring the Americans that his people were friendly toward the settlers. Although the Indians and most of the Americans were impressed by Tecumseh's grasp of events, one of the officials became impatient and interrupted him, stating "that he did not want him [Tecumseh] to be indulging in fine speeches." He asked if Tecumseh knew who was responsible for the recent deaths.

Assuming that he had an opportunity to undercut Black Hoof's influence, Tecumseh placed his hand on Black Hoof's shoulder and replied, "This is the man who killed your white brother!" Instantly pandemonium spread across the council ground. Jumping to his feet, Black Hoof denounced Tecumseh as a liar, and accused the Greenville Indians of the murders. The two men then withdrew from the others, ostensibly preparing to do battle. Meanwhile, warriors from both sides hurried forward to support their leaders. Fortunately, cooler heads prevailed and bloodshed was averted, but the meeting proved counterproductive. Although it seemed to ease American apprehensions, it widened the breach between the two parties of Shawnees. Ironically, a later investigation indicated that neither side was responsible for the deaths. The murders had been committed by a small band of Potawatomis.

Tecumseh's motivation for the false accusation remains unknown. Since he was confident that his people were innocent, he may have sincerely believed that Black Hoof's warriors committed the murders. By June 1807 the Indians at Greenville had become increasingly alienated from Black Hoof and his followers, and Tecumseh may have hypothe-sized that Black Hoof's warriors had killed the settlers in hopes that blame would fall on their rivals. Unquestionably, the accusations and suspicions leveled at the Indians at Greenville were taking their toll. Both Tecumseh and the Prophet realized that they were surrounded by people hostile to their cause, and throughout the summer of 1807 their replies to repeated government inquiries became more defensive in nature. When they were denounced as "rascals," "Devils," or British agents, it is not surprising that the Indians at Greenville viewed their situation with some paranoia. Certainly their past experiences with the Americans gave weight to their misgivings.

The *Chesapeake* affair heightened tensions in both the red and white communities. During July news reached Ohio that the crew of the British warship *Leopard* had fired upon and boarded the American frigate *Chesapeake*. Fearing that the United States and Britain were on the brink of war, officials in Ohio hoped to prevent the Indians from siding with the British. To preclude such a union, the new governor, Thomas Kirker, sent a delegation of frontiersmen to Greenville to meet with Tecumseh and the Prophet and to investigate their plans. The envoys were instructed to impress upon the Shawnees that any act of hostility would meet with swift and deadly retribution.

To the Americans' surprise, they "were treated with great hospitality and kindness" by the Indians. Tecumseh and the Prophet called the tribesmen to a general council, where Thomas Worthington and Duncan McArthur, two of the envoys, spoke at some length. After pointing out the difficulties engendered by the Indians' past relationship with the British, the Americans warned that if war broke out with Great Britain the Indians should remain neutral. If the tribesmen took up the hatchet they might "destroy a few families who are nearest to you; but you will suffer for it severely in the end."

One day later, on September 13, 1807, both Blue Jacket and the Prophet gave the Indians' formal reply. Blue Jacket assured the Americans that the Indians wanted no alliance with the British, who had "dealt treacherously with us in the past." As for the apparent rift between the Prophet's followers and the government, it was all the result of "a bad man [William Wells] . . . seated at Fort Wayne." If Wells were removed from office, all the problems would be ended. Tenskwatawa also assured the envoys that the Indians only wished to live in peace. After explaining his new faith to them, he discounted all the allegations that he was opposed to the government. He had moved to Greenville because Black Hoof and the acculturated Shawnees "had persecuted him" and had "produced a division in the nation." The Master of Life had chosen the site at Greenville as the place for him to settle, and there he intended to remain. But to assure Governor Kirker that he was a man of peace, the Prophet offered to send a delegation of chiefs to meet with state officials at Chillicothe.

Although Tecumseh took no part in the conference at Greenville, he led the party of Indians who accompanied the American envoys back to the capital. Among the other Indians in the party were such leading figures as Blue Jacket, the Panther, and the Wyandot chief Roundhead, but Tecumseh acted as "principal speaker" and dominated the meetings with the Americans. The tribesmen arrived at Chillicothe in mid-September and remained in the frontier village for about one week.

The Indians met with government officials upon several occasions, but the most important council was a lengthy session open to the general public. In this instance, Tecumseh delivered a speech which lasted almost three hours. Eager to prove that American claims to Ohio were fraudulent, Tecumseh spent considerable time and effort discussing past treaties between the government and the western tribes. According to the Shawnee, the agreements were only "pretended treaties," but since settlers now occupied these lands, the Indians were faced with a fait accompli. They would make no efforts to remove the Americans from former tribal lands in Ohio, but under no circumstances would they surrender any more territory north of the Ohio River. The Indians had no intentions of making war upon the United States, but they would defend their remaining lands with their lives. Although no verbatim record of Tecumseh's speech exists, white observers at the conference reported that both the Indians and the Americans were moved by Tecumseh's oratory, which they described as "bold, commanding, and impassioned." The speech also made a favorable impression upon Governor Kirker. He had earlier mobilized the state militia, but after listening to Tecumseh's speech he seemed assured that the Indians had no plans to attack the settlements and ordered his forces disbanded.

* * *

Tecumseh's speech at Chillicothe reflected the evolving nature of the Indian movement. The Prophet's religion still served as a focal point that attracted tribesmen from throughout the Old Northwest, but many of the permanent residents at Greenville were slowly shifting their attention away from a religious deliverance toward a political solution to their problems, with a primary focus upon land occupancy. Religious panaceas still appealed to many of the Prophet's more recent converts, but Tecumseh and other pragmatic tribesmen now realized that the protection of their remaining land-base was the most important issue facing the tribes. This concern for the retention of Indian territories indicated that Tecumseh's influence was increasing, but it also illustrated that Tecumseh and those tribesmen subscribing to his ideas had adopted (perhaps unconsciously) certain tenets of Euro-American land ownership. Traditionally, most of the tribes in the Old Northwest had believed that land could not be owned. Like the air men breathed, land was occupied or used; but after the inhabitants departed, land reverted to its original unoccupied status and might be settled by anyone. Land, therefore, was shared by all men but owned by none.

Tecumseh's insistence that the remaining Indian land-base continue as "Indian land" shows that he had accepted the Euro-American concept to some degree. Of course such a definition was forced on the Indians by the American purchase and occupation of former tribal lands in Ohio and by the Americans' claim to exclusive rights in the territory, including the right to exclude the tribesmen from the region.

For the Americans, the Greenville Treaty line was important in that it marked the boundary between Indian and American lands, a boundary the Indians supposedly were forbidden to cross. Originally both the Prophet and Tecumseh had ignored the line, and when they established their village following Tenskwatawa's visions, they erected it on lands earlier ceded to the Americans. Indeed, at first the Prophet seemed quite surprised at the American concern over the location of his town and he claimed to have settled at that spot only because "it had been appointed by the Master of Life." As late as April 1807, Tecumseh also had reiterated that neither the Master of Life nor his own people knew any boundaries, but by September his position had changed. He now was willing to accept a demarcation line between Indian and white territory, but he was determined to use that border as a defense against further American encroachment.

5

"The Moses of the Family"

During the autumn of 1807, while Tecumseh was meeting with Governor Thomas Kirker at Chillicothe, Tenskwatawa entertained two notable guests at Greenville. Unaware that Kirker already was conferring with the Indians, William Henry Harrison dispatched John Connor to Ohio to meet with "the chiefs and head men of the Shawanese tribe." Alarmed by repeated reports from William Wells that Greenville had become a center for British intrigue and that the Prophet was conspiring to attack the settlements, Harrison instructed Connor to deliver a message denouncing Tenskwatawa and urging the other Shawnees to drive him from their camp. Unwilling to believe that the holy man was the dominant force in the village, Harrison still assumed that the Prophet was subservient to more traditional Indian leaders.

Much to Connor's dismay, he arrived at Greenville while Tecumseh, Blue Jacket, and the others were in Chillicothe, and therefore was forced to deliver the message to Tenskwatawa. Although Harrison's speech denounced the Prophet as "a fool," the holy man was surprisingly calm in his reply. Perhaps the unexpected appearance of the American envoy caught him by surprise, and with Tecumseh and Blue Jacket absent he was uncertain of his response, for his answer was almost conciliatory in its character. After listening to Harrison's charges, Tenskwatawa replied that he was sorry that Harrison had received such false information. The governor's "impeachments" were untrue, and Harrison could "rest assured it was the least of our ideas to make disturbances, and we will rather try to stop such proceedings than encourage them." Although Connor privately questioned the Prophet's sincerity, he was much relieved by his moderate tone and returned to Vincennes at the earliest opportunity.

Shortly after Connor's departure, Tenskwatawa welcomed Main Poc, a Potawatomi chief from the Kankakee River in Illinois. Described by William Wells as the most influential Indian leader west of the Wabash, Main Poc was both a war chief and a celebrated shaman. Born without a thumb or fingers on his left hand, Main Poc claimed that the deformity was a special sign from the Master of Life, and his followers believed he possessed powerful medicine. Main Poc remained at Greenville throughout the fall of 1807, and met repeatedly with both the Prophet and Tecumseh. He seemed to subscribe to some of the Prophet's doctrines, but rejected others. An alcoholic, Main Poc refused to give up his taste for frontier whiskey or to accept Tenskwatawa's teachings that there should be peace among all the tribes. Nevertheless, Main Poc and the Prophet had much in common, and the latter evidently accepted the Potawatomi as an ally in spreading his movement in the West.

Tecumseh's relationship with Main Poc was more strained. Following the conference at Chillicothe, Tecumseh's attempts to politicize his brother's religious movement increased. For Tecumseh, the new concern over defending Indian lands posed additional problems of political organization. In the past, federal officials had gobbled up the Indians' lands piecemeal, purchasing small tracts from various tribal leaders until vast acreages had passed from Indian to white hands. Although Tecumseh argued that these treaties were fraudulent, the federal government used the transactions as a legal claim to the Indians' territory. Tecumseh therefore hoped to prevent such land sales in the future.

From the Shawnee's perspective, his new policy of land tenure would be based upon two precepts: common ownership of all the remaining Indian lands by all the tribes, and a political and military confederacy to unite the tribes under his leadership. Tecumseh's plans for land ownership reflected a "middle ground" between traditional Indian concepts of land tenure and those of the Americans. Tecumseh still agreed that the Greenville Treaty line and other established boundaries between Indian and white lands should stand, but he argued that all the remaining Indian land belonged to no particular tribe, only to all the Indians in general. Therefore individual tribes no longer had the right to sell their territories to the government. If such sales should take place, they would require the consent of all the Indians. Of course this permission would be almost impossible to obtain.

It was the second part of Tecumseh's policy that brought him into conflict with Main Poc. The Shawnee chief realized that in the past the traditional tribal political structure had proven ineffective. Because the tribes had acted independently, federal officials had been able to manipulate them, often playing one against the other to the government's advantage. Although the tribes had sometimes formed alliances, these combinations had been poorly organized and of short duration. Most Indian leaders remained tied to their tribal pasts and saw their world from a tribal perspective. In contrast, Tecumseh championed a stronger, pan-tribal confederacy in which the members would labor for the benefit of all Indians, rather than for particular tribal interests. Only a widespread confederacy under strong leadership could ever preserve the remaining Indian land-base. Such a concept was foreign to traditional tribal politics, but trying times demanded innovative leadership, and Tecumseh believed the tribesmen had no other acceptable choice.

Tecumseh's pleas for intertribal unity met with only a mixed response. Although many younger warriors readily subscribed to his views, Main Poc and other more traditional Indians were skeptical. Main Poc, for instance, had long warred against the Osages and he had no intention of making peace with his adversaries or of joining them in a political union. He was famous as a war chief and he informed Tecumseh that "the Great Spirit often told him that if he ever refrained from going to war and drinking spiritous liquor he would become a common man." Other leaders also seemed reluctant to accept Tecumseh's ideas, but many of the Indians settled permanently at Greenville listened attentively, and he also shared his ideas with the pilgrims who were drawn to the village by the Prophet's religion.

If Main Poc refused to wholeheartedly support Tecumseh's political confederacy, he did make one suggestion that both the Prophet and Tecumseh found agreeable. He invited the brothers to move their camp to a new site, on lands claimed by the Potawatomis near the juncture of the Wabash and Tippecanoe rivers. From Tecumseh's perspective, the invitation made sense. By the fall of 1807 their village again had filled with a multitude of religious converts, many of whom they could not feed. The pilgrims were forced to travel such distances that they exhausted their food supplies and arrived at Greenville half-starved. Although the permanent residents of the village had planted cornfields, their harvest was insufficient to feed the hundreds of visitors, and they had long ago depleted the neighboring forests of game animals. Moreover, their location at Greenville left them almost surrounded by enemies and vulnerable to American military expeditions. In contrast, the new site in Indiana lay amidst woodlands which still held some game, and the waters of the Wabash and Tippecanoe abounded in fish of several species. Because it was further west, the new location was more accessible to the tribes of Illinois and Michigan, people who had been especially responsive to the Prophet's message. Not only would converts have shorter distances to travel, but they also could send supplies of food or warriors, if either were needed. And, finally, a village on the Wabash or Tippecanoe would be far removed from the jealous influence of the village chiefs, and less accessible to the Long Knives.

Main Poc left Greenville in December and traveled to Fort Wayne, where William Wells attempted to interrogate the old Potawatomi about the Prophet's and Tecumseh's intentions. Aware that the chief held great influence in Illinois, Wells plied him with food and supplies, but Main Poc refused to answer his questions. After spending several weeks enjoying Wells's hospitality, the chief returned to his village.

Meanwhile, Tecumseh and the Prophet made plans to abandon Ohio for the new site on the Wabash. During the winter most of Tenskwatawa's religious converts returned to their homes, and in April 1808 the remaining inhabitants of the village near Greenville burned their wigwams and journeyed westward to the headwaters of the Mississinewa. There they constructed canoes, and while Tecumseh and a small party of warriors continued overland with the horses, the remainder of the Indians, including the Prophet, made preparations to descend the Mississinewa to the Wabash, and then float downstream to the Tippecanoe.

News of the emigration caused considerable alarm among government chiefs near Fort Wayne. Unsure of the Shawnees' destination, leaders such as Black Hoof, Five Medals, and Little Turtle were afraid that the two brothers might relocate near Fort Wayne in an attempt to undermine the chief's authority over their younger warriors. During the first week of April the government chiefs met in council at Fort Wayne, then dispatched Little Turtle and a small party of warriors to intercept the Shawnees and their followers on the Mississinewa. There Little Turtle interrupted the canoe construction to warn Tenskwatawa not to settle on the Wabash. If he dared to establish a new village, the government chiefs would destroy him.

Although Tecumseh and some of the warriors already had left the camp with the horses, the Prophet's followers still outnumbered Little Turtle's party. Not intimidated, Tenskwatawa berated the Miami leader, claiming that Little Turtle and the other government chiefs had no authority over him. The Master of Life had instructed him to move to the Tippecanoe and there he would build his village. Then, in a speech which reflected the growing influence of Tecumseh, the Prophet digressed from his theme of spiritual salvation to champion the new emphasis upon political unity. According to Tenskwatawa, although "the Indians in America were poor," it was the fault of Indian agents such as Wells and Harrison who were "always persuading the Indians to Sell their Land and by these means they made themselves great men by cheating the Indians." Harrison, he continued, "had found it necessary to persuade the Indians to not listen to him [the Prophet] as they well knew that when the Indians were united . . . they would no longer be able to buy the Indians' Lands." To prevent such evil, all the tribes of the West had

> unanimously agreed to meet him and remove the cause of their poverty[;] to effect this it only required the Indians to be united—they would then be able to watch the Boundary Line between the Indians and white people—and if a white man put his foot over it, the warriors could easily put him back.

Angered by the repudiation, Little Turtle and his party returned to Fort Wayne.

While Tenskwatawa was meeting with Little Turtle, Tecumseh accompanied the horses down the south bank of the Wabash. The Prophet and the remainder of the group arrived at the site of the new settlement during the last week in April. Within the next two months, the village, Prophetstown, was erected along the northwest bank of the Wabash, just below the mouth of the Tippecanoe. Several rows of bark wigwams spread over the river bottom and stretched up over the low bluff to an adjoining prairie. Anticipating the arrival of large numbers of converts, the Indians erected a large log-and-bark building called the "House of the Stranger" on a low shelf facing the river. At the other end of the village, on the prairie, two more structures were raised. In a clearing surrounded by several of the wigwams the tribesmen put up a long council house, where Tecumseh and the Prophet could meet with their followers. Nearby, a somewhat smaller building served as Tenskwatawa's medicine lodge.

Tecumseh took no part in the construction of the new village. While the Prophet and his followers labored on the Wabash, Tecumseh journeyed to Canada. His pilgrimage reflected an important change in the Indian movement's relationship with the British. At first, British Indian agents had been wary of the Prophet and his new religion, evidently confused over the holy man's motives. Since British Indian agents still maintained ties with Black Hoof and his followers, they initially heeded Black Hoof's warnings that the rapidly spreading revitalization movement constituted a threat to all established authority. During the summer of 1807, Deputy Superintendent of Indian Affairs William Claus denounced Tenskwatawa as a French agent and "a rascal," but he remained curious about the Shawnee and suggested that British Indian agents investigate the man. In the following months the British sent gifts to Greenville. The Prophet accepted these but declined invitations to come to Canada.

Since Tenskwatawa would not go to Canada, the British eventually sent agents to his village. During the spring of 1808 Frederick Fisher, a trader who also worked for the British Indian Department, met with the Prophet and Tecumseh at Prophetstown. Fisher reported to his superiors that the Indians now seemed more amenable toward the British, and Tenskwatawa indicated he was willing to journey to Canada. Accordingly, in mid-May Claus sent a Fox warrior to the Tippecanoe to inform the Shawnees that he would "be very glad to take [them] by the hand" and that he would welcome a delegation of their followers to Amherstburg, the British post opposite Detroit.

Although the Prophet originally intended to make the journey, by mid-May large numbers of new converts were assembling in his village and he was the focal point of their interest. He also remained the focal point for the government chiefs, who viewed the influx of warriors to Prophetstown with continued alarm. Little Turtle had failed in his initial attempt to prevent the Prophet from moving to the Wabash, but late in the spring another delegation of progovernment Miami and Delaware leaders rode to Prophetstown, intent upon demanding that the two Shawnee brothers remove their village from the Wabash Valley. Although they had planned to meet with Tenskwatawa, they were intercepted by Tecumseh, who denounced them in scathing terms and ordered them to leave the village. Cowed by the Shawnee's tongue-lashing, the government chiefs retreated up the Wabash.

Since Tenskwatawa was needed in Indiana, Tecumseh led the small party of warriors who finally rode to Canada. Like the Prophet's speech on the Mississinewa, Tecumseh's journey to Amherstburg reflected the changing nature of the Indian movement. Unquestionably, Tecumseh's role had increased in importance. Stronger ties with the British were essential if the movement hoped to prosper, and the Indians needed an articulate and convincing spokesman to present their case in Amherstburg. More significantly, the very decision to accept British assistance and cultivate political bonds with the Redcoats denoted another victory in Tecumseh's attempts to secularize his brother's religious movement. Although the Prophet had once railed against white men's food, clothing, and other technology, Tecumseh realized that such logistical support was necessary if the Indians were to defend their homelands. He also was aware of the strained political relations between the British and the Americans, and he hoped to use this friction to the tribesmen's advantage.

Tecumseh arrived at Fort Malden, near Amherstburg, on June 8, 1808, to find that Claus was temporarily absent from the post but would return in a few days. Still eager to speak with the agent, Tecumseh decided to wait at the Wyandot village near Brownstown, on the American side of the Detroit River. Claus returned to Amherstburg on June 11, and two days later he spent three hours conversing with Tecumseh. Claus's diary indicates that the British still saw the Shawnee chief as entirely secondary to Tenskwatawa, for neither Claus nor any of the other British officials referred to Tecumseh by his name, mentioning him only as "the Prophet's Brother."

Unfortunately, the substance of their conversation, which Claus mentioned was "taken down separately" from his diary, evidently was lost, and there is no verbatim record of the discussion. Yet other officers at the post were present at the conference, and from their correspondence strong indications of Tecumseh's proposals emerge. Not surprisingly, the Shawnee emphasized the political and military nature of the movement and suggested to the British that, if war erupted with the Americans, the Indians would make valuable allies. According to one British official:

> The Prophet's brother, who is stated to me to be his principle support and who appears to be a very shrewd intelligent man, was at Amherstburg while I was there. He told Col. Claus and Capt. [Matthew] Elliott that they were endeavoring to collect the different Nations to form one settlement on the Wabash about 300 miles southwest of Amherstburg in order to preserve their country from all encroachments. That their intention is not to take any part in the quarrels: that if the Americans encroach on them they are resolved to strike—but he added that if their father the King should be in earnest and appear in sufficient force they would hold fast to him.

In reply, Claus must have told Tecumseh what he had been telling all the Indians who had visited Amherstburg since the *Chesapeake* crisis. The British agreed that war might erupt, and if it occurred, an alliance between the Crown and the tribesmen would benefit both parties. He reminded the Shawnees that their British Father had been generous to them in the past and that it was the Long Knives, not the British, who now threatened the Indians' homelands. He agreed to send supplies of food and ammunition to Prophetstown, but probably cautioned Tecumseh against precipitating any contest. Following official British policy, Claus welcomed Indian support if war broke out between his country and the Americans, but he did not want to see his government entangled in a conflict solely of the tribesmen's making.

Unquestionably, Claus and other Indian agents were impressed with Tecumseh. Their description of him as a shrewd and intelligent man indicates that Tecumseh's proposals for political and military unification appealed to the Europeans, who saw his plans as much more logical and pragmatic than the religious manifestations of the Prophet. Since Lieutenant Governor Francis Gore was scheduled to visit Amherstburg within the next few weeks, Claus asked Tecumseh to remain in the region so that he could meet the official. Tecumseh agreed and returned to Brownstown, where he spent the next few weeks championing his plans among the Wyandots.

Ironically, while Tecumseh remained at the Wyandot village, Claus was visited by a delegation of Black Hoof's followers from Wapakoneta. Ostensibly loyal to the United States, Black Hoof still received British presents and attempted to maintain his ties with the Crown. Upon hearing that Tecumseh had been at Amherstburg, Black Hoof's people denounced Tecumseh, asserting that he had no authority to speak for the Shawnees. Although Claus now learned of the split in the Shawnee ranks, he evidently discounted its seriousness, for when Gore finally arrived at Amherstburg, Claus sent one of Black Hoof's supporters to summon Tecumseh to dine with the lieutenant governor. Not surprisingly, the Shawnee failed to deliver the message and Tecumseh did not arrive as expected. Finally, however, Tecumseh accompanied a party of Wyandots to the British post, and on July 11 he met with Gore, Claus, and various Indian agents. Although the contents of the meeting remain unknown, the British evidently assured him that they would send supplies and ammunition to the Tippecanoe. Following the meeting he attended a council at which Gore's formal message to the western tribesmen was translated for all the Indians. Tecumseh returned to Prophetstown in late July.

While Tecumseh was in Canada, the Prophet had been cultivating the Americans. Perennially short of supplies, Tenskwatawa had brazenly sent a delegation of his followers to Vincennes in June to solicit provisions from Harrison. The delegation carried a speech in which the Prophet promised "to live in peace with you and your people . . . it was never my intention to lift up my hand against the Americans." He also assured Harrison that as soon as his corn was planted, he would make a special journey to visit the governor. Obviously flattered, Harrison was duped by the holy man into providing food and farming implements for the delegation to carry to Prophetstown. Harrison also informed officials in Washington that he had transformed the Prophet and his movement into "a useful tool" for promoting American Indian policy.

When Tenskwatawa arrived at Vincennes in August 1808, the charade continued. The Prophet remained in the frontier village for over two weeks, meeting with Harrison and assuring him of the Indians' friendship. Although Tecumseh remained at Prophetstown, many other Indians accompanied the holy man, and Harrison was forced to feed the entire company. The Prophet took great pains to convince the governor of the piety of his movement, and he daily harangued his followers upon the evils of alcohol. Impressed by the devotion of Tenskwatawa's disciples, Harrison provided them with food, clothing, and even ammunition which they carried back to Prophetstown. After their departure, he again assured Secretary of War Henry Dearborn that the Prophet's influence would "prove advantageous rather than otherwise to the United States," and several weeks later he informed the Indiana legislature that "at no anterior period have our relations with neighboring tribes been placed on a better footing. . . . Our Indian frontier will be free from those alarms and apprehensions which have had so much effect in retarding its settlement."

At Prophetstown, "alarms and apprehensions" were of a different origin. Although Harrison had provided the Indians with foodstuffs, these stores were soon depleted and the harvest expected in the fall of 1808 failed to materialize. The Indians had spent the spring and summer in religious and political activities, and much of their corn crop failed. Meanwhile, the village continued to attract new disciples, and by October 1808 the population of Prophetstown had swollen to almost four hundred Indians, including men, women, and children. Desperately short of food, some Indians were attempting by mid-December to sustain themselves on the meager game that they scoured from the nearby forests. Other tribesmen resorted to eating their dogs and horses. To add to their miseries, the winter of 1808–1809 was particularly intense, and the snow that blanketed the ground in November remained until April.

This time Tecumseh did not share in his people's sufferings. Accompanied by a small party of warriors, Tecumseh spent the winter of 1808–1809 recruiting followers among the Wyandots and Senecas in Ohio. His efforts met with only limited success. Although he was able to convince several of the younger warriors to join his party, his attempts to lure large numbers to the Tippecanoe met with failure. The Ohio tribes had no knowledge of the food shortages at Prophetstown, but traditional tribal leaders generally were opposed to Tecumseh. Some of the Wyandot chiefs may have entertained the desire to move to Indiana, but they had no intention of sharing their followers with Tecumseh and the Prophet.

Championing this opposition was Tarhe, the old government chief who had thwarted the Prophet's witch hunt among the Wyandots in 1806. During late January 1809 Tecumseh met with the Wyandots and Senecas at Sandusky, where he spoke at some length, attempting to enlist the tribes. Discounting his connection with the new Indian movement, Tecumseh argued that the Ohio tribes should relocate because the region surrounding the Tippecanoe was a better land than Ohio. The soil was more fertile, game was more plentiful, and, most important, the region in Indiana was farther removed from the evil influence of the Long Knives. But Tarhe answered Tecumseh's speech with a warning to his kinsmen that Tecumseh and the Prophet only wanted to lure them to Prophetstown for their own purposes. If conditions on the Tippecanoe were as favorable as Tecumseh described, the Wyandots eventually would learn of them. In the future they might consider relocating in Indiana. But for the present they should remain at their villages in northern Ohio. Disgruntled, Tecumseh spent the next few weeks among the Wyandot and Seneca villages, but his endeavors were generally unsuccessful.

He returned to Prophetstown in February 1809, to find the Indians still short of food and now suffering from another of the white man's sicknesses. The disease (probably influenza), aided by the Indians' weakened condition, took a horrible toll among the villagers. Although the Shawnees, Kickapoos, and Wyandots seemed to have some natural immunity, the northern Indians, the Ottawas and Chippewas, were particularly susceptible to the malady, and by early spring many of them had died. The surviving Ottawas and Chippewas blamed Tenskwatawa for their losses, and in March they fled from Prophetstown, returning to their former homes in Michigan.

The desertions were a mixed blessing. Although the dissident Ottawas and Chippewas now alienated some of their kinsmen from Tecumseh and the Prophet, their withdrawal from Prophetstown ensured that the remaining Indians would have enough food to last until the fish began their spring runs in the Wabash. Still unhappy over his lack of success among the Wyandots, Tecumseh now decided to recruit new members for the movement among the tribes of Illinois. Early in April he rode west across the prairies to meet with the Sacs, Foxes, and Winnebagos in their villages along the Rock and Mississippi rivers. There the Shawnee leader found willing recipients for his offers of an anti-American confederacy. Many of these tribesmen were heavily influenced by pro-British traders from Prairie du Chien. Moreover, during the previous year federal officials had erected a new post, Fort Madison, at the mouth of the Des Moines River, and the Indians opposed the encroachment. Unlike the Wyandots, many leaders among these Illinois tribes gave tacit approval to Tecumseh's plans, and his speeches before their council fires seemed to arouse the younger warriors to a fever pitch. During May some of these young firebrands began to lurk around Fort Madison, sniping at the garrison and greatly alarming American agents both at the fort and at St. Louis. Although Tecumseh was eager to include these western tribesmen in his confederacy, he did not want them to precipitate a war. He remained on the Mississippi through July, recruiting more followers but counseling patience.

While Tecumseh enlisted supporters on the Mississippi, at Prophetstown Tenskwatawa again entertained large numbers of new disciples. He still preached his doctrine of religious revitalization, but the recent arrivals were also told that a political and military union was necessary, and they were advised to hoard their supplies of arms and ammunition. Alarmed by reports of the new militancy, Harrison sent several spies to the Tippecanoe who confirmed the rumors, but who also reported the defections of some of the Ottawas and Chippewas during the previous winter. Meanwhile, Tenskwatawa attempted to calm the Americans' suspicions. In May he journeyed to Fort Wayne where he met with John Johnston, who had recently replaced William Wells as Indian agent at the post. Aware that Johnston and Wells had been political opponents, the Prophet claimed that Wells had fabricated the reports of Indian hostility. The Shawnee also returned several horses which "hostile Indians" had brought to his camp, and so beguiled Johnston that the agent reported to Harrison that Tenskwatawa obviously had been much maligned. According to Johnston, "I have taken much pains and I have not been able to find . . . any grounds for the alarm."

Tenskwatawa next endeavored to hoodwink Harrison again, but this time the governor had seen enough of the holy man's protestations, and when the Prophet and about forty followers arrived in Vincennes late in June 1809, they received a cool reception. Tenskwatawa readily admitted he had met with unfriendly Indians at Prophetstown, but claimed that they had been influenced by the British and that he had made every effort to win them over to the Americans. Indeed, only his efforts had saved the frontier from being overrun by hostile war parties. Yet he had no answer when Harrison inquired why he had not reported such intelligence to Vincennes, and when the Shawnee finally left for Prophetstown, Harrison reported to officials in Washington that he now was convinced that Tenskwatawa was "a liar and a scoundrel."

Although Harrison had become persuaded that the Indian movement was hostile to the United States, he also believed that Tecumseh's and the Prophet's influence was declining. The recent defection of the Ottawas and Chippewas to Michigan seemed to indicate that many of the northern tribesmen no longer followed the Shawnees, and Tenskwatawa's continued inability to feed the residents of Prophetstown only strengthened the governor's convictions. Moreover, he received heartening information from another quarter. Many of the government chiefs from Indiana and

Ohio reported that the Shawnee brothers' magnetism had faded and that their young men had rebuffed all the Prophet's envoys. Although many of these chiefs were eager to ingratiate themselves with the government, and often supplied information designed to please federal officials, Harrison evidently accepted the reports at face value. Meanwhile, the steady influx of new white settlers into southern Indiana threatened to spill over onto lands still claimed by the Miamis, Delawares, and Potawatomis. Convinced that Tecumseh and the Prophet could not prevent another cession of Indian lands, the governor decided to negotiate a new series of treaties with the tribesmen. To ensure his success, he instructed several Indian agents to meet with influential government chiefs and to bribe them to support the negotiations.

The resulting Treaty of Fort Wayne, completed on September 30, 1809, transferred over three million acres of Indian lands to the United States. Signed by friendly chiefs among the Miamis, Potawatomis, and Delawares, the treaty provided the tribes with increased annuities and trade goods, some of which were distributed immediately after the Indians affixed their signs to the document. The Delawares and Miamis had legitimate claims to the ceded lands, but the Potawatomis had never occupied the region, and although they sometimes hunted over part of the territory, their title to the region was at best questionable. Although Harrison assured the treaty signers that "This is the first request that your new Father [President James Madison] has ever made of you and it will be the last, he wants no more of your land," thinking men on both sides of the negotiating table knew that such professions were spurious.

The treaty obviously caught Tecumseh unprepared. Of course Harrison tried to keep news of the proposed treaty from reaching Prophetstown, and he certainly did not invite Tecumseh to the proceedings, but the Shawnee chief eventually learned of the governor's intentions. Still, Tecumseh had spent the first part of the summer on the Mississippi and did not return to Indiana until early August. By then, preparations for the negotiations were well under way, and there was little he could do to stop them. In addition, he probably overestimated his influence among the treaty tribes. Since he had been so successful among the Sacs and Winnebagos, and since some of the Ottawas and Chippewas who had been alienated from the Prophet during the spring now were renewing their ties with the movement, Tecumseh evidently believed that his sympathizers among the Miamis, Delawares, and Potawatomis would prevent their tribal leaders from signing the document. The government chiefs might meet with the Long Knives, but they would never dare to agree to any land cessions.

The treaty jarred him back toward reality. Outraged by the agreement, both Tecumseh and the Prophet threatened to kill the government chiefs, who they claimed had betrayed their kinsmen. Tecumseh also attempted to prevent certain factions among the Weas and Kickapoos from signing supplementary treaties which relinquished these tribes' claims to the ceded region. But in these endeavors he also failed, and by December he was faced with a fait accompli: the lands had been legally transferred and both the Indians who signed the treaties and the federal government recognized the transaction as valid. But legal claims to the region did not guarantee its occupancy. Embittered, Tecumseh vowed that the lands still belonged to all the tribes. If American surveyors or settlers ventured into the region, they would risk their lives.

In retrospect, the Treaty of Fort Wayne was a temporary victory for Harrison, but its long-term ramifications worked to Tecumseh's advantage. He had repeatedly cautioned the tribes of Ohio and Indiana that they must stand together or lose their lands, and the recent cessions at Fort Wayne only seemed to confirm his warnings. Many tribesmen who had been suspicious of the Prophet's motives and reluctant to associate themselves with the Indian movement now were jolted from their complacency. Although Harrison had purchased other Indian territories in the past, these lands in Indiana were deemed especially valuable by several tribes. The threat of their immediate occupancy by the Americans also added to the Indian alarm. If white settlement poured into these regions, then all the tribal lands north of the Wabash would be vulnerable. Perhaps Tecumseh's warnings rang true. Perhaps his concepts of intertribal unity, so alien to traditional Indian politics, offered the only hope of retaining Indian homelands. Frightened, many tribesmen who earlier had followed their traditional village chiefs now reassessed their loyalties. They had refused his invitations in the past, but if Tecumseh or his emissaries again appeared at their village they intended to listen.

Following the treaty, the influence of the government chiefs deteriorated. Black Hoof did not participate in the negotiations, but pro-American leaders such as Little Turtle of the Miamis, Five Medals and Winamac of the Potawatomis, and Anderson of the Delawares affixed their signatures to the document. At first their followers seemed glad to share in the gifts and annuities distributed at the treaty site, but when the trade goods and whiskey were gone, many of the more reflective tribesmen accused their leaders of selling the people's birthright. In failing health, Little Turtle complained that many of his young men now refused to listen to his counsel and were being seduced by "British Indians." Five Medals registered similar complaints, and although Winamac continued to work in support of the government, his influence also declined. Winamac scurried from village to village attempting to negate Tecumseh's influence. Sometimes he was successful, but other Indians friendly to the government advised him not to remain too long in any one place. Warriors loyal to Tecumseh had vowed to take his life.

The Treaty of Fort Wayne also marked a turning point in Tecumseh's career. Prior to 1809 he had been willing to remain in the Prophet's shadow, obviously exercising a growing influence but still playing a secondary role. The treaty ended such abnegation. Now fully convinced that only assertive political and military leadership could protect the Indian landbase, Tecumseh cast off his mantle as "the Prophet's brother" to assume the dominant position in the movement. Before the Treaty of Fort Wayne most of the tribesmen who flocked to Greenville and Prophetstown came for religious reasons. After 1809 they came at Tecumseh's beckoning.

By the spring of 1810 the Indian reaction to the recent treaty was obvious. As soon as there was sufficient grass to feed their horses, hundreds of warriors arrived at Prophet-stown. In addition to Main Poc and a large party of Potawatomis, many Kickapoos from the Vermilion and Sangamon rivers took up residence in the village. They were joined by dissident Delawares and many younger Miami warriors who reported that they now found Little Turtle "contemptible beyond description." Tecumseh's efforts in western Illinois also were evident, for in late May over two hundred and forty Sacs and Foxes arrived from their towns along the Rock River.

The Sacs and Foxes remained at Prophetstown for about two weeks before journeying on to Canada. There they and other Indians met with the British, who supplied them with large stores of arms and ammunition. The British officials' generosity was indicative of their growing support for the Indian movement. During the winter of 1809–1810 they had sent several pack trains loaded with supplies to Prophetstown, and these foodstuffs, coupled with a bumper harvest during the previous fall, enabled Tecumseh and the Prophet to feed all the new arrivals.

While the Sacs and Foxes were in Canada, Tecumseh led a small party of his followers to the Shawnee and Wyandot towns still located in northwestern Ohio. Inspired by his recent success, and hoping that the Treaty of Fort Wayne might jar Black Hoof's people from their complacency, Tecumseh again attempted to enlist the support of the Shawnees along the Auglaize River. Although Black Hoof and other government chiefs refused to meet with him, Tecumseh did attract a considerable audience of younger warriors. Meeting with his kinsmen at Wapakoneta, Tecumseh assured them that warfare with the Long Knives now was certain. All the government's promises amounted to nothing, and if the Indians believed that they could live peacefully with the Americans, they were mistaken. Tecum-seh urged them to leave Ohio and go to Prophetstown, where they would join with other tribes from the West. According to the war chief, the unification of all the tribes was inevitable, and even if he were killed the movement would continue.

Many of the younger Shawnees responded favorably, but in the audience was Stephen Ruddell, the white man who had been captured as a boy and raised by the Shawnees. During their early years Ruddell and Tecumseh had been close friends, but after the Treaty of Greenville Ruddell had returned to Kentucky, where he became a Baptist minister. Sometime after 1800 he returned to the Shawnees on the Auglaize as a missionary, and he actively supported the government's programs to "civilize" the Indians. Although Ruddell listened to Tecumseh's speech, he adamantly opposed his former friend's movement, and he interrupted to say that Tecumseh was mistaken. According to Ruddell, the Great White Father loved his red children. He held up a recent letter from William Henry Harrison as proof of the government's fidelity. Angered, Tecumseh walked over to Ruddell, seized the letter, and threw it into the council fire, declaring that if Harrison were present he would suffer a similar fate. But Ruddell's interruption and Black Hoof's opposition detracted from Tecumseh's efforts, and although several young Shawnees accompanied him back to Prophetstown, most of Black Hoof's people remained tied to the Americans.

While Tecumseh labored among the Shawnees, other members of the Indian movement were active among the Wyandots. Here they finally achieved some success. Tarhe and other government chiefs remained friendly to the government, but recent events had worked to their disadvantage. During 1810 Wyandot lands along the Sandusky River had been invaded by white settlers, and Indian agents had failed in an attempt to remove the trespassers. Threatened by the invasion, some Wyandots believed that they should relocate along the Wabash in Indiana. Yet the recent Treaty of Fort Wayne indicated that the federal government might purchase such a future home before the Wyandots could resettle there. Meanwhile, the government had failed to honor promptly some of its treaty commitments to the tribe, and certain annuities and other supplies had not been delivered.

Tecumseh was particularly eager to bring the Wyandots into his confederacy. Especially venerated by the western tribes, the Wyandots had actively opposed the early American occupation of Ohio, and after the Treaty of Greenville they had retained a large beaded belt that had symbolized Indian unity during that period. The identify of Tecumseh's emissaries to the Wyandots remains unknown, but they skillfully played upon their audience's vanity. Chiding the tribe for remaining idle while its lands were overrun, they asked if the Wyandots had forgotten the Great Belt's significance. In response, many of the Wyandots admitted that most of the government's promises had been broken. Moved by the emissaries' appeal, they vowed to join with Tecumseh at Prophetstown. Others turned on their kinsmen who had cooperated with the Americans, and following the Prophet's teachings they accused these collaborators of witchcraft. In late June, while a large party of Wyandot warriors carried the Great Belt to Prophetstown, other new converts to Tecumseh's cause executed three pro-American Wyandots in northern Ohio.

Following his unsuccessful mission to the Shawnees, Tecumseh promptly returned to Prophetstown. There he found the village brimming with new residents, and Tenskwatawa embroiled in a controversy over the Kickapoos' salt annuity. Among the new residents of Prophetstown were large numbers of Kickapoos who had previously resided along the Wabash near the mouth of the Vermilion River. During the summer of 1810 they were scheduled to receive part of their annuity payments in the form of a salt ration, which the government attempted to distribute to them at Prophetstown. The Kickapoos at Prophetstown opposed the Treaty of Fort Wayne, and they believed that the salt was being offered as partial payment for the lands ceded by the treaty. When the government boat arrived at Prophetstown, the Kickapoos refused to accept the payment. Since Tecumseh was absent, the Prophet seemed unsure just what to do, and ordered the crew of the vessel to leave the salt on the river bank. The crew continued upstream to the Wabash-Maumee portage, but when they returned Tecumseh had arrived from Ohio, and he demanded that they reload the barrels of salt on the vessel. Angered by what he considered to be Harrison's attempt to force the salt upon the Kickapoos,

Tecumseh harangued the boat crew upon the evils of American Indian policy. He also seized the captain of the boat and several of the crew and "shook them violently," asking if they were Americans or Frenchmen. Since all of the crew were of Creole lineage, they finally were released and allowed to proceed downstream, but they arrived at Vincennes considerably frightened.

The Creole boatmen were not the only Americans of French descent to provoke the Indians' anger. Other Creole traders had been active at Prophetstown, and since the Shawnees and other tribes felt a special affinity for the French, these merchants generally conducted their business with Tecumseh's and the Prophet's blessing. During 1809 Harrison had sent a Creole trader, Michael Brouillette, to Prophetstown. Brouillette had ostensibly engaged in the Indian trade while secretly sending reports of the Indians' activities to the governor. Although both Brouillette and Harrison assumed that the trader's true purpose remained hidden, Tecumseh was aware of the man's intentions but tolerated his presence in the village.

Following the salt incident, such toleration ended. During the summer of 1810 Tecumseh met in council with hundreds of warriors visiting in his village, and he hoped to keep the substance of their conversations from reaching Harrison. Aware of Brouillette's true purpose, Tecumseh ordered the trader out of Prophetstown. Although Brouillette protested, the Prophet condemned him as "an American dog" and instructed his followers to pillage the trader's storehouse. Prizing his life more than his merchandise, Brouillette wisely returned to Vincennes.

Brouillette's departure left Harrison woefully lacking in intelligence about the Indians' intentions, and although Winamac and other pro-American chiefs provided him with some information, it often was inaccurate. The government chiefs continued to inform him that Tecumseh's influence was waning, but Harrison was not optimistic. Before his departure, Brouillette had estimated that Tecumseh could now raise at least seven hundred warriors and his strength seemed to be increasing daily. Moreover, settlers along the

Wabash reported that parties of Indians were brazenly stealing their horses, and Harrison feared that bloodshed was imminent. He was aware that a contingent of federal troops was en route from Pittsburgh for the express purpose of strengthening Vincennes' defenses, but he still remained unsure of the Indians' plans. Therefore in late June he sent another Creole, Touissant Dubois, to Prophetstown to inquire about the Indians' intentions and to gather any intelligence that was readily available.

Dubois met with the Prophet early in July, but the mission was generally unsuccessful. Tenskwatawa treated Dubois with cool civility, and answered his inquiries with the old cliché that the Indians had assembled only for religious reasons. When Dubois suggested that a delegation of Indians meet with Harrison in Vincennes, Tenskwatawa refused, complaining that the last time he had visited the governor he had been "ill treated."

Dissatisfied with Dubois's mission, Harrison sent another messenger, Joseph Barron, to ask the Prophet "and two or three of his principal men" to journey to Washington. Aware that similar trips had overawed government chiefs in the past, Harrison believed that if the Indians visited Washington "the knowledge which [they would] acquire of the strength and resources of the United States [would] prevent them in the future from attempting hostilities against us." Barron arrived at Prophetstown in late July and immediately ran into trouble. Since he entered the village unannounced, some of the women and children mistook him for a government scout preceding an American military column, and they incorrectly assumed that Prophetstown was about to be invaded. Panic ensued, and although Tecumseh and the Prophet were able to restore order, many of the Indians were considerably shaken.

Sorely angered by the disruption, Tenskwatawa received Barron in icy silence. He kept the messenger standing before him for several minutes before erupting in a denunciation of both Barron and Harrison. Declaring that he had long known that Brouillette and Dubois were American agents but had tolerated them in the village, the Prophet warned

Barron that his patience had ended. Charging that Barron also was spying for Harrison, he pointed to the ground between the messenger's feet and proclaimed, "There is your grave, look upon it!"

Fortunately for Barron, cooler heads prevailed. Aware that Barron had been sent as an official emissary from the government, Tecumseh intervened in his behalf, guaranteeing the messenger's safety. Barron then delivered Harrison's message, which was critical of the Indian movement but which assured the tribesmen that "the chain of friendship" could "easily be repaired." Harrison also warned the Indians that they could never defeat the Americans, for "Our blue coats are more numerous than you can count, and our hunting shirts are like the leaves of the forests or the grains of sands on the Wabash." To prove his point, Harrison invited the Prophet and several other Indians in the village to travel to Washington, where they could meet with the president and satisfy themselves of the overwhelming power of the United States.

Obviously surprised by the invitation, the Indians permitted Barron to remain overnight in the village while they prepared their formal reply. To safeguard the messenger, Tecumseh invited Barron to spend the night in his own lodge, where the two men talked for several hours after Tecumseh returned from the council. Tecumseh impressed Barron as "a bold, active, sensible man daring in the extreme and capable of any undertaking." The Shawnee assured Barron that he had no intention of starting a war, but he believed peace to be unlikely unless the Americans relinquished their westward expansion and acknowledged the Indians' common ownership of the remaining lands in the West. According to Tecumseh:

> The Great Spirit said he gave this great island to his red children. He placed the whites on the other side of the big water, they were not content with their own, but came to take ours from us. They have driven us from the sea to the lakes, we can go no farther. They have taken upon themselves to say this tract belongs to the Miamis, this to the Delawares and so on. But the Great Spirit intended it to be the common property of

all the tribes, nor can it be sold without the consent of all.
Our father tells us that we have no business on the Wabash,
the land belongs to other tribes, but the Great Spirit ordered
us to come here and we shall stay.

On the following morning Barron again met formally with
the Indians. The Prophet informed him that they remained
undecided about Harrison's invitation, but within a fortnight
Tecumseh would travel to Vincennes and personally deliver
their answer. He would not come alone. Tecumseh himself
stated that he would bring at least one hundred warriors to
Vincennes, and the Prophet warned that the number could be
much larger. Moreover, Tecumseh was coming as an equal,
and expected to be treated with respect. Relieved that the
conference had ended, Barron promptly withdrew from the
village.

Since Harrison was apprehensive about such large numbers of Indians entering Vincennes, he sent messengers to
Prophetstown instructing Tecumseh to bring only a small
party. Yet on August 12, 1810, Tecumseh, accompanied by
about seventy-five warriors, arrived at the frontier village.
The meetings with Harrison extended over the next few
days. Although Harrison had never before met Tecumseh, he
was immediately impressed with the war chief and reported
to Secretary of War William Eustis that Tecumseh already
had eclipsed the Prophet. According to Harrison, Tecumseh
was "the great man of the party [the Indian movement]" and
"the Moses of the family."

Tecumseh immediately confirmed the governor's assessment. Although he and his warriors were surrounded by
soldiers, Tecumseh refused to temper his accusations against
the government. In a series of speeches he catalogued the
Americans' past injustices and charged that the Long Knives
already had seized much of the Indians' land. Unless the
tribesmen joined together, they would be pushed into the
Great Lakes. He readily admitted that he and the Prophet
had "organized a combination of all the Indian tribes in
this quarter to put a stop to the encroachments of the white
people and to establish a principle that the lands should be

William Henry Harrison. A champion of westward expansion,
Harrison was Tecumseh's most powerful American adversary.
(© Mary Evans Picture Library/The Image Works)

considered common property and none sold without the
consent of all." As for those government chiefs who recently
had ceded lands at the Treaty of Fort Wayne, they would be
executed!

Tecumseh's proclamation caused considerable consterna-
tion on the part of Winamac, the Potawatomi sycophant who
was attending the conference as a guest of Harrison. Spying
Winamac, who was sitting in the grass near Harrison's feet,

Tecumseh denounced him in such strong terms that the Potawatomi feared for his life and began to recharge a pistol he had concealed in his clothing. Fearing bloodshed, Harrison attempted to intercede between the two adversaries and answered Tecumseh's charges by asserting that the United States always had treated the Indians with justice. Yet before Harrison could finish his reply Tecumseh interrupted him, and speaking in Shawnee he proclaimed Harrison a liar. Alarmed, one of the army officers who understood the Shawnee language ordered a small party of soldiers forward, and as the troops approached the council fire those warriors accompanying Tecumseh sprang to their feet, tomahawks in their hands. Harrison then rose from his chair and drew a dress sword from a scabbard on his belt, while white settlers in the audience seized firewood or other cudgels to defend themselves. Meanwhile, the soldiers cocked their weapons and prepared to fire. Finally, however, Harrison wisely ordered the troops to lower their weapons. Tempers cooled, and the conference was postponed until the following morning.

On the next day Tecumseh informed Harrison's interpreter that the Indians had meant no harm, but had been alarmed by the approach of the soldiers. The conference resumed, but Tecumseh again asserted his opposition to the recent treaty. According to the Shawnee, those lands ceded at Fort Wayne still belonged to the Indians. Any government attempts to survey them would be met with violence. Representatives from the Wyandots, Kickapoos, Potawatomis, Ottawas, and Winnebagos who had accompanied Tecumseh to Vincennes now spoke in his behalf, indicating that many of their people supported the Indian movement. Finally, Tecumseh asked Harrison to send the Indians' speeches to Washington, for until their plans had been completed neither he nor the Prophet would "accept of your invitation to go and visit the President."

The conference concluded on August 21. Tecumseh again warned Harrison not to meddle in intertribal politics. If the governor used his influence to spread dissatisfaction within the Indian ranks, he would be "doing them [the Indians] a great injury by exciting jealousies between them." Moreover, such interference would be futile for the Americans. The old government chiefs no longer spoke for their people. Now warriors from all the tribes were coming to the Tippecanoe, and according to Tecumseh, "I am alone the acknowledged head of all the Indians."

Surprised by Tecumseh's assertion, Harrison interrupted him to ask how the Kickapoos (many of whom were present) and other tribes would then receive their annuities, to which Tecumseh replied:

> Brother. When you speak to me of annuities I look at the land, and pity the women and children. I am authorized to say that they will not receive them. Brother. They want to save that piece of land. We do not wish you to take it. It is small enough for our purposes. If you do take it you must blame yourself as the cause of trouble between us and the Tribes who sold it to you. I want the present boundary line to continue. Should you cross it, I assure you it will be productive of bad consequences.

Harrison then said he would send the Shawnee's remarks to Washington but there was little chance that President Madison would agree with them. Saddened, Tecumseh turned to the governor and replied that he hoped the Master of Life would instruct the president not to demand the lands, for "he [the president] is so far off he will not be injured by the war; he may sit still in his town and drink his wine, whilst you and I will have to fight it out." Following this speech, the council ended. Late in the afternoon Tecumseh and his followers left Vincennes for Prophetstown.

6

To Tippecanoe

The conference at Vincennes seemed temporarily to ease the tensions between the Indians and the government. Although the basic differences between the two sides remained, the face-to-face confrontation between Tecumseh and Harrison apparently served as a catharsis for both leaders, and the autumn of 1810 ushered in a season of relative peace. In October Harrison again sent Michael Brouillette to Prophetstown to meet with Tecumseh and the Prophet, but this time the Creole's appearance at the village lacked the drama of his recent expulsion. Tecumseh was absent, but the Prophet listened quietly, and when Brouillette informed him that the president had not yet replied to Tecumseh's speech at Vincennes, the holy man seemed unaffected. He treated Brouillette with kindness, but he reiterated that the Fort Wayne Treaty lands must neither be surveyed nor be occupied by settlers. Tenskwatawa also assured the messenger that the confederacy was growing, but Brouillette reported to Harrison that the Kickapoos and Winnebagos recently had quarreled and the number of Indians at Prophetstown had declined.

Tecumseh was absent from the village because he again was conferring with the British in Canada. In early November he arrived at Amherstburg, accompanied by over 160 Potawatomis, Ottawas, Sacs, and Winnebagos, including 33 women and children. During mid-November he met repeatedly with Matthew Elliott, soliciting British assistance for the struggle against the Americans. He informed Elliott that he and his followers had seized power from the government

123

chiefs and "now managed the affairs of our Nations." They originally had planned to keep their political movement a secret, but Harrison's purchase of the lands at Fort Wayne had forced their hand, and they now openly avowed their purpose to unite all the western tribes against the Long Knives. Tecumseh assured his hosts that most of the northwestern tribes already were enrolled in the confederacy and that he intended to journey "towards the Mid Day" (to enlist the southern tribes). Indeed, he promised Elliott that before he again returned to Canada "the business will be done." According to Tecumseh the Indians did not want the British to take up arms against the Americans, but only to honor their promises of supplies and ammunition. The Shawnee assured Elliott that "We think ourselves capable of defending our country," but asked that the British "push forwards towards us what may be necessary to supply our wants."

The British commitment to the Indians was a matter of some confusion. Sir James Craig, governor general of Canada, was eager to maintain the tribesmen's allegiance. Like other officials in Canada, he realized that if war erupted between the United States and the British Empire, His Majesty's forces in Canada would desperately need the Indians' assistance. Yet he did not want Tecumseh and other Indian leaders to interpret British support as a carte blanche for action against the Americans, and most certainly he did not intend for his government to become involved in a war with the United States because of entangling alliances with the tribesmen. Therefore he wished local Indian agents to maintain the warriors' friendship but to restrain them from any overt military actions against the Americans.

Such policy was easier to formulate than to implement. Craig's directives to agents such as Matthew Elliott were confusing, and when the agents asked for clarification he often was tardy with his reply. The situation was further complicated by Elliott's personal ties with the tribesmen. Like many other agents, he had lived among the Indians for years, and he often identified with their cause. Moreover, Elliott had married a Shawnee woman, and his devotion to the tribesmen exceeded official British policy. Following his discussions with Tecumseh, Elliott wrote to his superiors for instruction, but in the meantime he furnished the Indians with ample supplies of clothing and ammunition. He also promised that additional trade goods would be sent to Prophetstown, and although he did not give the Indian movement his official blessing, evidence suggests that Tecumseh and other Indian leaders interpreted his generosity as tacit British approval of their confederacy. If Elliott and other agents supported their efforts, then surely their British Father must also be pleased with his children.

While Tecumseh was meeting with Elliott in Canada, American officials attempted to strengthen their ties with the government chiefs in Michigan and Indiana. In late September Governor William Hull met with friendly chiefs at Brownstown, the Wyandot village south of Detroit. Tecumseh originally had intended to attend this conference before meeting with Elliott, but when he learned that the proceedings would be dominated by pro-American leaders he boycotted the council and proceeded directly to Canada. Hull used the meeting to denounce Tecumseh and the Prophet, warning the assembled chiefs that Tecumseh recently had asserted that he alone was the sovereign leader over all the western Indians. Of course the government chiefs' reaction to Tecumseh's proclamation was what Hull had envisioned, and they sent a strongly worded protest to Prophetstown, admonishing Tecumseh and the Prophet not to meddle in the affairs of other Indians.

Hull reported to his superiors that the conference had been an unmitigated success, but his assessment was premature and far too optimistic. Although the village chiefs were jealous of Tecumseh's leadership, they obviously had been stirred by his warnings. Following Hull's departure the Indians met secretly and vowed to sell no more land to the government. Many then crossed over into Canada, where they discussed the conference with Elliott and other British agents. Although these chiefs had convinced Hull of their devotion to the United States, they complained loudly of American land policy to Elliott, and he warned officials in Quebec that Indian dissatisfaction seemed to be spreading.

A second conference, held at Fort Wayne, followed a similar pattern. In mid-October Indian agent John Johnston met with over 1,700 Potawatomis, Delawares, Shawnees (Black Hoof's people), and Miamis and attempted to distribute their yearly annuities. The Potawatomi, Delaware, and Miami annuities were comprised in part of payments for the Fort Wayne Treaty lands, and the government was eager for the Indians to accept the money and trade goods. The Potawatomis, Delawares, and Shawnees readily accepted their payments, but the Miamis at first refused to attend the conference and then balked at receiving the merchandise. Led by Peccan, a chief from the Mississinewa River, the Miamis complained that they had been coerced into signing the recent treaty and they no longer considered it valid. Johnston finally was able to persuade them to accept the annuity payment, but Peccan warned that the ceded lands could never be inhabited unless they were occupied by soldiers. Johnston charged that much of the Miami dissent had been instigated by former Indian agent William Wells, but he also reported that Tecumseh's influence among the Miamis had increased dramatically and that several of Tecumseh's followers had quietly monitored the proceedings.

Following his conference with Elliott, Tecumseh and many of his followers returned to Prophetstown, where they spent the winter quietly. By January 1811 heavy snows had again drifted around their wigwams, but this time they spent the season in relative comfort and security. Honoring their promises, Elliott and other British agents sent several pack trains of provisions to Prophetstown, and the Indian cornfields along the Tippecanoe had yielded an abundant harvest. During the winter Tecumseh met sporadically with small delegations of warriors from several of the western tribes, but the heavy snow and bitter temperatures kept most warriors tied to their lodge fires, and the harassment of the settlements was suspended. Harrison was so pleased by the apparent tranquillity that he reported to his superiors that Tecumseh's influence had diminished. Meanwhile, he made preliminary plans to survey the Fort Wayne treaty lands.

Spring brought an abrupt end to such optimism. As soon as the melting snow nurtured enough new grass to feed their horses, Potawatomi raiders struck at the settlements in southern Illinois. Most of the war parties were comprised of warriors loyal to Main Poc, and the old shaman ignored Tecumseh's pleas to restrain his followers. Reeling before the onslaught, white farmers abandoned their homesteads south of the Kaskaskia and Big Muddy, and Governor Ninian Edwards of Illinois appealed to Harrison for assistance in stopping the depredations. Harrison's initial investigations indicated that the attacks had originated from Potawatomi and Kickapoo villages in Illinois, rather than from Prophetstown, but in late April he sent William Wells and John Connor to the Tippecanoe to inquire about the incursions.

Both Wells and Connor met with Tecumseh, who admitted that some of his western followers had participated in the depredations, but denied that the raids had originated at Prophetstown. According to the Shawnee, he had counseled against the attacks, but his advice was unheeded. When Wells inquired if any of the raiders currently resided in the village, Tecumseh replied that several of the warriors had passed through Prophetstown en route back to their homes. Although none remained on the Tippecanoe, Tecumseh assured Wells that even if these warriors had been present they would not have been surrendered. Tecumseh did offer to relinquish several stolen horses, however, and he promised to inquire after other stolen livestock. Yet he did not want his cooperation in this matter to be misinterpreted. He "openly and positively avowed his determination to resist the encroachments of the white people," and when Wells chided him that his plans would never reach fruition, he ominously replied that if Wells was fortunate he might live long enough to see the contrary.

Wells's report of the conference seemed to confirm Harrison's apprehensions. Though the frontier had remained peaceful during the previous autumn and winter, it now erupted in a series of incidents that did not bode well for the Americans. In addition to Wells's intelligence, Harrison received reports from several agents that the tribes were meeting to plan attacks against the settlements. Informers among the Kickapoos advised him that Tecumseh had surrendered only a handful of the many stolen horses tethered in his village, and these animals had been relinquished merely to create a favorable impression upon the governor. Since Tecumseh had openly reiterated his defiance, such rumors probably were untrue, but they did little to assure Harrison of the Indians' good intentions. More foreboding, however, were reports from the Fort Wayne Treaty lands. There surveyors dispatched by Harrison to plot the newly acquired region had been threatened by the Weas, a tribe previously devoted to the government. The formerly peaceful Weas had acted so forcibly that the surveyors had abandoned their equipment and fled to Cincinnati.

The new militancy among the Wabash tribes reflected the continued efforts of Tecumseh. Following his meeting with Wells and Connor, Tecumseh journeyed to western Michigan, where he met with the Potawatomis and Ottawas. Meanwhile, messengers were sent to the Iowas and other tribes across the Mississippi, and to Mohawk villagers living in Ontario. Although these distant peoples sent few warriors to the Tippecanoe, those Iowa or Mohawk tribesmen who journeyed to Prophetstown passed through other Indian villages en route, creating the illusion that the confederacy was again expanding.

While Tecumseh was absent in Michigan, the Prophet became embroiled in another altercation with Harrison. In June 1811 Harrison sent a boatload of annuity salt up the Wabash to be delivered to several tribes. When the vessel reached Prophetstown, the crew attempted to leave several barrels of salt for the Kickapoos and other Indians in the village, but following Tenskwatawa's directives his warriors seized the entire cargo. When the captain of the boat protested, the Prophet replied that the seizure was justified. He reminded the officer that during the past year the Indians had refused to accept any of the annuity salt. The confiscation of the boat's current cargo only balanced the government's account with the Indians. Moreover, according to the Prophet, the salt was desperately needed. Although the number of fighting men residing in his village had recently declined, he boasted that within a few days Tecumseh would return "from the lakes" with a reinforcement of two thousand warriors.

Tenskwatawa's boasting was much exaggerated, but it produced a dramatic effect upon Harrison. Earlier reports had indicated that, if an Indian war erupted, Vincennes would be a primary target. Harrison had previously discounted such intelligence, but when news of Tecumseh's impending arrival at Prophetstown reached him, he evidently took the earlier rumors to heart. Writing to officials in Washington, he requested that troops be sent to reinforce nearby Fort Knox. He also forbade local merchants to supply any of Tecumseh's followers with ammunition, and when a small party of warriors from Prophetstown arrived in Vincennes to trade pelts for foodstuffs, Harrison prohibited local blacksmiths from repairing their weapons.

Convinced that "nothing but the great talents of Tecumseh could keep together the heterogeneous mass which composed the Prophet's forces," Harrison sent the war chief a message that reflected his growing apprehensions. Curiously, he accused Tecumseh of plotting his murder. The governor warned, "You shall not surprise us as you expect to do; you are about to undertake a very rash act; as a friend I advise you to consider well of it." If the Indians descended upon Vincennes, Harrison would muster his soldiers "as numerous as the mosquitoes on the shores of the Wabash." "Brothers," he cautioned the tribesmen, "take care of their stings!" Harrison informed Tecumseh that Tenskwatawa's recent seizure of the salt constituted a great insult to the government, but a peaceful solution could still be attained if Tecumseh and the Prophet would agree to go to Washington and visit the president. Tecumseh was welcome in Vincennes to discuss such a journey, but he must come alone. According to the governor, "If your intentions are good, you have no need to bring but a few of your young men with you. I must be plain with you; I will not suffer you to come into our settlements with such a force [a large party of warriors]."

Tecumseh received the message with some bewilderment. He had no intention of arranging Harrison's murder, but the governor's accusations indicated that the Americans were much alarmed. Unquestionably, Tecumseh wished to avoid a military confrontation. By the summer of 1811 most of the northwestern Indians had been brought into his confederacy, but he still hoped to enlist the support of the southern tribes. If war erupted with the Americans, he would be forced to remain in the Northwest. His confederacy would remain incomplete, and the western tribes would not all be unified against the Long Knives.

On the other hand, if he agreed to Harrison's demands and obediently journeyed to Vincennes, he would lose face among his followers. Moreover, the Americans might interpret such cooperation as a sign of Indian weakness and press for further concessions. Finally, in consultation with several of his advisers, Tecumseh decided upon a compromise. He would meet with Harrison in Vincennes, but he would be accompanied by a large party of his followers. Such a tactic would illustrate that the confederacy still wanted peace, but it also would indicate the strength of the Indian movement. In early July Tecumseh informed Harrison that he would arrive at Vincennes in eighteen days, "to wash away all these bad stories that have been circulated." According to the Shawnee, "When I come to Vincennes to see you, all will be settled in peace and happiness."

Tecumseh left Prophetstown in mid-July, accompanied by a large number of warriors. The chief and part of his entourage descended the Wabash by canoe, while the rest of the party journeyed overland. Intent upon maintaining the peace, Tecumseh traveled slowly and allowed several of the warriors to bring their families with them. He hoped that the deliberate pace and the inclusion of the women and children would convince the Americans that the large party of warriors intended no harm and would not attack the settlements. In addition, he ordered his warriors to halt about seventy miles upstream from Vincennes, where they camped for several days as a further insurance that their arrival would not surprise or alarm the Long Knives.

Their precautions had little effect. As soon as Tecumseh left Prophetstown spies brought news of his departure to Harrison, who was much alarmed at the size of the Indian party. The governor immediately alerted the garrison at Fort Knox and mustered militia units from the lower Wabash Valley. He also sent Captain Walter Wilson up the Wabash to intercept the Indians and to demand to know their purpose. Meanwhile, the panic-stricken editor of the Vincennes *Western Sun* warned his readers that Tecumseh and his "insolent banditti" intended to burn Vincennes and kill all its residents.

Wilson intercepted the Indians near Bosseron, about twenty miles north of Vincennes, where Tecumseh and his followers were camped along the east bank of the river. To Wilson's amazement, he found almost 300 warriors, accompanied by about two dozen women and children, who all planned to attend the conference. When Wilson inquired why Tecumseh had brought such a large party, the Shawnee assured him that he had asked only 24 warriors to accompany him, but the other Indians had come of their own volition. Yet he assured Wilson that all the tribesmen were peaceful. They were attending the conference only because they were devoted to the Indian movement.

Tecumseh arrived at Vincennes on Saturday, July 27. He found the frontier village in a state of readiness. Through Harrison's efforts, almost 800 regular army and militia troops patrolled the streets, obviously intent upon impressing the Indians. Yet Tecumseh refused to be intimidated. Although Harrison intended to begin the conference on July 29, Tecumseh informed him that the date was not suitable and the Indians would not assemble until Tuesday, July 30. Moreover, he inquired if Harrison intended to include large numbers of armed troops at the meeting, for if such were the case the Indians also would bring their muskets. When Harrison assured him that only a handful of dragoons would carry firearms, Tecumseh ordered his followers to leave their muskets in camp, but he did encourage them to bring their tomahawks, war clubs, and bows and arrows.

Starting under such inauspicious conditions, the council accomplished little. The two parties met for five days in an atmosphere of mutual suspicion. Secure in his military superiority, Harrison seized the initiative. He scolded Tecumseh for allowing such a large party of Indians to accompany him, and informed the chief that he would tolerate no more discussion of the Fort Wayne treaty lands. Such lands were now controlled by the government, and if Tecumseh wished to question the treaty "he might go and see the President and hear his determination from his own mouth." He further upbraided the Shawnee for the seizure of the annuity salt and again demanded that he surrender any of his warriors responsible for the recent raids in Illinois.

Tecumseh was surprisingly propitiatory in his reply. He completely ignored Harrison's complaints about the size of his party and even agreed to the governor's suggestions regarding a visit with the president. According to Tecumseh, in the near future "he would go and see the President and settle everything with him," but in the meantime he urged Harrison to keep settlers off the treaty lands. The lands were needed, he added, because "a great number of Indians were coming to settle at his town this fall and they must occupy the tract as a hunting ground." If frontiersmen moved into the region, his followers might inadvertently "kill the cattle and hogs of the white people which would produce a disturbance." As for the seizure of the annuity salt, such an affair was unimportant. Tecumseh pointed out that he had been absent when the incident occurred, but he chided the governor for complaining about the episode. He reminded the governor that in the previous year he had been angry when the Kickapoo salt was refused; now Harrison was angry when other barrels of annuity salt were taken. Perhaps, he suggested, it was impossible for the Indians to ever to please the Americans.

Harrison's other complaints received more serious consideration. Tecumseh admitted that some of his followers might have participated in the recent raids in Illinois, and he presented the governor with a large wampum belt to atone for their actions. Although he also promised that he would use his influence to prevent future attacks, he pointed out that those warriors responsible for the raids were not from his village nor were they under his personal control. Moreover, he informed Harrison that he had asked his followers to forgive all their enemies, and he urged Harrison to do the same. Indeed, according to the Shawnee, "the White people were unnecessarily alarmed at his measures." Of course he had attempted to unify the tribes of the Northwest, but "the United States had set him the example of forming a strict union amongst all the fires that compose their confederacy. . . . the Indians did not complain of it—nor should his white brothers complain of him doing the same with regard to the Indian tribes . . . they really meant nothing but peace." Tecumseh concluded his speech by informing Harrison that following the conference he planned to cross the Ohio River and enlist the support of the southern tribes. While he was gone, "he wished everything to remain in its present condition." When he returned, he would go to see the president.

On August 4 the conference ended. While most of the Indians returned to Prophetstown, Tecumseh and about twenty warriors rode south from Vincennes toward the Ohio. Somewhere near the mouth of the Wabash they crossed over into Kentucky, then proceeded on to Tennessee. They crossed the Tennessee River at Colbert's Ferry in northeastern Alabama, then met with several prominent Chickasaw leaders, including the mixed-blood George Colbert. Although the Chickasaws listened attentively and treated Tecumseh with respect, they were not receptive to his pleas. For centuries they had warred with the Algonquian-speaking tribes north of the Ohio, and they were reluctant to ally themselves with the Shawnees, Kickapoos, and other former enemies. Moreover, Colbert and many of the other mixed-bloods already had adopted many tenets of the white man's culture and they disliked the nativistic teachings of the Prophet. Colbert used his considerable influence to persuade his kinsmen to reject Tecumseh's offers, and although the Chickasaws provided a party of mounted warriors to escort the northern tribesmen through the villages, they refused to join the confederacy.

Tecumseh also fared poorly among the Choctaws. In late September he traveled among the Choctaw villages in central Mississippi, again promoting the Indian cause. He met with little success. Of all the southern tribes, the Choctaws traditionally were the most pro-American and anti-British. During the American Revolution they had refused British overtures, and many Choctaw warriors had assisted the colonists and their French and Spanish allies. In the years following the war the Choctaws had welcomed many

American missionaries into their midst, and Choctaw leaders had developed a close relationship with Indian agents from the United States. By 1811 many of the Choctaws actually had adopted the role then being urged by Indian agents upon the northern tribes: they were yeoman agriculturists, growing small fields of corn and raising hogs and other domestic livestock.

Although Colbert and other Chickasaw mixed-bloods had quietly opposed the Indian movement, they did not refute Tecumseh as actively as did many leaders among the Choctaws. Foremost among Tecumseh's Choctaw opponents was Pushmataha, a war chief closely tied to the Americans. Anticipating Tecumseh's arrival, Pushmataha and other progovernment chiefs met in council and advised their kinsmen against accepting the Shawnee's invitations. Primary accounts of Tecumseh's activities among the Choctaws are almost nonexistent, but Choctaw traditions indicate that Tecumseh traveled down the Six Towns trail into east-central Mississippi, passing through several Choctaw villages before reaching Mokalusha, the principal Choctaw town, near modern Philadelphia. During his journey into the Choctaw country, Tecumseh attempted to recruit new followers, but he was shadowed by Pushmataha, who followed him through the different villages, urging the tribesmen to remain friendly toward the United States. At Mokalusha Tecumseh spoke to a large, formal council, outlining the many injustices suffered by the Indians, but once again Pushmataha replied, and the Choctaws generally rejected the Shawnee's overtures. Following the Mokalusha council, similar meetings were held at Chunky's Town near modern Meridian, and at Moshulitubbee's Town on the Noxubee River. At these final conferences mixed-bloods David Folsum and John Pitchlyn joined in Pushmataha's rebuttal; and inspired by their leaders' denunciations, growing numbers of younger Choctaws adopted a militant opposition to the northern Indians. Aware that his efforts among the Choctaws had failed, Tecumseh was anxious to prevent any incidents that might lead to the intertribal violence he abhorred. Late in October he withdrew from the Choctaw villages and journeyed east, seeking recruits among his mother's people.

The Creeks provided him with some success. Scattered in small villages from central Georgia through Alabama, the Creek confederacy was united more by cultural and ceremonial ties than by any political connections. A schismatic people, the Lower Creeks, centered along the Chattahoochee and Flint rivers, were by 1811 under the influence of Indian agent Benjamin Hawkins and had adopted many of the white man's ways. In contrast, the Upper Creeks, whose villages stretched along the Tallapoosa and Coosa rivers in Alabama, were less acculturated and resented Hawkins's growing influence in the confederacy. The Upper Creeks were particularly angry over the recent construction of a federal road, championed by Hawkins, which bisected their lands. Although the road was intended to connect settled regions in Georgia with Mobile and New Orleans, it channeled American frontiersmen through the Creek homeland and encouraged these interlopers to form permanent settlements along the Tombigbee. Big Warrior, the dominant chief among the Upper Creeks, grew rich from tolls upon ferries and bridges along the route, but most of his people disliked both the road and the Americans who used it.

The Upper Creeks were susceptible to Tecumseh's overtures for other reasons. When the Shawnees fled to the South they settled among the Upper Creek villages, and Tuckabatchee, the Creek town near the confluence of the Coosa and Tallapoosa rivers, had always held a special appeal for the northern tribe. When Tecumseh left the Choctaws he crossed over to the Alabama River, then followed the stream east, passing through Creek villages at Autauga and the Hickory Ground (near modern Montgomery) before arriving at Tuckabatchee. Once again, documentary evidence of Tecumseh's activities is limited, but it suggests that he was received much more favorably here than among the Chickasaws or Choctaws. Many young Creeks were interested in his message, and when he reached Tuckabatchee several Creek warriors already had joined his retinue.

Tecumseh's entrance into the Creek nation did not go unnoticed. From his federal agency on the Flint River in Georgia, Hawkins dispatched William McIntosh, a mixed-blood of dubious reputation, to spy upon the Shawnee and to report upon his activities. Meanwhile, Tecumseh encouraged other

Creeks interested in his cause to assemble at Tuckabatchee, where he promised he would speak in council. Learning of Tecumseh's plans, Hawkins hurried to Tuckabatchee to attempt to neutralize the anti-American sentiment that seemed to be growing among the Upper Creek villages. He arrived before Tecumseh and found that Big Warrior was opposed to the northern Indians, but he also found that several thousand other Creeks had assembled to await Tecumseh's message.

Hawkins did not wait long, for after a few days Tecumseh and his party rode in from the west. Evidently they were surprised that the agent was in the village. Undoubtedly Tecumseh saw the recruitment of the Creeks as the capstone of his southern journey, and he seemed unwilling to jeopardize his efforts by speaking in Hawkins's presence. He spent several days in preliminary conferences with Big Warrior and other Creek leaders, and members of his party danced their war dances several times, but when asked to speak in council Tecumseh continually procrastinated. Frustrated by the delay, Hawkins eventually abandoned the council and returned to his agency. However, he did instruct several pro-American leaders to remain at Tuckabatchee and to use all their influence in countering the Shawnee's proposals.

Following Hawkins's departure, Tecumseh met in open council with the Creeks. The exact text of his speech remains unknown, although speculative accounts abound in a variety of secondary literature. Yet Creek oral traditions and "reminiscences" by mixed-bloods and early Indian traders generally agree upon the tone of his oration. The speech was delivered with a force and eloquence that greatly moved his audience. Even Big Warrior, who opposed Tecumseh and personally profited from the federal road, was temporarily shaken by the speech. Many younger Creeks also found much to agree with in Tecumseh's comments, and they too responded favorably.

Almost all of the accounts agree upon the content of the speech as well. In a carefully outlined statement Tecumseh listed the many injustices suffered by both the Creeks and the northern tribes at the hands of the Americans and their government. He pointed out that Indian homelands were being overrun by whites who killed the game and threatened the Indians' culture. Only if the tribesmen returned to the ways of their fathers could they ever resist such encroachment. The northern and southern tribes must join together in a unified front against the Long Knives. War between the Americans and the British was imminent, and the Creeks could be assured that when it erupted their British Father would provide the assistance they needed to defeat their enemies. Then their lost lands would be restored, and the Creeks could regain the happiness and prosperity of their forefathers.

While Tecumseh was attempting to spread his doctrine of political and military unification, other members of his party championed the religious ideology of the Prophet. Tecumseh was accompanied on his trip through the South by a holy man named Sikaboo, who had an excellent knowledge of the Muskhogean dialects and periodically served as an interpreter for Tecumseh and other members of the party. Some evidence indicates that Sikaboo may have been a Creek who earlier had journeyed to Prophetstown, although his name suggests that he was of Algonquian lineage. Regardless of his origin, Sikaboo also spoke to the Creeks, emphasizing the religious doctrines of Tenskwatawa and promising his audience the special blessings of the Master of Life.

Like Tecumseh he was successful. Among the Upper Creek towns were several mixed-bloods who aspired to religious leadership and harbored resentment against the Americans. Many of these individuals were of Loyalist, Scotch-Irish descent, and they were incensed over the ill treatment they believed the Americans had given their families. Typical of this group was Josiah Francis, a mixed-blood from Autauga, whose father, David Francis, operated a trading post at that location. The younger Francis was much taken with both Tecumseh and Sikaboo, and soon after listening to their pronouncements he claimed to have had a vision similar to Tenskwatawa's. Following Tenskwatawa's example, Francis began to proselytize among the Upper Creeks. He eventually won many followers and appointed "subordinate prophets" of his own, including Auttose or High-Head Jim, another religious leader of some prominence. Although Francis's movement did not peak until 1813, two years after Tecumseh's departure, its origins can be traced to the Shawnee's visit among the Upper Creek villages.

Following the conference at Tuckabatchee, Tecumseh evidently traveled through several of the other Creek towns, then returned to Big Warrior's village. There, in a final council, he met with many of his supporters and admonished them to prepare themselves for war against the Americans. They were not to strike precipitously but to await his word. When everything was ready the Creeks would join their northern brethren in a contest against the Long Knives. Big Warrior still remained aloof from the movement, and several progovernment Creeks advised their kinsmen against following Tecumseh, but many of the younger warriors supported his cause. When Tecumseh left the Creek villages in December, Sikaboo evidently remained behind, but about thirty Creek warriors accompanied the Shawnee back to Prophetstown.

In retrospect, Tecumseh's southern journey appears unsuccessful. Although some of the Creeks accepted his invitation, both the Chickasaws and the Choctaws were unmoved by his message. Unlike most of the northern tribes, the Chickasaws and Choctaws were primarily agriculturists whose way of life had not yet been threatened by the onrushing white frontier. Moreover, all of the southern tribes had begun to acculturate more rapidly than most Indians in the Old Northwest, and Tecumseh and the Prophet's emphasis upon nativism held little appeal for people who had incorporated many of the white man's ways into their culture. Unlike their northern brethren, most of the Chickasaws and Choctaws were not impoverished, nor did they see their white neighbors as an immediate threat. Led by acculturated mixed-bloods or by progovernment chiefs tied to the American cause, many of the southern Indians were more suspicious of Tecumseh than of the United States. After all, hadn't these northern tribes traditionally warred against the Chickasaws and Choctaws? Didn't Chickasaw and Choctaw scalps still hang in the lodges of some warriors who accompanied Tecumseh? And hadn't Chickasaw scouts guided Anthony Wayne's army north to Fallen Timbers? Intertribal unity was an alien concept for most of the tribes, and the Chickasaws and

Choctaws were reluctant to join any confederacy which allied them with their former enemies.

Even the Creeks contributed little to Tecumseh's cause. Many of the younger Creek warriors were initially stirred by the Shawnee's speeches, but most Creek leaders remained aloof from the movement, and the resentment which Tecumseh kindled was never channeled toward any productive response. A small party of Creeks accompanied him back to Indiana, but there is no evidence that large numbers of other Creeks ever joined his ranks. During the spring of 1812 many of Tecumseh's Creek companions returned to the South, where they killed several settlers near Nashville, but other Creeks, led by Hawkins and Big Warrior, retaliated and most of the raiders were killed.

Ironically, the intratribal violence precipitated by the return of Tecumseh's followers only exacerbated the factionalism in the Creek confederacy, and this led to the Creek uprising of 1813, a conflict that was as much a civil war among the Creeks as a war against the Americans. This disaster split the Creeks further, and although Andrew Jackson was forced to muster considerable military force to defeat the Creeks at Horseshoe Bend, the campaign took place during the winter of 1813–1814, after Tecumseh was dead and the northern tribes already had been defeated.

* * *

The Prophet fared even worse than Tecumseh. Prior to the conference in August 1811, Harrison had entertained plans to disperse the Indians at Prophetstown, and the meeting at Vincennes markedly strengthened his determination. He remained convinced that Tecumseh had planned to murder him during the Vincennes meeting and that only the obvious display of overwhelming American military strength had prevented the attempt. For Harrison, therefore, military power, not cooperation or diplomacy, now emerged as the cornerstone of American Indian policy in the Old Northwest. Since the tribesmen seemed to respect only force, he intended to use such an instrument to quash the Indian movement. He still would give lip service to negotiation, but he was convinced that American policy would be better served by bayonets.

Tecumseh's absence offered Harrison a rare opportunity to implement his theory. Although Harrison distrusted Tecumseh, he was acutely aware of the Shawnee's influence over the northwestern tribes. Shortly after Tecumseh left for the South, Harrison wrote to Secretary of War William Eustis:

> The implicit obedience and respect which the followers of Tecumseh pay to him is really astonishing and more than any other circumstance bespeaks him one of those uncommon geniuses, which spring up occasionally to produce revolutions and overturn the established order of things. If it were not for the vicinity of the United States, he would perhaps be the founder of an Empire that would rival in glory that of Mexico or Peru. No difficulties deter him. His activity and industry supply the want of letters. For four years he has been in constant motion. You see him today on the Wabash and in a short time you hear of him on the shores of Lake Erie or Michigan, or on the banks of the Mississippi and wherever he goes he makes an impression favorable to his purpose.

But while Tecumseh was away the Indian movement was vulnerable. Harrison reported to his superiors that Winamac had informed him that the British recently had sent large stores of supplies to Prophetstown. According to the governor, Tecumseh's absence "affords a most favorable opportunity for breaking up his Confederacy." If Harrison could attack Prophetstown "before his [Tecumseh's] return, then that part of the fabric which he considered complete will be demolished and even its foundations rooted up." The Indian movement would be broken.

Late in August, Harrison received a favorable reply. Eustis informed him that additional regular troops were being sent to Vincennes, and he authorized Harrison to call for volunteers from Kentucky. The governor was cautioned to maintain the peace if possible, but if the Prophet seriously threatened the frontier "he ought to be attacked." Interpreting the instructions as a mandate to march on Prophetstown, Harrison quickly assembled his forces and by late September over a thousand armed men, including regular troops, Indiana militia, and Kentucky volunteers, were camped in Vincennes and its environs. After first sending messages to government chiefs to keep their warriors clear of his path, Harrison issued his orders. On September 26, 1811, the American army marched out of Vincennes toward Prophetstown.

Harrison proceeded up the east side of the Wabash to modern Terre Haute, where the army stopped to construct a new post, a log stockade named Fort Harrison. During its erection a small party of Indians fired upon several members of the garrison. Yet other soldiers rushed to their defense, and the attackers quickly melted into the forest. Since no other incidents delayed the construction, by late October the fort was completed. While his soldiers were felling trees for the stockade, Harrison made a final, perfunctory effort at negotiation. He sent a small party of friendly Miamis to Prophetstown with the message that he would not attack if Tenskwatawa would disperse his warriors and surrender all of his followers who were guilty of depredations. Meanwhile, on October 29 the governor resumed his march up the Wabash. Two days later he crossed over to the west bank of the river and proceeded to the mouth of the Vermilion, where he halted long enough to erect Fort Boyd, a small blockhouse which would serve as a supply post for the final leg of his journey. On November 3 he continued his march and two days later he was within twelve miles of Prophetstown.

As Harrison proceeded up the Wabash, Tenskwatawa remained in a quandary. Scouts brought reports of the American advance, but the holy man seemed uncertain of his response. Before leaving for the South, Tecumseh had instructed him to avoid any confrontation with the Long Knives. The Indian movement remained incomplete, and both Tecumseh and the Prophet wished to avoid any open conflict until the southern tribes had been brought into the confederacy. But now the Long Knives had built a new fort inside the treaty lands and were marching on Prophetstown. If Tenskwatawa and his followers withdrew from the village, both he and Tecumseh would lose face. They would also lose the large stores of food and ammunition in the village. Therefore, when the delegation of

Miamis arrived at Prophetstown, Tenskwatawa informed them he would meet with Harrison and discuss the demands. The Miamis returned down the east bank of the Wabash, intending to intercept Harrison's advancing army.

Yet the Prophet also prepared for war. Certainly the warriors already assembled at Prophetstown wanted to attack the Americans, and their ardor had a profound influence upon Tenskwatawa. During October he sent riders to the Potawatomi and Kickapoo villages in Illinois, urging them to send warriors. He also assured the Indians in his village that they would strike the Long Knives. Although he remained uncertain about what actions to take, he prayed that the Master of Life would deliver up the Americans. After all, in the past Harrison's mistakes had proven to the Prophet's advantage. Perhaps the Master of Life was again using Harrison to implement a larger purpose, and in that case Tenskwatawa might gain a great victory over the Long Knives.

But when scouts brought news that Harrison had crossed over to the western bank of the river, the Prophet seemed confused. He had assumed that the governor would stay on the east bank and that the Wabash would help to protect the village from the Americans. Now, although his warriors wanted to strike the Americans as they forded Pine Creek, a day's march southwest of Prophetstown, he still procrastinated. But on November 6, when Harrison's army emerged from the forest just one mile east of the village, the Prophet was shaken from his vacillation. He hurriedly sent a delegation of warriors out to assure Harrison that he would meet with him on the following day to discuss the American demands. The Americans could camp along Burnett's Creek, a small stream emptying into the Wabash about two miles west of Prophetstown. Against the advice of many of his subordinates, Harrison agreed to these arrangements.

Both sides expected little from the negotiations. As Harrison withdrew to his campsite, he made preliminary plans to attack Prophetstown. The governor believed that the negotiations would fail, and if events proved him correct he intended to attack the village the following night, when the Indians had retreated to their lodges. Tenskwatawa made even more immediate plans. As the Americans retreated toward their bivouac, he met with his followers and promised them a great victory over the Long Knives. The Master of Life had assured him that they must strike the Americans before the next sunrise. The darkness would both hide the Indians and confuse their enemies. If the warriors could kill Harrison, the other soldiers would run and hide like frightened birds. There would be many new scalps hanging in the lodges at Prophetstown.

Anticipating an attack, Harrison camped on a slight elevation overlooking the prairie. On the west the campsite was protected by Burnett's Creek, which formed a deep ravine along the perimeter of the bivouac. On the east the camp fell off into a marshy grassland that stretched toward Prophetstown. Harrison formed his men into a hollow, irregular rectangle and occupied an open oak grove on the hillock. Sentries were stationed outside the camp's perimeter, and he ordered his men to sleep with their weapons. If the Indians attacked, the Americans would be ready.

Back at Prophetstown, Tenskwatawa and his advisers decided to strike the Long Knives in the predawn darkness. After midnight the Indians quietly surrounded the encampment while a party of handpicked warriors prepared to infiltrate the American lines. The infiltrators intended to kill Harrison and create a diversion within the American ranks while their comrades attacked the perimeter. Shortly after 4:00 A.M. on November 7, they began their penetration of the camp, but as they passed through the lines they were discovered by an American sentry. A few of the Indians had already entered the bivouac, but the sentry's shot roused the Americans from their bedrolls, and most of the infiltrators either fled or were shot. Harrison had already arisen when the attack began, and accompanied by an aide he mounted his horse and rode to the scene of the firing. Two of the warriors inside the camp encountered the governor, but in the confusion and darkness they killed the aide (Colonel Abraham Owen) and Harrison passed on in safety.

As soon as they heard the sentry fire, the warriors surrounding the American camp also began firing and the battle soon spread around the entire American perimeter. In many places the Indians had crept to within a short distance of the American lines, and their initial volleys took a heavy toll upon the soldiers. But the troops rallied and returned the fire, and the warriors' threats to the American lines were turned back. Still, the warriors fought with determination. The fighting raged for almost two hours before it slackened. But as dawn lightened the eastern horizon, the Indians began to disengage from the battle and retreat toward Prophetstown. Encouraged by the withdrawal, Harrison formed his men into regular ranks and ordered them to advance far enough to dislodge any warriors remaining on the perimeter. Shortly after sunrise all firing ceased. The Battle of Tippecanoe had ended.

Tenskwatawa took no part in the fighting. While the battle raged, he continued his prayers and incantations, still assuring his followers that the Master of Life would give them victory over the Long Knives. But as the warriors retreated he found that they blamed him for their failure. Although he had assured them that they would be invulnerable to American bullets, many of their kinsmen lay dead upon the prairie. Angered, the Winnebagos threatened his life, and though other warriors interceded in his behalf, the Prophet now found his influence broken. He attempted to rally his followers, informing them that he had new medicine that would give them a renewed power over the Long Knives, but they again threatened his life and he wisely ceased his protestations. Aware that Harrison would probably attack Prophetstown, the warriors began to desert the village. After hiding surplus food and other supplies in the nearby forest, the Indians packed their remaining possessions upon their horses and fled toward their former villages. By nightfall, Prophetstown was abandoned.

Harrison spent the remainder of November 7 securing his perimeter and caring for his wounded. On the following day, when the Indians failed to renew their attack, he sent a detachment of troops to Prophetstown. The soldiers found the town deserted. They encountered only one old woman, too old and sick to travel. The troops seized a large quantity of abandoned household items, and after searching the nearby forest they found much of the food the Indians had sequestered, almost five thousand bushels of corn and beans. Following Harrison's orders, they piled the foodstuffs amidst the wigwams, then burned everything. On November 9 Harrison left the Tippecanoe and marched back down the Wabash.

* * *

Although Harrison claimed the Battle of Tippecanoe as an overwhelming American victory, evidence suggests otherwise. On November 7 his troops numbered almost 1,000. He was opposed by a force of from 600 to 700 warriors. The Americans sustained 188 casualties, of which at least 62 were fatal. Indian casualties numbered about the same. The hostile warriors formerly residing at Prophetstown now were dispersed, and citizens in Vincennes slept easier. But that was small consolation for other white frontiersmen, who now found warriors from Prophetstown scattered throughout Illinois and Indiana. Before the Battle of Tippecanoe the hostile Indians seemed to be concentrated in one place. After the battle they seemed to be everywhere.

If the Battle of Tippecanoe was not a significant victory for Harrison, it was nevertheless a severe blow to Tecumseh and the Prophet. Prior to the battle Tecumseh had finally extended his influence throughout most of the northwestern tribes, and although he was still opposed by many of the government chiefs, his magnetism over the younger warriors had been spreading. He had left Indiana in the hope of bringing the southern tribes into the movement, but now even his efforts in the Northwest seemed broken. Prophetstown was destroyed, and most of his staunchest followers had returned to their old villages. The surplus food and other supplies finally accumulated on the Tippecanoe had been burned by his enemies. He now would be forced to spend considerable effort just to recoup his former position. November 7, 1811, had been a bad day for the Indian movement.

It also had been a bad day for Tenskwatawa. Although Tecumseh had gradually eclipsed him as a leader, the Prophet had continued to exert considerable authority. He had gambled that the Master of Life would deliver the Americans into his hands. If he had been successful, perhaps he would have regained his dominance over the movement. But in his failure he forfeited his remaining influence. Warriors who once had marveled at his power now scorned him. He still remained Tecumseh's brother, and that relationship probably saved his life following the Battle of Tippecanoe, but he no longer possessed any medicine. His days as a prophet had ended.

7

Red Ascendancy

Tecumseh returned to the Tippecanoe in January 1812 to find his movement in shambles. He had learned of the Indian defeat in southeastern Missouri, where he was visiting the Shawnee villages near Cape Girardeau, and as he crossed Illinois a series of earthquakes ominously shook the Ohio and Mississippi valleys. Yet he still was unprepared for the extent of the devastation at Prophetstown. Aware that he now would be forced to rebuild his movement, he turned on Tenskwatawa and denounced him for leading the warriors in the disastrous attack upon the Americans. In reply the Prophet attempted to defend his actions, but his paltry excuses infuriated Tecumseh, who seized his brother by the hair and threatened to kill him if he ever again jeopardized the Indian movement.

Few of Tecumseh's followers remained on the Tippecanoe. The Winnebagos, Potawatomis, and Kickapoos had all returned to their former villages, but Tecumseh found remnants of his Shawnee and Wyandot disciples still in the vicinity, and he established a temporary village on Wildcat Creek, east of the Wabash, about fifteen miles from Prophetstown. Some warriors were sent back to the Tippecanoe, where they scoured the surrounding forests for caches of food overlooked by the Americans. Other hunters rode east, seeking deer and other game in the thickets along the Mississinewa. The British also sent assistance. Shortly after Tecumseh returned from the South he met with two Delawares who had been sent by British Indian agents in

Canada. Tecumseh informed the messengers that his people desperately needed food and ammunition. The British had little food to spare, but they did supply a small quantity of lead and powder, and although Tecumseh and his followers sometimes faced empty cooking pots, they survived through the winter.

With their physical existence assured, Tecumseh began to rebuild his shattered confederacy. He first needed to prevent further attacks by his enemies. The danger seemed imminent. Encouraged by the recent battle, Winamac and other government chiefs made plans to assassinate both Tecumseh and the Prophet. Fortunately, when the assassination plot was disclosed to American Indian agents, the officials first hesitated, then disagreed among themselves over the plan. Frustrated by the vacillation, the government chiefs soon lost their enthusiasm for the murders, but their enmity continued and Tecumseh was anxious to distract them. He also was eager to preclude any further military expeditions by the United States.

To facilitate his plans, Tecumseh took great pains to placate Harrison. In January the governor sent a message to Tecumseh's village promising amnesty and renewing his offer to accompany a delegation of western warriors to Washington. According to the governor, both Tecumseh and the Prophet would be allowed to make the trip but would be forbidden to serve as leaders of the delegation. Although Tecumseh made no reply regarding the offer of amnesty, he did agree to go to the capital. He informed Harrison that he would be happy to make the journey but could not possibly leave before the following summer. If the governor would wait until his corn was planted, Tecumseh would be glad to speak to the president.

The Shawnee also encouraged his followers to appease the Americans. By March many of the Kickapoos and Winnebagos were again under Tecumseh's influence and he sent a delegation of these warriors to Vincennes. There they spent several days convincing Harrison and other officials that they had broken with Tecumseh. According to the Indians, the recent earthquakes had been a sign from the

Master of Life that they should live in peace with the Americans. They appeared ready to accept any terms offered by Harrison and promised to "lay down the tomahawk" and "do no more injury." The Winnebagos even offered to ride to the Mississippi and convince their kinsmen to make peace with the Long Knives. Harrison, of course, would have to furnish them with horses. Accepting their protestations at face value, Harrison was so optimistic that he reported to the Secretary of War: "I do believe, Sir, that the Indians are sincere in their professions of peace and that we will have no further hostilities."

Harrison's analysis was far too sanguine, but it was probably what his superiors wanted to hear. By the spring of 1812 the United States and Britain were on the brink of war, and the allegiance of the western tribes was critical to both sides. American officials were certain that the majority of the western Indians would not join them in a war upon the British, but they hoped that the tribesmen could, at least, be kept neutral. Harrison's assurances expanded the optimism in Washington, and Secretary of War Eustis instructed the governor to keep offering the olive branch. According to Eustis, it was "particularly desirable at the present crisis that measures should be adopted to re-establish the relations of peace and friendship with the Indians."

The British also were aware of the impending warfare, but in Canada a disagreement arose within the ranks of the British government. Governor General Sir James Craig and his successor, Sir George Prevost, still advocated a policy of Indian neutrality, but British Indian agents, those men responsible for British security in the West, adopted a more militant stance. Realizing that the Crown would desperately need the tribesmen to fend off an anticipated American invasion of Canada, agents such as Matthew Elliott continued to prepare the Indians for war. They assured the tribesmen that, if the Americans attacked, the British Father would expect his red children to take up the hatchet in his cause. Neutrality might be feasible in the polished board rooms of Montreal, but it seemed a dangerous luxury at Amherstburg.

While British and American officials jockeyed for a favor-able position among the western Indians, Tecumseh attempted to rebuild his broken movement. During February he had sent messengers to the tribes of Illinois and Wisconsin, inviting his followers to reassemble on the Wabash, where he would furnish them with lead and powder. Although many of the former residents of Prophetstown remained disenchanted with the Prophet, they still respected Tecumseh, and during March and April large numbers of Kickapoos, Winnebagos, and some Potawatomis arrived on the Tippecanoe. To accommo-date the warriors, Tecumseh moved his camp back to the old site at Prophetstown, where lodges were rebuilt and campfires rekindled.

The reappearance of large numbers of warriors on the Tippecanoe caused considerable concern at both Fort Wayne and Vincennes. Harrison's optimism deteriorated as reports reached his desk of the resurgence of Indian militarism. More-over, intelligence from Illinois was even more alarming. Although Tecumseh was able to keep the Indians on the Wabash at peace, Main Poc's followers were beyond the Shawnee's influence. In a pattern all too familiar, Potawatomi war parties again swept south, wreaking havoc upon Ameri-can settlements in southern Illinois. Meanwhile, the proposed visit of the western Indians to Washington also disintegrated. Harrison asked the warriors to assemble at Fort Wayne, but when the departure date arrived few Indians were there. Tecumseh and the Prophet remained in their village, ensconced with those Kickapoos and Winnebagos who had previously met with Harrison. Intimidated by the renewed threat, even the government chiefs refused to leave Indiana.

Yet Tecumseh's facade of friendship toward the Americans continued. During May both Tecumseh and the Prophet attended an American-sponsored conference on the Mississinewa River in eastern Indiana. The council, ostensi-bly organized by government chiefs at Fort Wayne, actually reflected the subtleties of British Indian agents at Amherst-burg. Aware that war was imminent, British officials met secretly with several warriors from Brownstown, a Wyandot settlement south of Detroit. Matthew Elliott hoped to use the

Wyandots as clandestine messengers to warn Tecumseh to prepare for war. They would also invite the Shawnee chief to Canada, where he would be supplied with additional stores of arms and ammunition. Since many of the Wyandots at Brownstown were friendly toward the United States, Elliott believed that warriors from the village would be able to travel freely to Indiana.

The pro-British Wyandots easily gained the Americans' confidence. First meeting with Governor William Hull's staff at Detroit, the Wyandots, led by mixed-blood Isadore Chaine, asked for permission to visit Tecumseh and the Prophet to "forbid them to make any further depredations on the Americans." Since the Wyandots traditionally held great influence among the western tribes, the American officials were delighted with the request and provided them with white wampum and supplies for the journey. Unknown to the Americans, however, Chaine and his companions also carried a black wampum belt from the British, a wampum belt signifying war.

The Wyandots arrived at Fort Wayne, where Chaine spent considerable time and effort winning the favor of Little Turtle, Five Medals, and Indian agent William Wells. Urged on by the government chiefs, Wells sent messages to Indian villages throughout Ohio and Indiana, asking the tribesmen to meet on the Mississinewa. By mid-May almost 600 warriors had assembled in eastern Indiana. Chaine played his role as a double agent to the hilt. He assured the assembled Indians that he had come to the Mississinewa solely to "clean your paths and wipe the blood off your land, and take the weapons that have spilled the blood from you, and put them where you can never reach them again." According to Chaine, the warriors should remain at peace, for even the British had "advised all the red people to be quiet and not meddle in quarrels that may take place among white people."

Taking their cue from the Wyandots, several tribesmen used the council as a forum to denounce Tecumseh and the Prophet. Potawatomis loyal to Five Medals admitted that some of their western kinsmen had attacked the settlements in Illinois, but "we have no control over these vagabonds, and consider them not belonging to our nation." According to the Potawatomis, the hostiles were "foolish young men" who no longer listened to their chiefs but "followed the counsel of the Shawnee, that pretended to be a prophet." Since Tenskwatawa had been "the cause of setting those people on our white brothers," the Potawatomis charged that he now should be responsible for stopping them. Indeed, if Tecumseh and the Prophet were truly inclined for peace, let them set a good example for the rest of the Indians.

Although Tecumseh had attended the conference hoping to project an image of friendship toward the Americans, he found the charges by the Potawatomis hard to swallow. At first concealing his irritation, he admitted that the recent Battle of Tippecanoe had been an "unfortunate transaction." "Had I been at home, there would have been no blood shed." But the affair was now "settled between us and Governor Harrison" and further recriminations over the battle served no purpose. Yet Tecumseh remained rankled over the Potawatomis' accusations, and he made charges of his own:

> We defy a living creature to say we ever advised any one, directly or indirectly, to make war on our white brothers. It has constantly been our misfortune to have our views misrepresented to our white brethren; this has been done by pretended chiefs of the Potawatomis.

In a final condemnation of Winamac, he added that such chiefs also were "in the habit of selling land to the white people that did not belong to them."

Afraid that the conference might deteriorate in a series of intertribal accusations, the Delawares interrupted Tecumseh to tell him, "We have not met at this place to listen to such words." Assuming the role of peacemakers, the Delawares pointed out that "we would tell the Prophet that both the red and white people have felt the bad effect of his counsels. Let us all join our hearts and hands together, and proclaim peace." The Miamis and even the Kickapoos seemed to agree, and the conference concluded with all the Indians apparently determined to cooperate with the Americans. The government chiefs seemed well pleased with the meeting, although some harbored reservations about Tecumseh's sincerity and eventually expressed their doubts to Indian agents at Fort Wayne.

Such skepticism was well taken. Unknown to either the government chiefs or American Indian agents, Chaine met secretly with Tecumseh and several of his followers and informed them that war between the British and the Long Knives was imminent. Chaine advised Tecumseh to keep his followers quiet. Hostile actions would only alarm the Americans and put them on their guard. Tecumseh was urged to return to Prophetstown and stockpile food and ammunition. Then, when he had secured his position on the Wabash, he should journey to Canada and meet with Matthew Elliott. Although American officials subsequently learned of Chaine's duplicity, by then his mission was completed. He easily eluded their custody and returned safely to Canada.

Following the Mississinewa conference, Tecumseh returned to the Tippecanoe, where he made preparations to visit Canada. By June 1812 he knew that Harrison again considered him hostile, but he still hoped to prevent another American expedition against Prophetstown. Although the Potawatomis continued their raids in Illinois, Tecumseh instructed his brother to keep the Indians on the Tippecanoe from attacking the Americans. In the meantime he would journey to Canada, meet with Elliott, and make plans for future military operations. Late in the summer he would return with additional supplies of arms and ammunition.

On June 17 Tecumseh arrived at Fort Wayne en route to Amherstburg. Surprisingly, he spent four days at the American post, conferring with Indian agent Benjamin Stickney. The reason for his lengthy delay remains unknown, but perhaps he hoped to allay Stickney's suspicions and minimize the possibility of American attacks upon Prophetstown. The Shawnee readily admitted that he planned to visit the British, but informed Stickney that such meetings were incidental to his purpose. The primary reason for his journey was to confer with the tribes near Detroit and arrange a lasting peace for all the western Indians. Tecumseh's explanation made little impact upon the agent, and he informed the

Shawnee that the government would interpret his trip as an "act of enmity," but Tecumseh left Fort Wayne on June 21, 1812. Stickney's reasons for allowing Tecumseh to continue his journey were known only to the agent, but he reported to his superiors that he believed it would not be "prudent" for him to detain the Shawnee.

While Tecumseh was on his way to Amherstburg, other events were shaping the future of the Old Northwest. Unknown to Tecumseh, an American army under the command of Governor William Hull also was marching toward Canada. Organized in Ohio, the army numbered about two thousand men and was designed to reinforce Detroit. If war erupted, Hull was ordered to protect American interests in Michigan, intimidate the surrounding Indians, and assist in an invasion of Canada. Confident in their numbers, in early July the troops skirted the western end of Lake Erie, where they learned that the United States had declared war upon Great Britain. On July 6 the army reached Detroit.

Tecumseh already had arrived in Canada. On July 1 the Shawnee and a party of warriors had crossed over to Amherstburg, where they found Main Poc and several other chiefs attended by large numbers of western Indians. Yet the Wyandots near Brownstown, the village across the river from Amherstburg, remained uncommitted, and these people were critical for both British and American Indian policies. If these Indians remained neutral, the Americans could more easily defend the land route between Detroit and Ohio. Moreover, the Americans might use the Wyandot villages as valuable sources of information about British troop movements. In contrast, if the Wyandots went over to the British, hostile forces would sit almost astride the southern approach to Detroit, and overland travel between the post and American positions in Ohio would be interrupted. Walk-in-the-Water and several other Wyandot leaders were opportunists ready to throw their support to whichever side seemed to be in the ascendancy. Although they met regularly with the British, they also were frequent visitors at Detroit, and American officials believed the Wyandots would remain friendly to the United States. To secure their allegiance, Tecumseh spoke

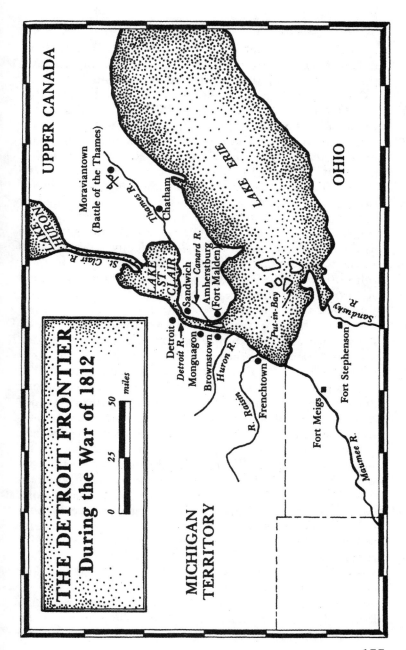

THE DETROIT FRONTIER
During the War of 1812

0   25   50
miles

UPPER CANADA

LAKE HURON

St. Clair R.

Moraviantown
(Battle of the Thames)

Thames R.

Chatham

LAKE ST. CLAIR

Sandwich
Canard R.
Amherstburg
Fort Malden

LAKE ERIE

OHIO

Detroit
Detroit R.
Monguagon
Brownstown
Huron R.

Put-in-Bay

Sandusky R.

Fort Stephenson

Frenchtown
R. Raisin

Fort Meigs

Maumee R.

MICHIGAN TERRITORY

repeatedly with Wyandot leaders, and by the time Hull reached Detroit most of the Wyandots at Brownstown seemed to embrace the British and Indian cause. Walk-in-the-Water brought his warriors to Amherstburg, where they participated in a series of councils at which the British explained their plans for defeating the Americans.

Upon arriving at Detroit, Hull made plans to invade Canada. Although he did not possess adequate supplies or equipment for a siege of Fort Malden (Amherstburg), Hull believed that a foray into Canada might capture valuable British provisions and enable his forces to gain a strategic advantage over the enemy. He also believed that many of the Canadians would rally to the American cause, and with this additional manpower he might gradually be able to gain control of the region. Although the British still could supply Amherstburg by water, Hull presumed he could surround and isolate the post, eventually forcing its surrender. Moreover, such a bold move on his part would intimidate the Indians and encourage them to leave the British.

Hull's army crossed over into Canada on July 12, seizing control of Sandwich, the settlement facing Detroit across the Detroit River. At first things went as Hull expected. The Canadian militia assigned to defend the village promptly retreated toward Amherstburg and the Americans landed almost unopposed. Colonel Duncan McArthur, one of Hull's subordinates, captured a large store of British supplies, and American forces overran the Canadian countryside as far south as the Canard River, where British forces still controlled the only bridges. Meanwhile, some of the Indians who earlier had joined with the British expressed second thoughts about their loyalties and began to desert into Michigan. Foremost among these turncoats was Walk-in-the-Water, who promptly led many of the Wyandots back to Brownstown.

Tecumseh tried to stop the desertions. Assisted by Main Poc, he met repeatedly with the warriors, but the surprise and initial success of the American invasion frightened many of the Indians and the majority followed Walk-in-the-Water to Michigan. There they met in council and informed

American agents that they would remain neutral in the conflict between the United States and Great Britain. Still, Tecumseh's efforts achieved some success. About three hundred of his most devoted followers remained in Canada, and Elliott admitted that only Tecumseh's personal influence "has kept them faithful—he [Tecumseh] has shown himself to be a determined character and a great friend to our government."

Hull soon lost the initiative. Although he still planned to attack Amherstburg, he lacked sufficient carriages to transport his artillery. Without artillery, he was unwilling to order his army to advance south of the Canard, and his hesitancy gave heart to his enemies. During mid-July a series of skirmishes took place along the Canard River, and in at least one of these engagements Tecumseh played a conspicuous part. On July 18 he led a party of warriors who fired upon an American reconnaissance patrol and who later attempted to ambush Colonel McArthur as the latter approached the Canard River seeking intelligence of British troop movements. American reinforcements drove Tecumseh and his warriors back across the river, but several days later another skirmish took place near Petit Côte, a nearby settlement, and several American troops were killed or wounded. Tecumseh's role in this second affair is unknown, but since he remained in the immediate region he probably was involved.

Other events also proved to Hull's disadvantage. On July 28 he learned that Fort Michillimackinac, the most strategic post in the upper Great Lakes, had fallen to the British and Indians. Located on an island in the Straits of Mackinac (the waterway connecting Lakes Huron and Michigan), the post had a garrison of 61 men commanded by Lieutenant Porter Hanks, an artillery officer. Isolated from other American garrisons, Hanks was unaware that war between the United States and Great Britain had erupted. Unfortunately for the Americans, British posts in the vicinity were better informed, and on July 17 Captain Charles Roberts, a British officer from nearby St. Joseph Island, surrounded the American fort with a force of over 600 British soldiers, traders, and Indians. Unprepared and horribly outnumbered, Hanks wisely struck his flag and surrendered.

The capitulation of Fort Michillimackinac had a profound impact on events in Upper Canada. The British force which captured the post included Indian agent Robert Dickson and at least 120 Sioux, Menominee, and other warriors from Wisconsin. Moreover, the fort sat astride the homeland of both the Ottawas and the Chippewas. With the post in British hands, many of these numerous northern tribesmen now rallied to the Crown, and Hull feared that thousands of hostile warriors soon would be descending upon him. Although news of the British victory brought jubilation from Tecumseh and other Indians at Amherstburg, it sent shock waves through the "neutral" Wyandots at Brownstown. Upon learning of the American defeat, Walk-in-the-Water again reassessed his relationship with the Long Knives. Wyandot messengers were dispatched to Tecumseh, and on August 2 the Shawnee accompanied a small force of British soldiers who crossed over into Michigan and, at Walk-in-the-Water's request, escorted the Wyandots safely back to Canada.

With the American invasion of Canada stalemated, the focus of the conflict shifted to Michigan. The redefection of Wyandots enabled British and Indian raiding parties to prey upon American commerce along the road from Detroit to Ohio, and by August 1812 that commerce was increasing. Although Hull had captured some British stores in Canada, Detroit still remained short of provisions. Attempting to remedy the situation, American officials in Ohio had sent a supply train commanded by Captain Henry Brush north toward Michigan. Meanwhile dispatches were forwarded to Hull, asking for a body of troops to escort the supply train from the River Raisin to Detroit. On August 4, 1812, Hull ordered Major Thomas Van Horne and 150 men to proceed to the River Raisin, rendezvous with the supply train, and escort it to its destination.

The Americans played into Tecumseh's hands. Accompanied by a small war party, he had remained near Brownstown after Walk-in-the-Water and the Wyandots returned to Canada, and on August 4 several of his warriors intercepted the dispatch rider carrying news of Van Horne's mission. Since his war party consisted of Matthew Elliott's son and only 23 warriors, Tecumseh sent a messenger to Amherstburg requesting additional forces. In response, on the following morning Colonel Henry Procter dispatched about 100 militia and regulars commanded by Brevet Major Adam Muir to Tecumseh's assistance. But Van Horne roused his men before dawn, and though they momentarily lost their way, they proceeded more rapidly than Muir had anticipated. Meanwhile, Tecumseh prepared an ambush near Brownstown, where heavy underbrush crowded upon the road as it forded a creek that flowed toward the Detroit River. Tecumseh also sent a handful of his warriors to monitor Van Horne's approach.

Events did not go as planned. Although Tecumseh's scouts tracked Van Horne's column, they could not resist attacking a ranger in advance of the main body, killing the man and taking his scalp. Their gunfire aroused the remainder of the Americans, who rushed forward, frightened the Indians away, and found their fallen comrade. As Van Horne was disposing of the body, a French Creole from the River Raisin arrived and warned the officer that Tecumseh and the British were planning to attack him near Brownstown.

But Van Horne ignored both the recent skirmish and the warning. Convinced that the attack was an isolated incident and the warning only an idle rumor, the officer foolhardily continued his march toward the River Raisin. At Brownstown, when Muir failed to appear, Tecumseh decided to attack the Americans on his own. Dividing his small party into two parts, he dispersed them in the thick underbrush on both sides of the road, facing the ford. Keeping the warriors concealed, Tecumseh waited until the Americans reached the opposite side of the creek before opening fire at almost pointblank range. The Indians' first volley threw Van Horne's men into confusion and the succeeding fire turned the confusion into panic. Since most of Van Horne's men were mounted, they reined their horses about and fled in a gallop toward Detroit. Some of the warriors followed them a short distance, but the Indians were on foot and were so vastly outnumbered that they were afraid to expose the actual size of their party. Although hardly a major encounter, the Battle of Brownstown was a humiliation to the Americans.

With only 24 warriors Tecumseh had turned back over 150 American troops and had achieved at least a great moral victory for the Indians. The Americans suffered 19 killed and 12 wounded. In contrast, Tecumseh lost only one warrior.

Four days later other scalps were taken. Since Brush's supply train still remained on the River Raisin, Hull dispatched another detachment of American troops to escort the provisions to Detroit. On August 7 Lieutenant Colonel James Miller and a force of over 600 regulars and militia paraded at Detroit, then confidently retraced Van Horne's route down the road toward Ohio. Spies brought news of the American plans and Procter rushed additional troops to the Brownstown region. Early on the morning of August 9, Muir assembled about 400 British troops and Indians north of Brownstown, where they anticipated Miller's advance, but this time the Americans moved so slowly that Muir decided to march out and meet them. During the early afternoon the British and Indians proceeded as far north as Monguagon, a small Wyandot village about five miles north of Brownstown. There scouts reported that the Americans were just over one mile away, and slowly advancing toward the British position. Muir instructed his men to conceal themselves in the underbrush on both sides of the road, while Tecumseh and his warriors took up positions on the left flank, in a field of standing corn along the west side of the roadway.

The afternoon was hot and humid, with almost no wind, and both the Indians and the British found the heat in their concealed and cramped quarters to be stifling. A small party of Potawatomis broke ranks and proceeded up the road, where they discovered and in turn were sighted by the approaching Americans. The Indians then fled back toward the cornfield, but unfortunately took new positions in the underbrush on the right side of the road, out of sight of the British. At about 4:00 P.M. the advance guard of Miller's column came into view and attracted the fire of the Indians. Upon hearing the gunfire, Miller ordered the rest of his men forward, and both the Indians and British opened a general fire upon the Americans. For once the Americans did not panic, formed regular ranks, and poured several volleys at their enemies. Although Tecumseh and the warriors in the cornfield held their positions, the American determination intimidated the Potawatomis, who decided to retreat down the right side of the road and join the British. But the British were unaware that any of their Indian allies had crossed the road, and when they spied men advancing toward their lines through the underbrush on their right flank, they mistook the warriors for Americans. The British then opened fire upon the Potawatomis, who returned the favor, so that in addition to the general battle another skirmish developed within the British position. To add to the confusion, Muir ordered his bugler to sound the call for a bayonet charge, but the signal somehow was misinterpreted by some of the British regulars, who thought Muir was ordering a retreat. Many of the British troops withdrew from their positions, and a general retreat became inevitable.

In the cornfield Tecumseh and his warriors stood firm, but as the British pulled back the Indians soon attracted all the fire from the Americans. Realizing that his allies had fallen back, Tecumseh also ordered a withdrawal. Yet the British and Indians retreated in different directions. Muir led his men southeast toward the Detroit River while Tecumseh and his followers retired on the opposite side of the road into the forest. The Americans elected to follow the Indians, and pursued them for some time before the warriors eluded their enemies.

Unlike Brownstown, the Americans claimed the Battle of Monguagon as a victory. Although their losses were heavier than their enemies' (18 killed and 64 wounded for the Americans; about 15 killed and 30 wounded for the British and Indians), the Americans had won the field. Ironically, however, Miller so feared another attack that he refused to advance any further without reinforcements. He sent messengers back to Hull asking for more men and rations, and when Hull had neither to spare, Miller remained at Monguagon. Afraid that the troops might be surrounded by the British, Hull then ordered Miller to retreat. On August 12, 1812, Miller struck camp and returned to Detroit. Brush and the supply column remained stranded at the River Raisin.

The Battle of Monguagon tooks its toll upon Tecumseh. In the retreat from the cornfield he was hit in the leg by American buckshot, and although the wound was not serious it was painful. With the other Indians he eventually returned to Amherstburg, where Elliott informed him that General Isaac Brock and a reinforcement of British troops were momentarily expected from the Niagara region. Brock arrived late on the evening of August 13 and soon met with Tecumseh. According to eyewitness accounts, the two men immediately liked each other, and Brock agreed to address the assembled Indians on the following morning.

At mid-morning on August 14, almost a thousand Indians met with the British commander, who assured them that he would lead them to victory over their enemies. Brock's bold, confident manner was well received by the warriors, who shouted their approval of Brock's promises. In reply, Tecumseh declared that the warriors were glad that their British Father had awakened from his slumber and had sent a soldier to lead his red children. They, in turn, were willing to "shed their last drop of blood" in their Father's service. Other Indian leaders echoed Tecumseh's sentiments, and after the conference Brock invited Tecumseh and several of the other war chiefs into his quarters, where he informed them of his plans to march against Detroit. According to one observer, Tecumseh was so pleased with the general's initiative that he paid Brock his ultimate compliment. After the general had outlined his proposals, Tecumseh turned to the other Indians and exclaimed, "This is a man!"

Captain John B. Glegg, Brock's aide-de-camp, who was present at the meetings between Brock and Tecumseh, recorded one of the most vivid descriptions of the Shawnee. According to Glegg, in August 1812 Tecumseh still was in the prime of his life, giving the impression of a man ten years younger.

> Tecumseh's appearance was very prepossessing; his figure light and finely proportioned; his age I imagined to be about five and thirty [he actually was forty-four]; in height, five feet nine or ten inches; his complexion, light copper; countenance, oval, with bright hazle eyes, beaming cheerfulness, energy,

and decision. Three small silver crowns, or coronets were suspended from the lower cartilage of his aquiline nose; and a large silver medallion of George the Third, which I believe his ancestor had received from Lord Dorchester, when governor-general of Canada, was attached to a mixed coloured wampum string, and hung around his neck. His dress consisted of a plain, neat uniform, tanned deer-skin jacket, with long trousers of the same material, the seams of both being covered with neatly cut fringe; and he had on his feet leather moccasins, much ornamented with work made from the dyed quills of the porcupine.

If optimism now reigned in the British and Indian camp, just the opposite infected the Americans. At Sandwich, Hull had continued to worry that the northern Indians might descend upon him from Michillimackinac, and he was disheartened by the inability of his troops to break through to Brush's supply column. Moreover, his continual delay in attacking Amherstburg had bred resentment in the ranks of the American army, and several of his subordinates, including Lewis Cass and Duncan McArthur, plotted to relieve him of his command. Although he had written back to Ohio asking for reinforcements, none were immediately available. Convinced that any further action in Canada was fruitless, on August 11 Hull ordered his army to abandon Sandwich and retreat across the river to Detroit. The withdrawal only intensified the resentment against him, but on August 14 he ordered McArthur and Cass to march to the River Raisin and rendezvous with Brush, who supposedly was again enroute up the river road. The combined forces were then to proceed toward Detroit.

While Hull vacillated at Detroit, Brock moved quickly at Amherstburg. Seizing the initiative, he occupied the deserted American positions in Sandwich, bringing artillery from Fort Malden to train upon Detroit. He also reorganized his troops, placing Tecumseh in command of all the Indians and ordering Procter to command the regular and militia forces. Leaving only a small garrison at Amherstburg, Brock moved the bulk of his army to a point just south of Sandwich, across the river from Spring Wells. Here the river was narrow, and though the position was close to Detroit it was out of range of American artillery. Aware that American morale had deteriorated, Brock sent a message to Hull on August 15 demanding that the Americans surrender Detroit. "It is far from my intention to enter into a war of extermination," Brock wrote, "but you must be aware, that the numerous body of Indians who have attached themselves to my troops will be beyond my control once the contest commences."

Brock neither expected Hull to surrender nor anticipated that Tecumseh's warriors would massacre the Americans, but he knew that Hull and his men were frightened of the Indians, and he believed that the threat of an Indian attack would further demoralize his enemies. As Brock expected, Hull refused his demands, and late in the afternoon of August 15 the British batteries began firing upon the American positions. Hull answered in kind, and although the barrages had little effect, the battle for Detroit was under way.

Determined to attack the American fort, Brock conferred with Tecumseh about the terrain across the river. Taking a piece of bark, the Shawnee sat down and drew a detailed map of Detroit and its environs. Brock then explained that he wanted the Indians to cross over to Michigan during the night and quietly surround the village. The British would follow in the morning, and while the British troops marched against the fort, Tecumseh and his warriors would attack the town from the opposite direction. Tecumseh agreed to the plan, and in a short time brought the Indians forward to lead them across the river. Impressed by the chief's strong leadership, Brock took off a scarlet sash he had been wearing and presented it to Tecumseh. The pleased Shawnee accepted the gift, but later gave it to Roundhead, a Wyandot war chief who had remained consistently loyal to the Indian movement.

The invasion went as planned. At dawn Tecumseh and the Indians infiltrated the northern and western approaches to Detroit while Brock's forces crossed from Canada and approached the Americans' southern perimeter. Meanwhile

the British batteries at Sandwich resumed their bombardment of the fort. Hull attempted to protect both the town
and the fort, but he had insufficient forces. Almost 400 of his
troops were absent with Cass and McArthur, leaving just
over 1,000 men to defend the American position and protect
a large number of women and children. In addition, many of
the Michigan militia proved unreliable, and as the British
started their advance some of the militia either deserted or
surrendered. Facing the Americans were well over 1,100
British regulars and militia, and about 600 Indians. Fearing
for the safety of his women and children, Hull decided to
surrender. Late in the morning he sent a messenger to Brock
asking for terms, and shortly after noon on August 16 the
American flag was lowered. The Redcoats marched into the
fort and Detroit belonged to the British.

Ironically, while Hull was surrendering, Cass and McArthur
were only three miles away on their return from another
unsuccessful attempt to join with Brush's supply column. On
the previous day they had proceeded as far south as the Huron
River, but when they did not encounter Brush they returned to
Detroit. Upon hearing the artillery barrage during the morning
of August 16, they sent out a scout, who incorrectly informed
them that the post already had fallen. Convinced that their
position was untenable, they then followed Hull's example
and laid down their arms. Meanwhile, unaware that he was
supposed to be marching toward Detroit, the hapless Brush
remained at the River Raisin.

Although Hull's fear of the Indians probably was justified,
Indian conduct following the surrender of Detroit posed only
minor problems. During the previous evening Tecumseh had
enjoined his warriors to treat all captives as prisoners of war.
Some horses were seized and a small amount of American
property was stolen, but no American civilians or military
personnel were harmed. Eventually all of the Americans
captured at Detroit were either paroled or transported to
Montreal, where they were exchanged for British troops
made prisoner by the Americans.

American civilians along the River Raisin fared less well.
Immediately after the fall of Detroit, Brock dispatched

Matthew Elliott to the River Raisin, where he demanded that Brush also surrender. Although Brush theoretically was under Hull's command and was now obligated to follow British orders, he refused to be intimidated and ordered his supply train back to Ohio. Brock then dispatched a force of regulars and Indians to march as far south as the rapids of the Maumee River to assert British control over north-western Ohio and to capture any supplies that Brush had abandoned.

Led by Major Peter Chambers and Tecumseh, the detachment consisted of a handful of British troops and a large party of Indians. They stopped first at the River Raisin, where the British destroyed an abandoned American blockhouse but where the Indians began to pillage the American settlement. The depredations were initiated by the Wyandots, former residents of the region, who surged into their American neighbors' cabins to seize anything of value. Fortunately, most of the settlers acquiesced in the plunder and only two lives were lost. Disgusted by the looting, both Tecumseh and Round-head attempted to stop it, but they were only partially successful. When order was finally restored the British and Indians proceeded on to the Maumee. There they burned another American blockhouse before returning to Canada.

Detroit was not the only post besieged by the British and Indians. In mid-August Potawatomi warriors near Chicago learned of American reverses in Michigan, and on August 15, as the American garrison prepared to evacuate Fort Dearborn, it was attacked by a large war party. The battle took place along the shores of Lake Michigan about two miles south of the fort, and when the fighting ended 53 of the 96 Americans were either dead or mortally wounded. The remainder were prisoners. Other Potawatomis, inspired by the fall of Detroit, congregated at Fort Wayne, and late in August they began to destroy abandoned American settlements in the region. On September 5 they launched an unsuccessful attack upon the post, then surrounded the stockade. Although the Americans were trapped they refused to surrender, and the Potawatomis sent messengers to Canada asking for additional men and British artillery.

In response, Henry Procter, who had succeeded Brock at Amherstburg, sent Major Adam Muir with three cannons, about 250 regulars and militia, and over 800 Indians to assist in the siege. Yet the expedition was difficult to organize and provision, and Muir's forces did not leave Canada until September 14, much later than anticipated. The Indians, whose numbers had increased with recent arrivals from Michillimackinac, were led by Tecumseh, Main Poc, Roundhead, and another Wyandot war chief, Split Log. But unknown to both the British and the Indians, on September 13, one day before the detachment set out, William Henry Harrison and an army of over 2,200 men had arrived at Fort Wayne from Ohio. Faced with such overwhelming numbers, the Potawatomis abandoned their siege and retreated into northern Indiana.

Muir's expedition had reached the Maumee River by the time news came of the American reinforcements. On September 25, while Muir paused to consider the intelligence, scouts rushed into camp with reports that most of Harrison's army, now commanded by General James Winchester, was proceeding down the Maumee Valley and would reach the camp within thirty-six hours. Although they were outnumbered, Muir and Tecumseh decided to fight. On the following day the British and Indians assembled their forces just above the mouth of the Auglaize and prepared to meet the Americans. But Winchester anticipated an attack and came on very slowly, and on the evening of September 26 he camped about eight miles upstream from the British and Indian position. Afraid that the larger American force might try to flank him during the night, Muir retreated downstream to the mouth of the Auglaize, where he attempted to reassemble his forces. But during the retreat the Indians scattered through the surrounding forests, and on the morning of September 27 some of them failed to rejoin the British. While Tecumseh searched for the missing warriors, Muir conferred with Roundhead over the best location to meet the Americans, but the two could come to no agreement, so once again Muir retreated a short distance down the river.

The repeated retreats disillusioned both the British and the Indians. Late in the afternoon Muir loaded his cannons on boats and shipped them down the Maumee toward Lake Erie. Although he still was willing to oppose Winchester's forces, he had become so apprehensive that he no longer would risk the capture of his artillery. The departure of the field pieces did little to instill confidence in the Indians. Late in the evening on September 27 they assured Muir that they would fight, but they met in council throughout the night, and shortly before dawn they informed the officer that large numbers of warriors had decided to return to Canada. Ignoring Tecumseh's pleas, most of the Ottawas and Chippewas from the Michillimackinac region abandoned the camp and retreated down the river. Tecumseh and Roundhead still wanted to meet the Americans, but Muir now believed his situation was hopeless. The chiefs assured him that Main Poc and other medicine men had experienced dreams assuring them of victory, but Muir was not moved. With the Americans advancing less than two miles away, Muir ordered a general retreat, and the British and Indians fled down the Maumee Valley. They arrived back at Detroit early in October.

The failure of Muir's expedition had an unsettling effect upon Tecumseh. He had admired and respected Brock, but in September the general had been forced to return to the Niagara frontier to prepare for an expected invasion by the Americans. With Brock's departure, Colonel Henry Procter had assumed command of British forces in the Detroit region. Unfortunately, Procter lacked Brock's decisiveness and had little rapport with the tribesmen. To Tecumseh and many of the other Indian leaders, Muir's retreat was indicative of the change in command and did not bode well for the warriors. Late in October they received news which only added to their apprehension. On October 13, 1812, General Isaac Brock was killed while leading a counterattack against the Americans at Queenstown. The report saddened Tecumseh, and in November when Matthew Elliott led a large party of Indians back to the Maumee on a foraging expedition, the Shawnee remained at Detroit. In addition to his depression over Brock's death, the gunshot wound he had received at Monguagon still plagued him, and he needed some time to recover.

* * *

While Tecumseh fought the Long Knives near Detroit, the Prophet remained on the Tippecanoe. Information about the declaration of war first reached the Wabash in early July, but Tenskwatawa took pains not to alarm the Americans. He seemed genuinely frightened that the government might launch another expedition against his village, and during mid-July he traveled to Fort Wayne, where he remained for ten days, pleading his friendship for the United States. He presented Indian agent Benjamin Stickney with a large belt of white wampum and assured him that the Indians at Prophetstown would remain at peace. Although the British had asked him to take up the tomahawk, Tenskwatawa declared, he would not listen to them. He even promised Stickney he would send to Canada for Tecumseh, so that both he and his brother could attend a government-sponsored council with friendly Indians in Ohio.

Stickney accepted the Prophet's protestations but remained skeptical of the man's sincerity. Such skepticism was well taken. Even while he remained camped at Fort Wayne, the Prophet secretly received a messenger from Tecumseh at Amherstburg. Carrying a huge wampum belt, painted red, to symbolize "the King's Great Broad Axe," the messenger called the tribes to prepare for war. Tecumseh's instructions were to rally the warriors at Prophetstown and to send all the women and children west to the Winnebago villages in Illinois and Wisconsin. The warriors were then to attack Vincennes, and if they failed to capture the town they were to follow their families to the west. Eventually Tecumseh would join them and they would continue their fight against the Long Knives.

Yet Tecumseh's instructions, issued shortly after Hull invaded Canada, assumed that the British and Indians would remain on the defensive. During August, as news reached the Tippecanoe of the continued British and Indian successes,

Tenskwatawa again took matters in his own hands. Rather than retreat to the Winnebagos, he prepared a scheme to attack and capture Fort Harrison, at modern Terre Haute. On September 4, in an ill-conceived plan, a war party of Kickapoos and Winnebagos from Prophetstown attempted to gain entrance to the fort through a ruse. When they failed, they set fire to the stockade and fired upon the garrison. Led by Captain Zachary Taylor, the Americans extinguished the flames and repulsed the attack. Most of the war party then returned to the Tippecanoe, although some of the warriors rode south into southern Indiana, where they killed several settlers near the small village of Pigeon Roost.

The failure of the attack upon Fort Harrison disheartened the Prophet, and he was further unnerved by events at Fort Wayne. Shortly after Harrison's arrival broke the Potawatomi siege of that post, Harrison sent part of his army in a wide sweep through northeastern Indiana, destroying Indian villages and burning cornfields. Prophetstown escaped the forays, but the attacks illustrated the village's continued vulnerability, and during October most of the Winnebagos and Kickapoos returned to their homes in Illinois. His manpower depleted. Tenskwatawa hid much of his food supply in the surrounding forest, and late in October he led his remaining followers up the Tippecanoe Valley into northwestern Indiana, where they formed winter camps amidst the swamps between the Iroquois and Kankakee rivers.

The Prophet's retreat came none too soon. In mid-November over 1,200 Kentucky militia marched up the Wabash and burned all the Indian villages clustered near the mouth of the Tippecanoe. Led by General Samuel Hopkins, the militia scoured the surrounding forests, where they discovered and confiscated Tenskwatawa's hidden provisions. In anger the Prophet sent a war party to harass his enemies. On November 22 the warriors ambushed and killed eighteen Kentuckians, but Hopkins's army was far too large to confront and the Indians were forced to flee back up the Tippecanoe.

The warriors returned unscathed, but their skirmish was a hollow victory. Once again the Prophet and his followers found themselves with winter approaching and almost no provisions. Faced with the bleak prospect of an extended period without food, Tenskwatawa decided to abandon his camp and seek sustenance from his British Father. In mid-December he led his few remaining followers to Canada.

8

Death on the Thames

The Prophet's arrival at Amherstburg must have caught Tecumseh by surprise. By December 1812 his leg finally had mended and he was planning to leave Canada. His departure had Procter's blessing. Although the British had accumulated large stores of supplies, they were hard pressed to feed the multitude of Indians who now flocked to the Detroit region. To lessen their burden, they suggested that many of the warriors return to their home villages and reassemble in the spring, when a major campaign against the Americans would be started. In the meantime, the warriors could carry some provisions back to their homes, but they should supplement the foodstuffs with hunting. During December some of the tribesmen from northern Indiana and southern Michigan followed the British advice and returned to their villages. Tecumseh planned to join them, and in the spring bring them back to Amherstburg.

Tenskwatawa had little interest in Tecumseh's mission. Since his sole purpose in journeying to Canada was to seek British food and protection, the Prophet was reluctant to return to Indiana. Yet, after the debacle at Tippecanoe, he was even more reluctant to oppose his brother, and following some discussion he agreed to accompany Tecumseh westward. The two Shawnees, attended by Main Poc and a party of warriors, left the Detroit region late in December and returned to the Indian country between the Wabash and Lake Michigan. There they spent the winter of 1813, evidently traveling among the Indians' winter camps and preparing their followers for the coming offensive.

Since both Tecumseh and the Prophet were absent from eastern Michigan, they took no part in the Battle of Frenchtown. Following the retreat of Tecumseh and Muir from the Maumee River, Winchester slowly proceeded down the Maumee Valley and eventually established a camp near the rapids. In January 1813 he received reports from American settlers that there was only a token British force at the River Raisin. Disobeying Harrison's orders, Winchester led about a thousand regulars and militia to Frenchtown, a small village on the river. Although the Americans easily routed the small detachment of British and Indians they found there, on January 22 Procter and Roundhead counterattacked and the Americans were defeated. Winchester was captured, and upon Procter's promise that prisoners would be treated generously, the American officer ordered his troops to surrender.

But Procter failed to keep his promise. Following the surrender, several of the Indians murdered some American prisoners and the British officers failed to intercede. On the next day, other Americans, wounded in the earlier action, also fell victims to the tribesmen's vengeance. Although Procter later condemned the killings, he failed to prevent them, and the survivors blamed both Procter and Matthew Elliott for the slaughter.

While Procter, Roundhead, and Winchester battled on the River Raisin, Tecumseh traveled among the tribes of Illinois and Indiana. He assured them that in the spring the British would supply them with arms and ammunition so that they again could make war upon the Long Knives. In March he returned to Amherstburg, where he informed Procter that he would soon bring several hundred warriors to Canada. According to Tecumseh, the Indians were currently assembling with the Prophet on the upper reaches of the Tippecanoe, but they remained short of food and needed provisions to make their journey. In late March he returned to Indiana, collected his followers, and started toward Amherstburg. En route the Indians met a small train of pack horses laden with food that Procter had dispatched from the Detroit region. Tecumseh and the Prophet arrived in Canada on April 16, accompanied by a large party of western Indians.

In Ohio, Harrison also was collecting his forces. Following Winchester's defeat, he advanced to the rapids of the Maumee, where he began the construction of a new post to be used as a base for the liberation of Detroit and the invasion of Canada. The stockade, Fort Meigs, near the present town of Maumee, was completed in April.

Aware of Harrison's intentions, Procter was eager to attack Fort Meigs before the Americans received any reinforcements. While awaiting Tecumseh and the western warriors, he mustered his forces and made preparations to march to the Maumee. When Tecumseh arrived, the Shawnee met with the many Indians now assembled at Amherstburg and again enjoined them to attack the Long Knives. After a series of celebrations the warriors donned their paint, and on April 24 the British and Indians left Canada for the Maumee.

Although ships carried the regulars, militia, and artillery across Lake Erie, Tecumseh and almost twelve hundred warriors traveled overland, skirting the western end of the lake and arriving at Swan Creek, near the mouth of the Maumee River, on April 27, 1813. There they rendezvoused with Procter's forces, and during the morning the British and Indians met in council to discuss their plans for attacking Fort Meigs. Both Procter and Tecumseh were confident of success. Not only did their combined followers outnumber the Americans, but Procter had brought considerable artillery, including two 24-pounders, a howitzer, mortars, and several smaller cannons. In addition, two shallow-drafted gunboats had accompanied him from Canada, and they could ascend the Maumee as far as Fort Meigs. Harrison might be protected by log walls, but the stockade could not withstand a prolonged bombardment. Moreover, Procter's artillery officers informed him that they could lob explosive shells inside the pallisade, creating havoc among the defenders. While the British artillery shelled the fort, Tecumseh and his warriors would surround the stockade and harass the garrison with small-arms fire. They would prevent the Americans from fleeing and also intercept any reinforcements. Procter was so sure of victory that as the council ended he made a promise to the Prophet. When the war was over, he said, the Prophet and his followers would be free to establish new homes in eastern Michigan. Harrison, if he survived the battle, would be Tecumseh's personal prisoner.

On the next day the British and Indians advanced to the ruins of old Fort Miami, on the opposite bank and about two miles downstream from Fort Meigs, where they established a permanent encampment. On horseback, Tecumseh and Procter then reconnoitered the American position, drawing some fire from one of Harrison's cannons but escaping unharmed. Procter ordered his engineers to construct two batteries: one just opposite Fort Meigs on the northern shore of the river, and another on the south bank on a hill overlooking the fort. Rainy weather hampered the emplacement of the guns, but by May 1 the artillery was in position. Meanwhile, other omens seemed favorable. A war party of Winnebagos and Kickapoos attacked a herd of American livestock tethered under the walls of the fort, killing many of the hogs and oxen and stampeding the horses, and on April 30 four Ottawa boys (the oldest only fourteen) intercepted a small party of Americans carrying dispatches from the Sandusky region. Although the Americans outnumbered the boys, the Ottawas fired from ambush and the Americans promptly fled, abandoning their documents. The dispatches proved to be of little military value, but the rout of Americans by the youngsters brought jubilation to the Indians.

But Harrison, unknown to Tecumseh and Procter, was making preparations of his own. Aware of the British intentions, Harrison used the three days while Procter was positioning his batteries to construct a series of earth walls or traverses inside the American stockade. Designed to limit the effectiveness of exploding bombs and artillery shells, the traverses eventually crisscrossed the American compound and offered considerable protection to the garrison. Since Harrison masked his labors with rows of tents, the British were unaware of the traverses until the morning of May 1, when they opened fire upon the pallisade.

Harrison's strategy proved effective. Although the British bombarded Fort Meigs for four days, they caused little significant damage. The American soldiers took cover in the trenches excavated to produce the traverses, and they covered their powder magazine with several feet of soil to protect it. The British then positioned two more batteries, but to little purpose, and though the Indians kept up a steady fire at any American foolish enough to show himself above the walls, they too proved ineffective. In the four days of bombardment, with the expenditure of considerable ammunition, the British and Indians killed only six Americans, and many tribesmen complained about the uselessness of the British batteries. Still hoping that Harrison might capitulate, Procter sent a messenger into the fort on May 4 to demand surrender. Undaunted, Harrison replied that, if Procter captured Fort Meigs, "it would be under circumstances that will do him more honor than a thousand surrenders."

Harrison was confident that his men could withstand the siege, and he had other reasons for optimism. He knew that reinforcements were en route from Kentucky. During April General Green Clay and over 1,200 Kentucky militia had marched north across Ohio to the Auglaize, where they constructed barges and floated down that stream to its junction with the Maumee. Late on May 4 they had proceeded downstream to within a few miles of Fort Meigs, but halted to await daylight before descending through the rapids to the stockade. When messengers brought news of their approach, Harrison sent several men in a canoe up the river in the darkness with instructions for Clay. He should descend the Maumee in the morning, but with his force divided into two detachments. One party should first land opposite the fort, seize and spike the British cannons, then retreat across the river before the British and Indians could counterattack. The second party should land upstream, attack any warriors who surrounded the stockade on the south bank of the river, and then break through to Fort Meigs. Meanwhile, Harrison planned to lead a sortie to capture and destroy the British battery on the hill just east of the fort.

Clay followed Harrison's instructions, but the outcome was disastrous. Early on the morning of May 5, Clay's force traversed the rapids, and Lieutenant Colonel William Dudley and almost 800 men landed across the river from the post, captured the British cannons, and attempted to spike them. The attack so surprised the small party of British and Indians at that location that the latter offered little resistance. Elated over their success, the Kentuckians refused to retreat and ran pell-mell after the Indians, who fled through the forest toward the British and Indian encampment. Aroused by the gunfire, Tecumseh and Major Adam Muir rallied their forces in the camp and rushed forward to meet the Americans. Indeed, as Dudley's men proceeded through the trees they encountered growing Indian resistance, until they paused, hesitated, then began to fall back toward their landing. As Tecumseh and his warriors pressed forward, the American retreat became a rout, and many of the Kentuckians threw their weapons aside and fled madly toward the river. By that time another body of British troops had marched rapidly up the river, recaptured the cannons, and seized the American boats. As Dudley's men appeared on the river bank, now hotly pursued by the Indians, they found their escape blocked. A few managed to snatch some of the boats and paddle frantically across the river, but most were either killed or captured. Of the 800 men who had landed, only about 150 reached the safety of Fort Meigs.

While Dudley's men were chasing the Indians through the forest, Clay and the remainder of his forces landed above the fort on the south bank of the river. There they encountered some Indian resistance, but with assistance from Harrison's sortie they scattered their enemy and reached Fort Meigs in safety.

Across the river, the survivors of Dudley's defeat faced less favorable circumstances. After their capture they were marched downstream toward the Indian encampment. On the way they were harassed by the warriors, and many of the prisoners were stripped of their clothing and other possessions. But the worst was yet to come. At the ruins of the old British fort, the Indians formed two long lines stretching out from the gate, and they forced their captives to run the gauntlet. Although some of the prisoners were felled by musket fire or tomahawks as they passed between the Indian lines, the majority reached the fort and temporary refuge.

Unfortunately, however, their safety was short-lived, for some of the Indians followed the Americans into the enclosure and began a random slaughter. British officers nearby offered half-hearted protests, but really did little to stop the killings.

At first Tecumseh was ignorant of the carnage. He had remained with Muir at the recaptured British battery, and he learned of the abuse only after the prisoners had been forced to run the gauntlet. Angered, he seized a horse and rode quickly toward the encampment, evidently joined en route by Matthew Elliott. When he arrived at the fort, almost forty Americans were dead and the killings still continued. Galloping through the gates, he ordered the warriors to sheathe their knives and condemned them for cowardice. The slaughter ended as the guilty parties withdrew, shamed by Tecumseh. According to the American survivors, he then lashed out at Procter and other British officers who had failed to intercede in behalf of the prisoners.

Ironically, Dudley's defeat proved costly for the British. At first the British and Indian victory seemed so substantial that many of the warriors believed their enemies were vanquished. Harrison's army had been beaten and the Long Knives would now be forced to withdraw up the Maumee Valley. Of course the Americans still occupied Fort Meigs, but they no longer constituted a threat to British and Indian security. Besieging fortified positions was tedious, and the warriors had had their fill of it. Moreover, the capture of Dudley's boats had proven an extra bonus. The vessels were loaded with provisions, and in the aftermath of the victory the Indians plundered large quantities of weapons and clothing. Burdened with their new-found wealth, the Indians began to desert the encampment. Although Tecumseh urged them to remain, by May 7 most of the warriors had departed. Procter's Canadian militia also wished to withdraw, so on May 9 the British lifted the siege and sailed for Canada. The first Battle of Fort Meigs had ended.

Tecumseh, the Prophet (who had watched the battle from a safe distance), and about forty other warriors accompanied the British back to Amherstburg. During June the Shawnee brothers established a village on the Huron River, south of Detroit, where they and other Indians settled as a defense against any American incursions into the region. Yet the concept of remaining on the defensive troubled the Shawnee chief. He had joined with the British not to defend Canada but to secure permanent tenancy of Indian lands in Ohio, Indiana, and Illinois. As long as Procter remained at Amherstburg, Harrison and other American leaders would be free to build their forces in these regions. Unlike the British, the Indians were fighting for their homelands. If the war remained a stalemate, they would lose. Tecumseh needed a series of decisive victories if the Indians were to dictate terms to the Americans.

Procter was much more cautious. Meeting with Tecumseh at Amherstburg, he pointed out that he once again was short of provisions. American raiders on Lake Erie had disrupted his supply lines, and without supplies he was at the mercy of the Americans. Indeed, control of the lake was critical, for if the Americans could cross Lake Erie they might place an invasion force between Amherstburg and Niagara, effectively cutting off the Detroit frontier from the rest of Canada. British spies reported that the Americans were building a new naval force at Presque Isle, on the Pennsylvania shore of the lake, and the British made plans to attack the shipyard; but during the summer of 1813 changes in the British command created indecision, and the American shipwrights continued unmolested.

In early July the Indians forced Procter's hand. British agent Robert Dickson and almost 600 Indians arrived at Amherstburg from Michillimackinac, and they were eager to strike the Americans. Procter realized that these western warriors had to be utilized or they would become discontented and return to their homes. Moreover, they would be easier to feed in the field, where they could forage for part of their food. As a prelude to an attack upon Presque Isle, Procter proposed that the British and Indians move against American settlements near Sandusky. If they were successful, they might then combine with British naval units and attack the American shipyards. But Tecumseh and the other Indian leaders disagreed. Still smarting from the withdrawal after Dudley's defeat, Tecumseh and Roundhead argued for another attack upon Fort Meigs. Procter countered that he no longer had adequate vessels to transport his siege guns, but Tecumseh claimed they would not be needed. The Indians had their own plan for defeating the Long Knives.

Thus in mid-July a small force of British regulars and about 1,000 Indians again left Canada for Fort Meigs. Crossing Lake Erie in small gunboats and canoes, they were discovered by American scouts, who warned the garrison. During the night of July 20 the British and Indians ascended the river, and by dawn on the following morning they had surrounded the pallisade. This time Procter made no attempt to use his artillery. Although he had brought several six-pounders, he fired only a few rounds at the stockade. A small party of warriors did surprise some American pickets stationed outside the fort, and killed six of them, but neither the British nor the Indians made any sustained assault on the post. Meanwhile, General Green Clay, who now commanded the fort, remained optimistic. Since the earlier siege Fort Meigs had been both reinforced and resupplied.

On July 23 Tecumseh initiated his plan to lure the garrison out of the pallisade. Early in the morning he led almost 300 Indians up the opposite side of the river, in full view of the fort, on an apparent raid toward American posts on the Auglaize. During the next two days, while some warriors kept up a sporadic fire at the garrison, most of the other Indians secretly joined Tecumseh and his party in the forest, about two miles south of the stockade. Tecumseh knew that reports of the siege had now reached American officials, and that Clay expected reinforcements would soon arrive from other posts in Ohio. Tecumseh hoped to stage a sham battle, within hearing of the fort, to trick Clay into believing that these reinforcements had been ambushed. Tecumseh speculated that Clay would then order a major sortie to assist the reinforcements, and the Indians would be able to surround Clay's men in the forest. If large numbers of Americans could be killed or captured, Fort Meigs would be forced to surrender.

Tecumseh sprang his trap late in the afternoon on July 26, but the snare came up empty. The ruse itself was well planned and executed. Tecumseh assembled his men along the Sandusky road, as it passed through the forest about a mile from the fort, and instructed them to sound their war cries and fire their muskets. The warriors even moved up and down the road to indicate that the battle was surging back and forth, but the Americans refused to leave the stockade. When the "battle" started, many of the junior officers and enlisted men urged Clay to send assistance, but the general suspected chicanery. Unknown to Tecumseh, an American messenger who knew that no reinforcements were in the vicinity had slipped through the Indian lines early in the morning and entered Fort Meigs. Refusing to take the bait, Clay ordered his men to remain inside the stockade and after about an hour the sham battle ended. Bitterly disappointed, Tecumseh led his warriors back to their encampment. Even the weather seemed to mirror the Indians' mood, for as the warriors retreated through the forest they were deluged by a violent thunderstorm.

Some of the Indians wanted to return to Canada, but Tecumseh refused to admit that the mission had failed. After a conference with Procter, a decision was made to attack Fort Stephenson, a small post on the Sandusky River. Unlike Fort Meigs, Fort Stephenson contained only a small garrison, and both Procter and Tecumseh believed it could not withstand an assault by the combined British and Indian forces. On July 28, abandoning the camp on the Maumee, the British troops set sail for Lake Erie and Sandusky Bay. Tecumseh and the Indians traveled overland, and both parties rendezvoused near Fort Stephenson on August 1, 1813.

The American stockade on the Sandusky River was so small that Harrison earlier had ordered it abandoned, but due to some confusion over the orders it remained garrisoned by about 200 men, commanded by Major George Croghan. Although only twenty-one years old, Croghan made up in stubbornness what he lacked in experience, and he was determined to hold the post or die trying. During the afternoon of August 1, Procter sent Matthew Elliott, Major Peter

Chambers, and Robert Dickson under a flag of truce to demand the fort's surrender. They were met by Lieutenant Edmund Shipp, who conveyed Croghan's refusal. When Dickson warned that, if the Americans resisted, the Indians might kill the survivors, Shipp, again speaking for Croghan, replied that if the British captured Fort Stephenson there would *be* no American survivors. The two parties then retired to their respective positions, and the British artillery began firing at the fort.

The barrage continued throughout the night and most of the following morning, but it had little effect. Although the stockade was not large, it recently had been renovated and Procter's six-pounders were not heavy enough to breach the walls. Frustrated, Procter ordered a frontal attack late in the afternoon. The British regulars, supported by the Indians, would advance to the moat surrounding the pallisade and would hack through the stockade with axes. The remaining regulars and their Indian allies would then pour through the breach and overwhelm the garrison. By 5:00 P.M. the attack was underway and the leading British troops, hidden by dense smoke, plunged into the dry moat, carrying ladders and axes. So far the British advance had been unopposed, and Procter assumed that the Americans' attention was focused upon a party of Indians who had kept up a steady fire of the opposite side of the stockade. Tecumseh and other warriors supporting the assault followed in the wake of the regulars, awaiting the breach in the pallisade.

Both Procter and Tecumseh misjudged their adversary. Croghan was well aware of the British advance, but he ordered his men to remain concealed and not to fire until they received a specific command. Meanwhile, the Americans brought their single cannon, a six-pounder loaded with grapeshot, to bear on the moat where the British axemen now were scrambling up their ladders. Finally, at a signal from Croghan, the Americans opened fire and the British regulars in the moat were devastated. Caught in the moat without any protection, they were mowed down like wheat in a hailstorm. Those who survived the initial volley scrambled up the opposite side of the moat and fled back toward safety, while their comrades fired from the smoke, attempting to cover the flight.

For the most part, Tecumseh and the Indians remained completely out of the action. They were more than willing to risk their lives fighting from the protection of the forest, but they considered an open advance upon a well-defended position to be suicidal. European and American commanders were willing to take such calculated losses since their ties to their troops were only of a professional nature, but among the tribesmen many members of the war parties were relatives or life-long friends. For Tecumseh and other war chiefs, there was no disassociation from their "troops." Calculated losses in pursuit of offensive objectives were always too high if those losses included one's sons or brothers.

Regardless of the Indians' participation or lack of it, the battle was disastrous for the British. Fort Stephenson remained unscathed and the Americans lost only one killed and seven wounded. In contrast, the British suffered almost 100 casualties. Indian losses were very small, but the psychological impact of two consecutive failures took a heavy toll upon the tribesmen. Following the battle Procter assembled his forces downstream from the fort and loaded the British survivors on the gunboats. Tragically, his army was now so diminished that he did not have sufficient men to sail all his gunboats back to Amherstburg, and he was forced to leave one of the vessels behind. Late in the evening of August 2, the British set sail for Canada and the Indians retreated overland toward the west. Many of the western warriors failed to return with Tecumseh to Amherstburg. Dejected over their lack of success, large numbers of Sacs, Foxes, Menominees, and Chippewas deserted the British and Indian cause and returned to their homelands.

While some warriors were leaving Tecumseh, others were joining the Americans. Earlier in the war several of Black Hoof's people had served as scouts for the American cause, but in August 1813, following the unsuccessful British and Indian attacks upon Fort Meigs and Fort Stephenson, about 200 friendly Shawnees, Delawares, and Wyandots from Tarhe's town met with Harrison in Ohio and promised to assist him against his enemies. Intent upon splitting the British and Indian alliance, Harrison late in August sent a party of friendly Wyandots and Senecas to meet with the Wyandots at Brownstown, offering them an opportunity to make peace with the United States. Harrison believed that if Walk-in-the-Water's people defected, many other Indians would follow.

Although Harrison intended his speech to be read privately to the Wyandots, when the messengers arrived at Brownstown they found Tecumseh, the Prophet, and even Matthew Elliott in attendance at the council. The American Wyandots, speaking for Harrison, informed their kinsmen that the American navy was ready to leave Presque Isle and would soon be loose upon Lake Erie. They charged that the British were deceiving their allies by not informing them of recent British reverses which threatened the Crown's position in Upper Canada. Reminding their audience that Tecumseh and Procter had repeatedly failed to capture American posts in Ohio, the American Wyandots asked their kinsmen to "take pity on [your] women and children" and to "step forward and take him [Harrison] by the hand."

Harrison's emissaries were rebuffed by Roundhead. Speaking for the British Indians, the Wyandot war chief chided the Americans for remaining in their forts. "We are happy to learn your Father [Harrison] is coming out of his hole as he has been like a ground hog under ground and will save us much trouble in traveling to meet him." He advised the American Wyandots "to remain at home and take no part in this war." Meanwhile Elliott furnished them with copies of dispatches illustrating recent British victories on Lake Champlain; they should give the documents with Elliott's "compliments" to Harrison. Since all the Indians seemed to reject the American proposals, the council ended and Tecumseh, Roundhead, and Elliott left the Wyandot village.

They should have remained at Brownstown. After Tecumseh's departure Walk-in-the-Water secretly informed the American messengers that he was willing to abandon both the British and Tecumseh. Aware that the British now seemed on the defensive, Walk-in-the-Water anticipated an American invasion of Canada, and if such a campaign occurred he intended to support the stronger side. According to the Wyandot, if Harrison and a large army advanced up the western end of Lake Erie, he would advise his warriors to desert the British and assist the Long Knives. Moreover, if he were sure of an American victory, he promised to seize several strategic locations and hold them until relieved by Harrison's forces. Pleased with the promises, the American Wyandots carried the message back to Harrison.

A political realist, Walk-in-the-Water reflected the growing pessimism in the Indian camp. Although large numbers of warriors remained near Amherstburg, most were aware of a subtle change in their British allies. Procter still remained reluctant to initiate offensive operations, but his reticence now seemed tinged more by fear than by caution. Recent reverses along the Niagara frontier threatened his lifeline with Montreal, and his repeated requests for more men and supplies remained unanswered. He was hard pressed to feed the warriors still encamped near Amherstburg, and he needed additional artillery if he hoped to defend Upper Canada. By late August Procter realized that he had lost the opportunity to attack the fledgling American fleet as it lay at Presque Isle, but he pinned his hopes on the *Detroit*, a large brig just launched at Amherstburg. The British desperately needed a naval victory on Lake Erie, for Harrison was amassing an army for the invasion of Canada, and open supply lines were essential for British defenses.

While Procter waited in Canada, shipwrights at Presque Isle completed the construction of the American fleet, and early in August 1813 Captain Oliver H. Perry launched his vessels on Lake Erie. Since Perry was woefully short of experienced sailors, he spent about a fortnight training his crews, but during the last week of August he suddenly appeared off Barclay's Point at the mouth of the Detroit River. The American fleet remained near the point for about two days, while Tecumseh and many of the Indians paddled over to Bois Blanc Island to observe the warships. Procter earlier had boasted of British naval power and Tecumseh expected

Captain Robert H. Barclay, commander of the British fleet at Amherstburg, to challenge Perry. When the British remained in port, Tecumseh crossed back to Amherstburg and inquired why the British fleet had failed to attack the Americans. Procter replied that, although the *Detroit* was finished, she was lacking in armaments, and until the ship was completely rigged with artillery she would stay under the protective guns of Fort Malden. Tecumseh relayed the information to the other Indians, but as Perry's squadron withdrew into Lake Erie, Procter's influence over the Indians further deteriorated. From Tecumseh's perspective, the Americans had thrown down the gauntlet and Procter had refused to accept it.

In September the British finally answered the American challenge. Although his fleet still was undermanned, Barclay persuaded Procter to arm the *Detroit* with part of the artillery from Fort Malden. On September 9, 1813, the British sailed down the Detroit River into Lake Erie, and one day later they encountered Perry's ships near Put-in-Bay, among the Bass Islands. After a naval battle lasting three hours, the Americans emerged victorious. The entire British fleet was either sunk or captured, and control of Lake Erie now belonged to the Long Knives.

Tecumseh was aware that a naval battle was in progress, and like many other warriors he proceeded to the Point Pelée region. There the Indians could hear the artillery and could see the clouds of powder smoke which drifted north over the lake, but they could not ascertain which side won the battle. Afterwards they received no official information regarding the battle's outcome, but the failure of the British fleet to return to Canadian waters seemed ominous. Moreover, on September 12 some of the warriors reported that Procter appeared downcast, and had ordered his aides to assemble several trunks, barrels, and other packing containers.

Procter learned of Perry's victory on September 12, and immediately decided to abandon Amherstburg and retreat toward Niagara. Since the British had lost control of Lake Erie, his decision was a wise one, but it was poorly implemented. Instead of immediately informing Tecumseh of his intentions, Procter asked Matthew Elliott to call the Indians together in council on September 18, when he would advise them about future British policy. Meanwhile, he ordered his soldiers to dismantle parts of Fort Malden, and he packed many of his personal possessions in crates and barrels, obviously intending to ship them east. Procter's actions infuriated Tecumseh, who met with Elliott and demanded to know of the British plans. The substance of their conversation remains unknown, but since Elliott and Procter had often quarreled, it seems doubtful that the agent defended the officer. Indeed, by September 1813 Procter's haughtiness had so alienated many of his subordinate officers that these soldiers criticized their commander in the presence of Tecumseh and other Indians.

On September 18, 1813, Procter met with the Indians in council and formally informed them of Perry's victory. He also announced that Harrison and a large army were preparing to invade Canada. In response, he proposed to abandon Detroit, Sandwich, and Amherstburg and retreat to the Niagara frontier, where he would join with other British forces. If Tecumseh and the other Indians would accompany him, they would be well supplied and could further assist the British in the defense of Canada.

Tecumseh's reply ranks as one of the most inspiring speeches ever delivered by an American Indian. Clad in buckskin, and wearing an ostrich plume in his hair, he stood before the assembled British and Indians with a wampum belt in his hands. Turning to Procter, he stared at the officer, then commanded:

> Father, listen to your children! You have them now all before you.

> The war before this, our British father gave the hatchet to his red children, when our chiefs were alive. They are now dead. In that war, our father was thrown on his back by the Americans, and our father took them by the hand without our knowledge; and we are afraid that our father will do so again at this time.

> Summer before last, when I came forward with my red brethren, and was ready to take up the hatchet in favor of our

British father, we were told not to be in a hurry, that he had not yet determined to fight the Americans.

Listen! You told us, at that time, to bring forward our families to take this place; and we did so; and you promised to take care of them, and that they should want for nothing, while the men would go and fight the enemy. That we need not trouble ourselves about the enemy's garrison; that we knew nothing about them, and that our father would attend to that part of the business. You also told your red children, that you would take care of your garrison here, which made our hearts glad.

Listen! When we were last to the Rapids, it is true we gave you little assistance. It is hard to fight people who live like ground hogs.

Father listen! Our fleet has gone out; we know they have fought; we have heard the great guns; but we know nothing of what has happened to our father with one arm [Barclay]. Our ships have gone one way and we are very much astonished to see our father tying up everything and preparing to run away the other, without letting his red children know what his intentions are. You always told us to remain here and take care of our lands; it made our hearts glad to hear that was your wish. Our great father, the king, is our head, and you represent him. You always told us, that you would never draw your foot off British ground; but now we see you are drawing back, and we are sorry to see our father doing so without seeing the enemy. We must compare our father's conduct to a fat animal, that carries its tail upon its back, but when affrightened, he drops it between his legs and runs off. [Here Tecumseh's speech was momentarily interrupted by laughter from both the warriors and the ranks of British soldiers.]

Listen Father! The Americans have not yet defeated us by land; neither are we sure that they have done so by water; we therefore, wish to remain here, and fight our enemy, if they should make an appearance. If they defeat us, we will then retreat with our father.

At the battle of the Rapids last war, the Americans certainly defeated us; and when we retreated to our father's fort at that place the gates were shut against us. We were afraid that it would now be the case, but instead of that we now see our British father preparing to march out of his garrison.

Father! You have got the arms and ammunition which our great father sent for his red children. If you have an idea of going away, give them to us, and you may go and welcome.

As for us, our lives are in the hands of the Great Spirit. We are determined to defend our lands, and if it be his will we wish to leave our bones upon them.

Tecumseh's speech had an electrifying impact upon his audience. Although Procter remained momentarily dumbfounded, the Indians erupted in a frenzy of war cries, grabbing their weapons and brandishing them at the British. While Elliott intervened to restore order, Procter asked to meet again in three days to answer Tecumseh's speech. Tecumseh agreed and the council ended.

During the next three days Procter and Elliott met repeatedly, attempting to formulate a policy acceptable to both sides. Obviously, both men were deeply concerned over their relations with the Indians. Although Elliott conferred with Tecumseh and other Indian leaders, he found them implacably opposed to Procter's proposals. Moreover, Elliott feared that the split held the gravest of consequences for the British. At best, if Procter continued with his plans, the Indians would abandon the British and retreat into Michigan. Such a withdrawal would leave the Crown's forces woefully outnumbered. At worst, the warriors might even turn on their former allies. Although Tecumseh opposed such actions, Elliott knew that some of the warriors had become so embittered by Procter's proposals that they wanted to kill the general and all his advisers. They had even threatened Elliott's life, and he had served as their friend and confidant for almost forty years.

In the face of these alternatives, it is not surprising that Procter was willing to compromise. On September 21 he met privately with Tecumseh and attempted to explain why his retreat was a necessity. Spreading maps upon a table, Procter pointed out that the British and Indians were particularly vulnerable to American naval forces, and that Perry not only might land troops on the northern shores of Lake Erie, but also might sail up the Detroit River to Lake St. Clair, then ascend the Thames to deposit American forces across the road from Sandwich to Dundas. In either instance, both the British and Indians would be cut off from their supplies and vulnerable to the Americans. To prevent such an occurrence, Procter proposed to retreat to Chatham on the Thames River, a point he understood to be upstream from the head of navigation and Invulnerable to Perry's squadron. There the British and Indians would muster their forces, and if Harrison dared to follow them, they would defeat the Long Knives.

After listening to Procter's explanation and examining the British maps, Tecumseh agreed to the proposal. Undoubtedly he was reluctant to leave the Detroit region, but he was a war chief with many years of experience, and he understood the British position. Moreover, he had little choice. Although he had threatened to abandon his allies, Tecumseh knew that his warriors desperately needed the Crown's supplies. Without British arms and ammunition, they could never recapture their homelands. A stand at Chatham would provide his people with another opportunity to defeat Harrison, and the British and Indians might regain the initiative. Tecumseh presented the compromise to the assembled Indians, and after some discussion it was accepted.

The British evacuation began in late September. After shipping most of his supplies on to Sandwich, Procter burned the shipyards at Amherstburg on September 22. On the following day he also put Fort Malden and other public buildings to the torch. The British army remained at Sandwich until September 27, then it started east, marching along the southern shore of Lake St. Clair toward the mouth of the Thames.

Dispirited, many of the Indians refused to accompany the British. Although Tecumseh and Roundhead argued that the withdrawal to the Thames was a strategic necessity, many of the warriors believed that the British already were beaten. Led by Main Poc, large numbers of Potawatomis, Sacs, Foxes, Ottawas, and Chippewas crossed over into Michigan, where they seized American property and awaited the outcome of the coming battle between the British and Americans. If Harrison prevailed, these warriors could flee toward Lake Michigan, avoiding any confrontation with their enemy. If Tecumseh and Procter were victorious, Main Poc's warriors planned to fall upon the retreating Americans. In either case, the Indians in Michigan risked little, and they enjoyed considerable opportunities for plunder.

About 3,000 Indians, including many women and children, accompanied the British toward the Thames. Most of these Indians were loyal to Tecumseh and many had been associated with him since Prophetstown. They included many Kickapoos, Winnebagos, Potawatomis, Wyandots, and Shawnees. At first Tecumseh did not participate in the retreat. Saddened by the reverses, he remained behind, awaiting the approach of Harrison's army. He did not wait long. Late in the afternoon on September 27 both Tecumseh and Elliott watched from horseback as the Americans landed near Amherstburg, then moved forward and occupied the village. As dusk fell, the Shawnee retreated to Sandwich, where he spent the night before following the other Indians.

On October 1 Tecumseh reached the mouth of the Thames, where he encountered some of the retreating tribesmen. To his dismay, he learned that the desertions had continued; en route from Amherstburg, almost half of the remaining 3,000 Indians had abandoned the British and returned to Michigan. He also learned of a loss of a more personal nature. Roundhead, the Wyandot war chief who had first joined with the Shawnees at Greenville, had been killed while scouting Harrison's army. For Tecumseh, Roundhead's death only accentuated the declining Indian fortunes. Old friends, like old hopes, seemed to be dying.

On the following evening Tecumseh arrived at Chatham, where he expected to find the British well entrenched to oppose the Americans. He was disappointed. He discovered most of the British army camped on the north side of the river, with the Indians on the opposite bank, yet few preparations were under way to meet Harrison's forces. Indeed, Procter had proceeded upstream in his carriage, ostensibly searching for a better place to fight. Enraged, Tecumseh denounced the British as cowards and demanded that the British troops cross over to the south bank of the Thames to assist the Indians in opposing Harrison's oncoming army. But the British troops had no boats and refused to join the warriors. Finally, on October 3, a message was received from Procter proposing a withdrawal up the river to a point just below Moraviantown. There the terrain afforded better opportunities for defense, and he again promised to stand and meet the Americans.

Again Tecumseh had little choice. On October 4 the British troops on the north side of the river packed their gear and marched toward Moraviantown. The Indian withdrawal was much slower. Many of the warriors were encumbered by their families, and the women and children were exhausted. To protect their retreat, Tecumseh and a party of warriors remained behind and destroyed two bridges over McGregor's Creek, a tributary of the Thames that joined the river at Chatham. Taking cover in the underbrush, they planned to ambush Harrison's army as it advanced from the west, providing their women and children with ample time to reach Moraviantown. After their families had withdrawn to safety, the warriors would retreat and rejoin the British.

While the British and Indians withdrew up the Thames, Harrison mustered his forces at Sandwich. He had landed at Amherstburg, but was forced to wait for four days until Colonel Richard M. Johnson arrived with a force of mounted militia. In the meantime, Harrison moved on to Sandwich and dispatched about 700 troops to Detroit to protect American citizens from Main Poc and his warriors. Johnson reached Sandwich on October 1, and on the following day Harrison led a force of 3,000 regulars and militia along the shores of Lake St. Clair, in pursuit of their enemies. Two days later Harrison had proceeded as far as Chatham, where part of the American force encountered the Indians.

When the vanguard of Harrison's army reached McGregor's Creek, they found that the beams spanning the stream were intact but that Tecumseh and his warriors had destroyed the crossties, leaving the bridges without flooring. Suspecting an ambush, the troops advanced in battle formation, and as they approached the bridges Tecumseh and the Indians opened fire from the underbrush on the opposite bank. At first the Americans fell back, but they returned the fire and Harrison trained his artillery on the Indian position, sending several rounds across the river into the underbrush. Outnumbered and hopelessly outgunned, Tecumseh pulled his warriors back and surrendered the bridges. Harrison's men repaired the spans and crossed into Chatham, bivouacking that night about five miles east of the village.

For the Indians, the skirmish at McGregor's Creek was a sorry affair. They suffered ten dead and several wounded, including Tecumseh, who sustained a slight flesh wound on his left arm. The Americans lost only three dead and six wounded. In addition, Harrison's men captured large stores of supplies abandoned by the warriors. The defeat further dampened the Indians' spirits. Following the skirmish, Walk-in-the-Water and most of the remaining Wyandots from Brownstown defected to the Americans.

As Harrison's men camped for the night, Tecumseh and the war party withdrew up the Thames, then forded the river to join the other British and Indians just below Moraviantown. There, around the campfires, Tecumseh spent the evening reminiscing with his followers. They had traveled many miles since Prophetstown, but Tecumseh was convinced that the end was near. Indians who survived the Battle of the Thames later agreed that on the eve of the battle Tecumseh appeared to have a premonition of his death. He did not act depressed, but he did seem reflective, aware that his cause was lost. His father and two of his brothers had died fighting the Long Knives. If the Master of Life willed it, he would join them.

October 5 dawned bright and sunny, and with it came a resurgence in Indian morale. Tecumseh spent the morning conferring with Procter, rallying his warriors, and providing for the evacuation of the Indian women and children. The British and Indians decided to make their stand about two miles west of Moraviantown, on the north side of the Thames, where the road from the west passed between the river and a series of swampy thickets. Procter and the British formed two lines across the road while Tecumseh and the Indians took up positions in the thickets on the British right. Opposite the Indians flowed the Thames, whose deep waters would protect the left flank and channel the Americans toward the British guns.

At noon scouts brought reports that Harrison's army had marched upstream, forded the Thames, and would soon be approaching. The news seemed to cheer Tecumseh. Faced with the prospect of battle, the Shawnee war chief again was in his element. As the British and Indians took their places, he accompanied Procter in an inspection of the lines, reassuring his followers that they soon would defeat the Long Knives. Although Procter seemed less optimistic, Tecumseh attempted to buoy his spirits: "Father, tell your men to be firm, and all will be well." The Shawnee then dismounted and took his place among the warriors.

In mid-afternoon Harrison's army approached the British and Indian position. Aware that the Indians were well entrenched in the thickets, Harrison decided to attack Procter's regulars first, believing that if the British retreated it would both demoralize the Indians and allow American forces to sweep around their flank. Harrison ordered part of his infantry to advance slowly toward the Indian lines, but he sent his mounted militia and other forces in a charge at the British center, focusing on a six-pounder which the British had positioned in the road.

The British lines collapsed. Their resistance, from start to finish, lasted no more than five minutes. Envisioning the battle as already lost, most of the regulars fired two or three volleys, then abandoned their position and fled toward Moraviantown. The crew of the six-pounder retreated so precipitously that they forgot to discharge their weapon. From behind the British lines Procter momentarily attempted to rally his forces, but he too had little taste for American gunpowder, and after a few half-hearted efforts he galloped past his men down the road toward Moraviantown.

In the thickets the Indians continued to fight. Although Johnson's mounted militia swept through the British positions, the warriors repulsed Harrison's infantry, even advancing from the underbrush to force the soldiers back toward the road. Tecumseh was stationed near the eastern end of the Indian line, and he witnessed the British flight. He must have been angered, but he refused to follow his allies and he encouraged his warriors to keep their places. Yet, with the collapse of the British position, the American units who had first attacked Procter now turned toward the thickets, falling upon Tecumseh and those Indians near the former British lines. Into this area drove Johnson's horsemen, and though they could not penetrate the underbrush, they crowded its fringes, pouring their fire in upon the warriors. Infantry units also advanced toward the thickets, adding their numbers to the forces now confronting the Indians. Tecumseh and his warriors fought back valiantly, but in the ensuing battle Tecumseh fell, with a mortal gunshot wound in his chest. Demoralized, the Indians slowly disengaged from their enemy, and after thirty minutes the fighting ceased. The Battle of the Thames was over. Tecumseh was dead. The Indian movement had ended.

9

Tecumseh in Retrospect

The Battle of the Thames resulted in a significant American victory. The sizes of the opposing armies in the affair are difficult to ascertain. The Indians must have numbered somewhere between 700 and 800 warriors, while approximately 450 British troops either assembled across the road or assisted Procter at his "command post" behind the British lines. In contrast, Harrison's army seems to have consisted of about 3,300 soldiers. The losses sustained by both sides also remain uncertain. Harrison reported that he suffered 12 killed and 22 wounded, with British losses numbering the same. Yet many British troops either deserted or were captured, for when Procter assembled the remnants of his army at Ancaster he could muster only 246 men. Indian losses are even harder to calculate. Following the battle the Americans found the bodies of 33 warriors dead upon the field, but evidence suggests that many more were carried away by their comrades. In late October, when the Prophet attempted to rally the survivors, he could gather no more than 375 warriors. Of course not all of the remaining 700–800 Indians had fallen, for many returned to Michigan, but Indian losses in the affair were certainly substantial, probably approaching 70–80 warriors.

The British and Indian defeat signaled the collapse of Tecumseh's confederacy. Although some warriors remained in Canada, they lost their enthusiasm for further resistance and only half-heartedly supported the British. Further west, in Michigan, Main Poc tried to rally Tecumseh's followers

197

but his efforts also failed. After Tecumseh's death most tribesmen accepted the inevitable. They would be forced to accommodate the Americans.

The events surrounding Tecumseh's death and the fate of his body have been the subject of considerable controversy. At first neither British nor American authorities were sure he had been killed. Although Indians straggling into Ancaster reported that Tecumseh had fallen, Procter at first discounted their reports and did not officially inform his superiors of the Shawnee's death until October 23, almost three weeks after the defeat. The Americans were even more cautious. Private correspondence by American military personnel mentions Tecumseh's death as early as three or four days following the battle, but Harrison's initial reports were strangely silent regarding Tecumseh's fate. Although Harrison described his victory in great detail to Secretary of War John Armstrong on October 9, and even discussed Tecumseh's speeches in a note to Governor Return J. Meigs of Ohio on October 11, neither letter mentioned Tecumseh's death. In fact the first official American notice of the Shawnee's passing emerged from a letter by Lewis Cass, written on October 28, which stated that Tecumseh had been killed and that his body had been identified.

According to Cass, "subsequent information" had confirmed the identity of Tecumseh's body, but that confirmation was hardly definitive. Indeed, American reluctance to report the Shawnee's death was based on considerable confusion over the fate of Tecumseh's corpse. Following the battle, many of the Indian bodies were mutilated by white frontiersmen. Although Anthony Shane and John Connor identified one of the fallen Indians as Tecumseh, their superiors remained uncertain. Both Harrison and Simon Kenton also examined the body, but they could make no positive identification.

Captured British soldiers were of little assistance. Although several evidently identified a fallen warrior as Tecumseh, the corpse had been mutilated before the American authorities saw it. Decades later Indian survivors of the battle all agreed that Tecumseh had fallen, but they disagreed over the fate of his body. Some stated that they had buried Tecumseh at a secret location in the forest. Others admitted that his body had been left on the battlefield, but claimed that it had not been mutilated. To add to the confusion, local residents in the Thames Valley asserted that Tecumseh's body was among the many corpses buried by British traders after the Americans withdrew toward Detroit. Of course several of these residents also argued, with considerable pride, that Tecumseh was buried at a specific location on their property.

If Tecumseh's death and the fate of his body were shrouded with uncertainty, at first there seemed to be a general consensus about the American personally responsible for his death. Shortly after the battle, several of the participants claimed that Colonel Richard M. Johnson, the commander of the mounted Kentucky militia, had shot and killed Tecumseh with his pistol. Following Procter's retreat, Johnson and the Kentucky militia had attacked the Indian lines where the latter abutted the British position, and in the attack Johnson, while wounded, killed an Indian warrior who was advancing toward him. Johnson was then forced to withdraw from the battle to seek medical attention for his injuries. The body which Shane, Connor, and the British prisoners supposedly identified as Tecumseh was found in the immediate area where Johnson had shot and killed the Indian.

To Johnson's credit, he evidently never claimed that he personally was responsible for Tecumseh's death, but he did little to discourage such claims by his supporters, and he accepted the nickname "Old Tecumseh" with considerable pride. He served in both Congress and the Senate during the 1820s and 1830s, and in 1836 he campaigned for the vice-presidency with the following slogan.

> Rumpsey dumpsey, rumpsey dumpsey,
> Colonel Johnson killed Tecumseh!

Yet Johnson was not the only American who claimed responsibility (or honor) for Tecumseh's death. In the years that followed the Battle of the Thames, almost a dozen other participants in the battle made similar assertions, and although their credentials seem more spurious than Johnson's, several of their claims were championed by Johnson's political opponents.

In retrospect, a few facts regarding Tecumseh's death emerge from the confusion. Unquestionably Tecumseh was killed in the Battle of the Thames. He fell as the mounted Kentucky militia attacked that part of the Indian position closest to the former British lines. As the Kentuckians advanced, Johnson killed an Indian. The evidence indicates that Tecumseh's body was probably one of several Indian corpses discovered lying in the vicinity of Johnson's action. Shane's and Connor's claims to have identified Tecumseh's body may very well be true, for other accounts mention that one of the fallen warriors had a bandage on his left arm (Tecumseh's wound from Chatham) and seemed to have sustained a broken leg which had mended much earlier in his life (Tecumseh's leg had been broken on a hunting trip in Kentucky). Soon after the battle ended (and before Harrison or Kenton viewed the body) all the Indian corpses in the immediate vicinity were severely mutilated by American frontiersmen. The bodies later were buried by residents of the region. Tecumseh was killed in this part of the battlefield. His body probably was mutilated by the Americans and later buried by British citizens. Whether he fell at the hands of Richard M. Johnson remains open to speculation.

* * *

The confusion surrounding Tecumseh's death is typical of the mythology associated with the Shawnee warrior. More than any other Indian in American history, Tecumseh has achieved an almost legendary status. The real Tecumseh has been overshadowed by a folk hero whose exploits combine the best of fact and fiction. These mythological accounts begin with Tecumseh's birth, suggesting that his father, Puckeshinwa, had a white parent and that Tecumseh was a twin to Tenskwatawa. Of course the boys' father was not a half-blood, and Tecumseh was at least six years older than the Prophet, but since both white lineage and the mystique of a multiple birth were deemed desirable in nineteenth-century

America, both bits of misinformation were incorporated into several of the biographies. Other apocrypha are associated with the death of Puckeshinwa. Although almost all historical evidence indicates that Puckeshinwa fell at the Battle of Point Pleasant, some of Tecumseh's biographers have accepted a fictitious, if romantic, account that the warrior was murdered by white hunters on the Mad River in Ohio. One of the most recent biographers even embellishes the story with verbatim speeches by Methoataske, Tecumseh's mother, as she accompanied her son on yearly pilgrimages to Puckeshinwa's grave.

Another prominent legend associated with Tecumseh is his supposed love for Rebecca Galloway, the daughter of John Galloway, an old Indian fighter who settled in modern Greene County, Ohio. According to accounts handed down by the Galloway family, Tecumseh became enamored of Rebecca while visiting the family, and repeatedly returned to court the "young, golden-haired girl with deep-blue eyes." Although there is not one fragment of evidence to support this "romance," local legends abound of Tecumseh sitting at the feet of the frontier maiden, receiving instructions in English and listening as she read extended passages from the Bible, Shakespeare, and world history (Tecumseh supposedly preferred Exodus, *Hamlet*, and Alexander the Great). Galloway family traditions assert that Tecumseh asked for her hand in marriage, and Rebecca agreed, on the condition that Tecumseh would give up his life as an Indian and "adopt her people's mode of life and dress." Of course Tecumseh refused, and the two parted, never to meet again. This story is so patently fictitious that it taxes the credulity of all but the most gullible adherents of nineteenth-century romanticism, but it has been included in several of the more reputable Tecumseh biographies and even forms the basis for a historical drama performed each summer before large audiences of tourists near Chillicothe, Ohio.

Similarly, Tecumseh's efforts in recruiting warriors for his movement have been the object of considerable exaggeration. The Shawnee war chief did journey throughout Ohio, Indiana, Illinois, Michigan, and perhaps part of Wisconsin

soliciting support for his confederacy, but in the years following his death numerous white frontiersmen claimed to have
encountered him as far east as New York and as far west as
Oklahoma. He also is reputed to have made repeated trips
into the South, seeking assistance from the Five Southern
Tribes. Many of these fabricated expeditions reflect attempts
by white frontiersmen to enhance their own reputations
through fictitious associations with the Shawnee chief. Caleb
Atwater's account of Tecumseh among the Iroquois is a
classic example. Atwater, a minor political figure from Ohio,
claimed that he accompanied Tecumseh, the Prophet, and
two Winnebagos on a recruiting journey to New York in
1809. Although there is no primary evidence to corroborate
Atwater's story, he asserts that he served the party as an
interpreter. Atwater fails to explain why Tecumseh would
have asked an American frontiersman (with close ties to both
state and federal governments) to assist him in building his
anti-American movement, and there is no evidence to imply
that Atwater had any mastery of either Shawnee, Iroquois,
or Winnebago (three very separate and distinct Indian lan-
guages); yet Atwater's story is commonly cited to prove that
Tecumseh was active among the Iroquois.

Accounts of Tecumseh's activities among the Osages also are
unsubstantiated. Many of Tecumseh's biographers assert that
he visited the Osages during the fall of 1811 as he returned
from the South, but their accounts are based upon a spurious
report by John D. Hunter, who claimed to have been a prisoner
among the Osages during this period and who supposedly
witnessed Tecumseh speaking to his captors. Hunter's claims
seem questionable. Once again there is no contemporary evidence to support Hunter's story, and when queried about the
visit, Colonel Auguste P. Chouteau, who was married to an
Osage woman and whose family was intimately associated
with the tribe for decades, admitted that he had never heard
any of the Osages mention the incident. Moreover, in 1811,
at the time of Tecumseh's supposed visit, the Osages were
still bitterly involved in warfare with the Potawatomis and
Kickapoos, two of Tecumseh's staunchest allies. Since Shawnee
warriors from the Cape Girardeau settlements sometimes

assisted the Potawatomis and Kickapoos in this warfare, it is highly unlikely that Tecumseh would have been received favorably by the western tribe.

Most of Tecumseh's alleged recruiting trips into the South also are difficult to corroborate. Tecumseh certainly journeyed south in August 1811, and there is ample evidence to indicate he met with the Chickasaws, Choctaws, and Creeks during the next few months, returning to Indiana sometime in early January. Most of Tecumseh's biographers assert that he visited the southern tribes on several other occasions, specifically in 1809 and during the first three months of 1813. These additional trips seem highly unlikely. Although Tecumseh's whereabouts, on a daily basis, are hard to ascertain, for 1809 there is enough primary evidence to indicate that he did not have the opportunity to make a trip to the South. In addition, there are no contemporary accounts documenting any southern trip during this year. For the early months of 1813 the evidence is even more firm. To counter allegations that he visited the southern tribes during this period, there are letters by British and American officials mentioning that both Tecumseh and the Prophet spent the first three months of the year in northwestern Indiana, rallying warriors from nearby tribes for the spring offensive against the Americans.

Tecumseh's itinerary on his trip to the South during the fall of 1811 remains uncertain as well. There is ample evidence that he passed through the Chickasaw and Choctaw villages, and that he made considerable efforts to bring the Creeks into his movement. Some biographers argue that he also visited the Cherokees and Seminoles, although evidence for his contacts with these two tribes is much more speculative. Following his sojourn through the South, he recrossed Tennessee and part of Kentucky before meeting with some of the Shawnees still living near Cape Girardeau in eastern Missouri. Letters by officials at St. Louis indicate that he then passed over into Illinois on his way back to Prophetstown.

Of course there are many other legends associated with the Shawnee chief. Both the Creeks and the Shawnees believed that Tecumseh predicted the great 1811 earthquake, warning his Creek followers that the earth's trembling would be a sign that he had returned to his home and that the Master of Life favored his movement. Whether Tecumseh actually did predict the earthquake is more a theological than a historical problem, but if he made such a prediction he certainly miscalculated the onset of the tremors. The most severe shocks occurred while he was in either Missouri or Illinois, long before he returned to the Tippecanoe. Similarly, there is no evidence to substantiate claims that Tecumseh ever was appointed to the rank of brigadier general in the British army. Brock evidently did present him with a sword and a scarlet sash, and may have even given him a red officer's coat, but the British general certainly did not have the authority to make the Shawnee chief a fellow officer, and British military records make no mention of such an appointment.

Tecumseh's personal appearance also has been altered through the years. Although he often is described as a tall, lean, handsome man with light skin, contemporary evidence suggests that his height was no more than five feet ten inches, and that his complexion matched that of other Shawnees. Most of his contemporaries mentioned that Tecumseh had pierced the septum of his nose, affixing a silver ring or other small ornaments that hung down toward his upper lip, but some of his biographers do not mention this ornamentation, and twentieth-century artists, when completing hypothetical portraits of the Shawnee, invariably fail to include this jewelry in their paintings. Of course such adornment is seen as undesirable or even "barbaric" by modern Americans, and in attempting to enhance the image of Tecumseh it is not surprising that his biographers or painters would delete the jewelry, but ornamentation of this type was quite common among the Shawnees in the early decades of the nineteenth century.

Perhaps the most accurate portrait of Tecumseh is the Le Dru–Lossing portrait, a composite of the work of two early-nineteenth-century artists. The portrait is based upon a pencil sketch of Tecumseh by Pierre Le Dru, a Creole trader who encountered the Shawnee at Vincennes in the years preceding the war. Le Dru's drawing portrays Tecumseh in a turban (common among the Shawnees during this period) adorned with an eagle feather. Le Dru also includes several small silver ornaments suspended from the septum of Tecumseh's nose. Le Dru's sketch of Tecumseh's head was later incorporated into a bust of the Shawnee chief drawn by an unnamed British officer who met him at Detroit after the fort had been captured by the British. The officer adorned Tecumseh with a British medal (which he sometimes wore), and even dressed him in a red officer's coat, which Tecumseh might have worn on certain ceremonial occasions but which was not his standard attire. Years afterward this portrait was published in a book by Benson Lossing.

Tecumseh's legendary status is indicative of his position in the history of Indian-white relations. More than any other Indian in American history, Tecumseh was admired by the white men (both British and American) who knew him, and he has continued to receive accolades from historians. British officers were almost unanimous in their praise. In 1812 Brock reported that "a more sagacious or a more gallant warrior does not I believe exist. He has the admiration of everyone who conversed with him." Other British officers, including Matthew Elliott and even Procter, echoed Brock's views, and when Tecumseh stopped the slaughter of prisoners after the first Battle of Fort Meigs, Major John Richardson commented that in Tecumseh "nought of the savage could be distinguished save the color and the garb," for the Shawnee was "a savage such as civilization herself might not blush to acknowledge as her child."

Even the Americans, men who opposed Tecumseh, extolled him. Lewis Cass described him as "a man of more enlarged views than are often found among the Indian chiefs; a brave warrior, and a skillful leader, politic in his measures, and firm in his purpose." John Johnston, who served as an Indian agent among the Shawnees, ranked Tecumseh as "among the great men of his race, [who] aimed at the independence of his people by a nation of all the Indians, North and South, against the encroachments of the whites. Had he appeared fifty years sooner he might have set bounds to the Anglo-Saxon race in the West." Even Harrison, as noted earlier, admitted that Tecumseh was "one of those uncommon geniuses, which spring up occasionally to produce revolutions and overturn the established order of things. . . . No difficulties deter him. . . . Wherever he goes he makes an impression favorable to his purpose."

Since his death, Tecumseh's image has grown accordingly. Biographers from Benjamin Drake to Glenn Tucker have presented an Indian whose qualities were limited only by the bounds of the biographer's imagination. Although the following characterization by ethnologist James Mooney is more stilted than most, it typifies the historical image of Tecumseh.

> Of commanding figure, nearly six feet in height and compactly built, of a dignified bearing and piercing eye, before whose lightning even a British general quailed; with the fiery eloquence of a Clay and the clear-cut logic of a Webster, abstemious in habit, charitable in thought and action, brave as a lion, but humane and generous withal—in a word, an aboriginal knight—his life was given to his people.

Of course Tecumseh possessed many of these qualities. In real life he was a magnetic leader who commanded the loyalty of large numbers of followers. He was a brave man, dedicated to his people, yet humane to his enemies. His attempts to forge the tribesmen into a pan-Indian confederacy reflected a farsighted approach to the problems of Indian land tenure, and the failure of his political movement should not detract from his goals or his efforts. Tecumseh also was a dynamic orator, although he always spoke in Shawnee and the translations of his speeches probably did not reflect their impact upon his followers. Yet Tenskwatawa, the Shawnee Prophet, initiated the Indian movement. For five years, from 1805 until late in 1809, his religious teachings were the magnet that attracted large numbers of tribesmen first to Greenville, then to Prophetstown. Only after the Treaty of Fort Wayne did Tecumseh emerge as the dominant leader, and even then he based his political confederacy upon his brother's religious movement.

If Tecumseh's confederacy originated in the religious teachings of the Shawnee Prophet, why have white men, both Tecumseh's contemporaries and historians, championed

Tecumseh as the primary force behind the movement? The answer is obvious. From the Anglo-American perspective, Tenskwatawa was a strange man whose concepts of religious revitalization seemed incongruous. Since the British and Americans never understood the Prophet's teachings, they dismissed his religious movement as entirely secondary to Tecumseh's political confederacy, and they assumed that Tecumseh had dominated the movement from its inception. Moreover, unlike Tecumseh, there was little about Tenskwatawa to romanticize. He was a disfigured holy man whose personal qualities were unappealing. Discounting his sincerity, his critics described Tenskwatawa as a charlatan who rode his brother's coattails. Never a warrior, the Prophet was pictured as a coward who refused to fight at Tippecanoe and who abandoned his brother at the Battle of the Thames. Although he survived the War of 1812, he was ignored by historians, and in November 1836 he died quietly in his lodge in Kansas. In retrospect, however, Tenskwatawa's religious movement was typical of Indian reactions to white aggression. Sorely oppressed, the tribesmen often turned to holy men. The Delaware Prophet, Handsome Lake, Kanakuk, and Wovoka all offered deliverance. Tenskwatawa was not unique. His solution was undeniably Indian.

Tecumseh was different. If white men, both past and present, could have designed an "ideal Indian" they would have designed Tecumseh. His attempts at political and military unification seemed logical to both the British and the Americans, for it was what *they* would have done in his place. Although such a system of centralized leadership seemed foreign to the Indians, it was common within the framework of Anglo-American political traditions. Tecumseh's boast that "I am alone the acknowledged head of all the Indians" may have frightened the village chiefs, but it stirred the hearts of Harrison, Brock, and other Anglo-American leaders, and it continues to appeal to modern Americans.

More than any other prominent Indian, Tecumseh exemplifies the European or American concept of the "noble savage." Many of Tecumseh's personal qualities are easily identified with such an image. He was a brave and honest man, physically strong, and dedicated to his people. Moreover, his kindness toward prisoners particularly appealed to Americans, although such generosity reflected European concepts of warfare more than the usual treatment of captives on the American frontier. Since his death, both his contemporaries and historians have embellished these qualities and given him others which have further enhanced his noble-savage image. Many of these newer attributes are apocryphal; but since they were associated with the image, and since Americans wanted to believe in them, they have been accepted as fact. Even the events surrounding Tecumseh's death contributed to his personification as the noble savage. He fell, fighting, in the last great battle of his times, and the uncertainty surrounding his body only added to his mystique.

And so, as Tecumseh passed into history, he also passed into legend. The man and the myth became one. As the threat of Indians diminished, the noble savage became safer and more fashionable. Tecumseh emerged as the "bravest of the brave," the "Greatest Indian." And if white Americans were melancholy over his fall, they also took pride in his passing, for in conquering the red champion they could assure themselves that they were worthy of his kingdom.

Study and Discussion Questions

Chapter 1: The Shawnees

1. A "sense of place" has always been important to Native American people. Why were the Shawnees so attached to the Ohio Valley?

2. What was the role of the Shawnees in the contest between the British and French for control of the Ohio Valley?

3. What was the Shawnee relationship to the Iroquois Confederacy?

4. What does the colonists' expansion onto Shawnee lands in the upper Ohio Valley illustrate about the relationship between the colonies and the British government?

5. How did the outcome of the Battle of Point Pleasant create potential problems for the Shawnees in the decade following Dunmore's War?

Chapter 2: Learning the Warrior's Path

1. What does Tecumseh's ancestry illustrate about intertribal relationships and tribal affiliations in the Ohio country and trans-Appalachian West during the late 18th century?

2. What does Tecumseh's upbringing indicate about the role that families and kinship groups played in Shawnee society?

3. Why did the Shawnees ally with the British against the Americans during the American Revolution?

4. Why were the British able to maintain considerable influence among the Shawnees and other Ohio tribes in the decade after the American Revolution?

5. Why were the Americans eager to exert control over the Ohio Country in the immediate post-Revolutionary period?

6. Why were the Americans so unsuccessful in their initial military campaigns against the Ohio tribes? How did Anthony Wayne's campaign differ from these earlier military efforts?

7. What do the defections within the Indian ranks prior to the Battle of Fallen Timbers illustrate about the structure of Native American politics and leadership during this period?

8. What was the impact of the Treaty of Greenville upon the tribes of Ohio, Indiana, and Illinois?

Chapter 3: A Culture Under Siege

1. Why did Europeans and Euro-Americans have difficulty understanding Shawnee political structure? How did Shawnee political structure differ from that of the Europeans?

2. In what ways did women influence Shawnee life?

3. How did the fur trade change Shawnee life?

4. Discuss how different concepts of land use and land ownership caused friction between the Shawnees and the Americans.

5. Why did federal officials encounter difficulty in dispensing justice between Indians and whites on the American frontier?

6. Discuss Black Hoof's attempts to adopt the Americans' lifestyle.

7. Why did the Shawnees believe that their society was plagued by witches and sorcerers?

Chapter 4: Red Messiah

1. How did Tenskwatawa's (the Shawnee Prophet's) earlier life seem to add credence to the validity of his vision experience and subsequent transformation?

2. How and why did Tenskwatawa's new religious doctrines combine traditional Shawnee religious beliefs with religious and cultural values from Europeans and Americans?

3. Why were Tenskwatawa's teachings so attractive to Native Americans in the Midwest?

4. What was Tecumseh's initial reaction to his brother's transformation and teachings?

5. How did the actions and policies of William Henry Harrison strengthen the Shawnee Prophet's influence?

6. Why did Tenskwatawa particularly condemn the Moravian Delawares? What made these Delawares such a ready target for the Prophet's followers?

7. Why was Tecumseh so critical of interpreters and agents such as William Wells?

8. Why did Black Hoof oppose Tecumseh and the Shawnee Prophet?

Chapter 5: The Moses of the Family

1. How did Tecumseh's relationship with Main Poc illustrate the problems Tecumseh encountered in recruiting other tribal leaders into his confederacy?

2. Why were the British initially uncertain about supporting Tecumseh and the Shawnee Prophet?

3. What role did logistical problems (food, ammunition, and other supplies) play in Tecumseh's attempts to maintain his confederacy?

4. How did the Treaty of Fort Wayne prove advantageous to Tecumseh's plans?

5. Discuss how the conference between Tecumseh and William Henry Harrison at Vincennes in August 1810 cause Harrison to change his opinion of the Shawnee chief?

Chapter 6: To Tippecanoe

1. Discuss the influence of local British Indian agents such as Matthew Elliott on the tribes. How did their opinions sometimes differ with those of their superiors in Canada? Why?

2. Why did Tecumseh meet with Harrison at Vincennes in July 1811?

3. Discuss Tecumseh's success in recruiting Chickasaw and Choctaw warriors into his confederacy.

4. How did Tecumseh and the Shawnee Prophet contribute to the civil war that erupted among the Creeks in 1813–1814?

5. What was Harrison's motivation for his campaign against Prophetstown?

6. Why did the Shawnee Prophet attack Harrison at Tippecanoe? Should he have retreated instead of launching the attack?

7. Why was Tecumseh so angry with his brother over the Battle of Tippecanoe?

Chapter 7: Red Ascendancy

1. Why were the British and Indians able to gain the ascendancy during the opening months of the War of 1812?

2. Discuss Isaac Brock as the British military commander in the West. What was his relationship with Tecumseh?

3. What did the military encounters at Brownstown, Monguagon, and near Fort Dearborn illustrate about Native American military tactics?

4. What was the Americans' ultimate motivation for invading Canada?

5. Why did William Hull surrender Detroit to the British and Indians? What particular roles, both actual and psychological, did the Indians play in Hull's decision?

Chapter 8: Death on the Thames

1. Why did the British attacks upon Fort Meigs and Fort Stephenson fail? Why didn't the Indians participate in a frontal assault, and try to "storm the walls"?

2. Discuss how British and Indian goals differed in fighting the War of 1812 in the West. How did these goals influence both groups' strategies?

3. Why was the American naval victory on Lake Erie such a blow to the Indian and British cause?

4. Why did Black Hoof's followers and some other Indians support the Americans against Tecumseh and the British? Were they rewarded for their loyalty to the Americans?

5. Why were Tecumseh and many of the other Indians critical of Henry Procter's ability as a military leader?

6. Discuss the role of Walk-in-the-Water and the Brownstown Wyandots in the War of 1812. Were they realists or opportunists?

7. In Tecumseh's speech to Procter on September 13, 1813, he pointed out that "when we retreated to our father's fort at that place the gates were shut against us." To what was he referring? Why had the Indians grown suspicious of their British allies?

Chapter 9: Tecumseh in Retrospect

1. Why was Tecumseh so admired by both his American and British contemporaries?

2. Why have many Americans accepted the myth that Tecumseh was of partial Euro-American ancestry?

3. Why has the myth of a romantic relationship between Tecumseh and Rebecca Galloway gained such credulity?

4. Did Tecumseh's plans for a grand Indian alliance incorporating Native Americans from many tribes in an effort to contain American expansion have any chance for success? Why or why not?

5. Several other figures in American history have also achieved legendary status in which "the man and the myth" have been combined. Who? What do all these figures have in common?

A Note on the Sources

Primary materials focusing upon Tecumseh and the Shawnees during the period of Tecumseh's life are relatively few, and are scattered through the holdings of many depositories. Of course Tecumseh left no personal papers. The largest collection of manuscript materials concentrating upon the Shawnee chief is the Tecumseh Papers, in the Draper Manuscripts at the State Historical Society of Wisconsin. These papers, available on microfilm, contain the investigations of Lyman C. Draper, an early historian of the Old Northwest who was particularly interested in the history of the frontier in this region. The Tecumseh Papers include both Draper's and Benjamin Drake's correspondence with many of Tecumseh's contemporaries. They also include long accounts by Stephen Ruddell and Anthony Shane, former captives among the Shawnees who knew Tecumseh rather well. Other important collections with the Draper Manuscripts are the William Henry Harrison Papers, the Simon Kenton Papers, the Thomas Forsyth Papers, and Draper's Notes. Portions of several other collections in the Draper Manuscripts also contain material on the Shawnees during Tecumseh's lifetime.

Among the many useful state and regional depositories is the Great Lakes–Ohio Valley Indian Archives, at the Glenn A. Black Laboratory of Archaeology in Bloomington, Indiana. The archives include source materials compiled by Erminie Wheeler-Voegelin and her staff and used by the Indian Claims Commission; these consist of copies of primary documents from a wide variety of sources. Since the documents are filed chronologically for each tribe, the archives provide a unique opportunity for initial research upon most tribal subjects. Also valuable are the George Winter Papers at the Tippecanoe County Historical Society in Lafayette, Indiana. The Winter Papers contain materials relevant to Tenskwatawa's doctrines. The Eyewitness Account File at the Tippecanoe Battleground Historical Association, in Battle Ground, Indiana, offers some interesting insights into the military action at that location, while several collections of papers and manuscripts held by the Indiana Historical Society Library and the Indiana State Library, both located in Indianapolis, include documents focusing upon Tecumseh and his activities.

In Ohio, the Cincinnati Historical Society holds several series of manuscripts—including the William Henry Harrison Papers, the John Johnston Papers, and the Frank J. Jones Collection—that center upon Indian affairs in western Ohio during Tecumseh's era. The Ohio Historical Society, located at Columbus, contains considerable materials relevant to Tecumseh and the Shawnees; although its collections also are too numerous to enumerate, especially important are the papers of several early governors, including Thomas Kirker, Return J. Meigs, Edward Tiffin, and Thomas Worthington. All of these documents are available on microfilm.

The Burton Historical Collections at the Detroit Public Library contain significant materials focusing upon Indian affairs in Michigan and Upper Canada during the War of 1812. Of primary importance are the John Askin Papers, the Lewis Cass Papers, the William Henry Harrison Papers, the George Ironside Papers, the Benson J. Lossing Papers, the Tecumseh Papers, and the Benjamin F. Witherell Papers. Located nearby, the William L. Clements Library at Ann Arbor holds the Lewis Cass Papers, the Michigan Papers, and the War of 1812 Papers—all of which include manuscripts pertaining to Indian affairs on the American-Canadian frontier. The Thomas Forsyth Papers, at the Missouri Historical Society in St. Louis, contain a series of letters documenting the impact of the Indian movement upon Indian-white relations in Illinois.

Especially significant among the many records incorporated in the National Archives in Washington are documents found within Record Group 75 (Records of the Bureau of Indian Affairs) and Record Group 107 (Records of the Office of the Secretary of War). In Record Group 75, materials relating to Tecumseh are most prevalent in the Records of the Michigan Superintendency (M1) and the Records of the Secretary of War Relating to Indian Affairs (M271 and M15). More important is Record Group 107, which contains the Letters Received by the Secretary of War, Main Series (M221), the Letters Received by the Secretary of War, Unregistered Series (M222), and Letters Sent by the Secretary of War Relating to Military Affairs (M6).

Among the depositories of pertinent British documents is the Public Records Office in London, where the Records of the Colonial

Office, especially the Original Correspondence of the Secretary of State with both Upper and Lower Canada (Series 42), are particularly important. In Canada, the archives of the Fort Malden National Historical Park contain materials on Indian activities during the War of 1812, while the Public Archives of Canada incorporate considerable correspondence focusing upon Indian affairs in the Great Lakes region. The Public Archives include Manuscript Group 19, which contains the papers of John Askin, William Claus, and the McKee family, all of whom were associated with the British Indian Department. Record Group 8 embraces the C Series of the British Military and Naval Records, documents focusing upon military action during the war, while Record Group 10 is comprised of correspondence and other materials compiled by the Indian Department. Within the latter record group, the Records of the Governor General and the Records of the Superintendent's Office are especially significant.

Numerous biographies of Tecumseh have been written, but many are full of errors and mythology. Herbert Goltz's studies of the Shawnee leader are a notable exception. Although neither work has been published, Goltz's master's thesis, "Tecumseh: The Man and the Myth" (University of Wisconsin–Milwaukee, 1966), and his doctoral dissertation, "Tecumseh, the Prophet, and the Rise of the Northwest Indian Confederation" (University of Western Ontario, 1973), present balanced accounts of Tecumseh's life and discuss the legends associated with the Shawnee chief. Of the published biographies, John Sugden's *Tecumseh: A Life* (New York, 1997) is the most documented and detailed. Sugden presents Tecumseh in heroic terms, and although he often qualifies such assertions with "probably," he includes some information (e.g., about Tecumseh among the Osages and Cherokees) for which there is very scant or questionable evidence. Still, the Sugden volume is a "must read" for any serious student of Tecumseh's life. One of the earliest published biographies, Benjamin's Drake's *Life of Tecumseh* (Cincinnati, 1858) remains a valuable source book. Drake interviewed many frontier residents who had known Tecumseh, and he incorporated materials from his interviews into the narrative. Some of Drake's information is incorrect, but his biography, although it was published in the nineteenth century and is relatively brief, is more accurate than many of those written by later historians. Among such subsequent biographies are John Oskisson's *Tecumseh and His Times* (New York, 1938), Bil Gilbert's *God Gave Us This Country: Tekamthi and the First American Civil War* (New York, 1989), and Glenn Tucker's *Tecumseh: Vision of Glory* (Indianapolis, 1956). For almost three decades Tucker's volume remained the "standard" study of Tecumseh, but the book is replete with apocryphal material and presents a romanticized image of the Shawnee chief. The late Alvin M. Josephy Jr.'s chapter on Tecumseh in *The Patriot Chiefs* (New York, 1958) is well written but also includes questionable accounts, while Carl F. Klinck's edited volume, *Tecumseh: Fact and Fiction in Early Records* (Englewood Cliffs, N.J., 1961), contains selections of both primary and secondary materials focusing upon the Shawnee.

The most important sources for early Shawnee history include Charles Callendar's chapter, "Shawnee," in Bruce E. Trigger, ed., *Northeast,* volume 15 of *Handbook of North American Indians* (Washington, D.C., 1978); and Richard White's sweeping and perceptive *The Middle Ground: Indians, Empires, and Republics in the Great Lakes Region, 1650 –1815* (New York, 1991). Shawnee participation in the colonial struggle for the Ohio Country during the middle decades of the eighteenth century is detailed in Randolph C. Downes's *Council Fires on the Upper Ohio* (Pittsburgh, 1940), and more recently in Michael McConnell's scholarly, well-documented *A Country in Between: The Upper Ohio Valley and Its Peoples, 1724–1774* (Lincoln, Neb., 1992). McConnell examines events in this region from a Native American perspective. Shawnee tribal movements during these years and in the early nineteenth century are admirably traced in Helen M. Tanner's *Atlas of Great Lakes Indian History* (Norman, Okla., 1987).

Shawnee involvement in Pontiac's Rebellion is dramatically chronicled in Francis Parkman's classic *The Conspiracy of Pontiac* (Boston, 1851) and in Howard Peckham's less lurid, but more accurate *Pontiac and the Indian Uprising (*Princeton, N.J., 1947*)*. More recently, Gregory Dowd has published *War Under Heaven: Pontiac, the Indian Nations, and the British Empire* (Baltimore, 2002), which argues that in addition to political and economic reasons, the Indians opposed the British because the latter treated them disdainfully and because the tribespeople were heavily influenced by Native American religious leaders. Indian activities during Dunmore's War are described in documents contained in Reuben G. Thwaites and Louise P. Kellogg, eds., *Documentary History of Lord Dunmore's War* (Madison, Wisc., 1905), and in Jack M. Sosin, "The British Indian Department and Dunmore's War," *Virginia Magazine of History and Biography,* vol. 64 (January 1966), 34–50.

Shawnee participation in the American Revolution is admirably documented in three volumes edited by Louise P. Kellogg and published in Madison, Wisconsin: *Frontier Advance on the Upper Ohio, 1778–1779* (1908); *Frontier Defense on the Upper Ohio, 1778–1779* (1912); and *Frontier Retreat on the Upper Ohio, 1779–1781* (1917). Good secondary accounts of Indian-white confrontations during this period can be found in Jack M. Sosin's *The Revolutionary Frontier* (New York, 1967), and in Colin G. Calloway's *The American Revolution in Indian Country* (New York, 1995). Calloway devotes an entire chapter to the Shawnee's efforts to preserve their control over the upper Ohio Valley. Documents relating to Indian-white relations in the postwar period can be found in *American State Papers: Indian Affairs* (2 vols., Washington, D.C., 1832–1834); *American State Papers: Military Affairs* (7 vols., Washington, D.C., 1832–1861); William Henry Smith, ed., *The St. Clair Papers* (2 vols., Cincinnati, 1882); and Richard C. Knopf, ed., *Anthony Wayne: A Name in Arms* (Pittsburgh, 1960). John Sugden's *Blue Jacket: Warrior of the Shawnees* (Lincoln, Neb., 2000) provides a good account of the Shawnee participation in the border warfare of the 1790s, while both Wiley Sword's *President Washington's Indian War* (Norman, Okla., 1985) and Alan D. Gaff's *Bayonets in the Wilderness: Anthony Wayne's Legion in the Old Northwest* (Norman, Okla., 2004) offer detailed discussions of American military strategy in the 1790s. Reginald Horsman's *Matthew Elliott, British Indian Agent* (Detroit, 1964) and Larry B. Nelson's *A Man of Distinction Among Them: Alexander McKee and British Affairs Along the Ohio Country Frontier, 1754–1799* (Kent, Ohio, 1999) provides insights into the influence of local British Indian agents among the Shawnees and other Ohio tribes during this period, while Colin Calloway's *Crown and Calumet: British-Indian Relations, 1783–1815* (Norman, Okla., 1987) presents an excellent overview of British Indian policy during these years. In contrast, Reginald Horsman's *Expansion and American Indian Policy, 1783–1812* (East Lansing, Mich., 1967) discusses the impact of the westward movement upon the Shawnees and other tribes.

In addition to Callender's chapter on the Shawnees in *Handbook of North American Indians,* a comprehensive study of Shawnee culture is James Howard's *Shawnee: The Ceremonialism of Native Indian Tribe and Its Cultural Background* (Athens, Ohio, 1981). Vernon Kinietz and Erminie Wheeler-Voegelin, eds., *"Shawnese Traditions": C. C. Trowbridge's Account,* Occasional Contributions from the Museum of Anthropology of the University of Michigan, No. 9 (Ann Arbor, 1939), includes Trowbridge's interviews with Tenskwatawa and Black Hoof during the early 1820s. Clarence W. Alvord's *Civilization and the Story of the Absentee Shawnees* (Norman, Okla., 1936) incorporates observations of Shawnee life, as do Leonard Hill's *John Johnston and the Indians in the Land of the Three Miamis* (Piqua, Ohio, 1957) and Henry Harvey's *History of the Shawnee Indians from the Year 1681 to 1854* (Cincinnati, 1854). Harvey's volume discusses the efforts of Quaker missionaries among Black Hoof's followers, as do Paul Woerhmann's *At the Headwaters of the Maumee* (Indianapolis, 1971) and Gerrard Hopkins's *A Mission to the Indians from the Indian Committee of the Baltimore Yearly Meeting* (Philadelphia, 1862). R. David Edmunds, "Forgotten Allies: The Loyal Shawnees and the War of 1812," in David Curtis Skaggs and Larry L. Nelson, eds., *The Sixty Years War for the Great Lakes, 1754–1814* (East Lansing, Mich., 2001), 337–352, examines the role of Black Hoof's followers during the war, while Steven Warren's *The Shawnees and Their Neighbors, 1795–1870* (Urbana, Ill., 2005) provides a comprehensive, in-depth analysis of Black Hoof's followers, Shawnee removal, and subsequent Shawnee nation building in the West. Both Lucy Murphy's *A Gathering of Rivers: Indians, Métis, and Mining in the Western Great Lakes, 1737–1832* (Lincoln, Neb., 2000), and Susan Sleeper-Smith's *Indian Women and French Men: Rethinking Cultural Encounter in the Western Great Lakes* (Amherst, Mass., 2001) focus on the changing economic and political roles of Native American women in this region during the eighteenth and early nineteenth centuries.

A complete discussion of Tenskwatawa and his religious movement can be found in R. David Edmunds, *The Shawnee Prophet* (Lincoln, Neb., 1983). Other works with significant materials upon the holy man include James Mooney's *The Ghost Dance Religion and the Sioux Outbreak of 1890,* Fourteenth Annual Report of the Bureau of American Ethnology (2 vols., Washington, D.C., 1896); Benson Lossing's *The Pictorial Field Book of the War of 1812* (New York, 1869); and John Tanner's *Narrative of the Captivity and Adventures of John Tanner During Thirty Years Residence Among the Indians of the Interior of North America* (New York, 1830). Additional insights into Native American revitalization movements can be found in Anthony F. C. Wallace's "Revitalization Movements," *American Anthropologist,* vol. 58 (May 1956), 264–281; and in Wallace's *The Death and Rebirth of the Seneca* (New York, 1970). Also see Robert F. Berkhofer Jr.'s "Protestants, Pagans, and Sequences Among the North American Indians, 1760–1800," in Deward E. Walker's *The Emergent Native Americans: A Reader in Cultural Contact* (Boston, 1972), which offers several models for understanding Indian responses to white aggression. Gregory Dowd's *A Spirited Resistance: The Native American Struggle for Unity, 1745–1815* (Baltimore, 1992) traces the close relationship between Indian religious revitalization and political resistance to Euro-American hegemony during these years and argues that Tecumseh's movement was the final chapter in a long historical process that started in the mid-eighteenth century.

Several volumes of published documents illustrate the spread of the Indian movement. Of primary importance is Logan Esarey, ed., *Messages and Letters of William Henry Harrison* (2 vols., Indianapolis,

1922). Esarey's volumes not only chronicle the growing influence of the Shawnee Prophet, they also illustrate the emergence of Tecumseh and contain many of the latter's speeches. In Clarence E. Carter, ed., *The Territorial Papers of the United States* (27 vols., Washington, D.C., 1934–), specific volumes that focus upon Ohio, Indiana, Michigan, and Illinois provide evidence of the Indian movement in these states. Ninian W. Edwards's *History of Illinois from 1778 to 1833 and the Life and Times of Ninian Edwards* (New York, 1975) is especially useful on the activities of Tecumseh's followers in Illinois. Scattered through the forty volumes of the *Collections of the Michigan Pioneer and Historical Collections* (Lansing, Mich., 1874–1929) are selections from both British and American documents that reflect Indian activities in the Detroit region.

Good secondary accounts of Tecumseh's activities in the years preceding the War of 1812 can be found in Wallace Brice's *History of Fort Wayne* (Fort Wayne, Ind., 1868), Moses Dawson's *A Historical Narrative of the Civil and Military Services of Major General William H. Harrison* (Cincinnati, 1824), and John Dillon's *A History of Indiana* (Indianapolis, 1859). All these nineteenth-century works are rather antiquated, but they offer useful details of Indian-white relations in Indiana. Among the books cited earlier, Woehrmann's *At the Headwaters of the Maumee* presents a good discussion of American Indian policy during this period, while Horsman's *Matthew Elliott,* and Calloway's *Crown and Calumet* focus upon the actions of the British Indian Department. A doctoral dissertation by George C. Chalou, "The Red Pawns Go to War: British–American Indian Relations, 1810–1815" (Indiana University, 1971), provides a fine overview of events during these years.

Tenskwatawa's witch hunt among the Delawares is described in Lawrence Henry Gipson, ed., *The Moravian Indian Mission on the White River* (Indianapolis, 1938); in John Heckewelder, *A Narrative of the Mission of the United Brethren Among the Delaware and Mohegan Indians* (New York, 1971); and in Henry E. Stocker, *A History of the Moravian Mission Among the Indians on the White River in Indiana* (Bethlehem, Pa., 1917). In *The Delaware Indians: A History* (New Brunswick, N.J., 1972), Clifford Weslager discusses the role of this tribe throughout the War of 1812 period. R. David Edmunds's *The Potawatomis: Keepers of the Fire* (Norman, Okla., 1978) illustrates that some Potawatomis were among Tecumseh's staunchest supporters, while other members of the tribe remained loyal to the government. In "Main Poc: Potawatomi Wabeno," *American Indian Quarterly,* vol. 9 (Summer 1985), 259–272, Edmunds traces the career of this influential, yet dubious ally of

Tecumseh during this period. A. M. Gibson's *The Kickapoos: Lords of the Middle Border* (Norman, Okla., 1963) and Burt Anson's *The Miami Indians* (Norman, Okla., 1970) offer accounts of the interaction of these tribes with Tecumseh and his movement.

Although materials describing Tecumseh's southern trip are sketchy and sometimes contradictory, the most detailed discussion of these activities among the Chickasaws, Choctaws, and Creeks can be found in Henry S. Halbert and T. H. Ball's *The Creek War of 1813 and 1814* (Chicago, 1895). Other older secondary sources on this subject are Thomas Woodward's *Woodward's Reminiscences of the Creek or Muskogee Indians* (Montgomery, Ala., 1859), Albert James Pickett's *History of Alabama* (2 vols., Charleston, S.C., 1851), and Wesley Whickar's "Tecumseh and Pushmataha," *Indiana Magazine of History,* vol. 18 (December 1922), 315–331. Frank Owsley's *Struggle for the Gulf Borderlands: The Creek War and the Battle of New Orleans* (Gainesville, Fla., 1981) provides a good synopsis of Tecumseh's efforts among the southern tribes, while Joel Martin's *Sacred Revolt: The Muskogee Struggle for a New World* (Boston, 1991) examines the Creek War as a religious upheaval within the tribe. Both Claudio Saunt's *A New Order of Things: Property, Power, and the Transformation of the Creek Indians, 1753–1816* (Lincoln, Neb., 1999) and Robbie Ethridge's *Creek Country: The Creek Indians and Their World* (Chapel Hill, N.C., 2003) examine changes within Creek political, economic, and social structures during this period and place the Creek War in an ethnohistorical perspective.

A complete account of the Battle of Tippecanoe can be found in Edmunds's *The Shawnee Prophet,* while Alameda McCollough, ed., *The Battle of Tippecanoe: Conflict of Cultures* (Lafayette, Ind., 1973), contains several accounts by participants of the battle and includes additional information about leading figures on both sides.

Published primary materials concerning American activities during the war can be found in Esarey's *Messages and Letters of William Henry Harrison* and in the *Collections of the Michigan Pioneer and Historical Society.* Documents and accounts revealing the British perspective on the conflict are included in William Wood, ed., *Select British Documents of the War of 1812* (3 vols., Toronto, 1920–1926); and in Alexander Clark Casselman, ed., *John Richardson's War of 1812* (Toronto, 1902). Good accounts of Indian warfare on the Detroit frontier during 1812 are incorporated in "The Robert Lucas Journal of the War of 1812," *Iowa Journal of History and Politics,* vol. 4 (July 1922), 342–437, and in Milo M. Quaife, ed., *War on the Detroit: The Chronicles of Thomas Vercheres de Boucherville and the Capitulation by an Ohio Volunteer* (Chicago, 1940). Harlow

Lindley's *Fort Meigs and the War of 1812* (Columbus, Ohio, 1975) offers some diaries and other records documenting the British and Indian invasion of northern Ohio.

A balanced secondary account of the War of 1812 in the Great Lakes region can be found in Alec Gilpin's *The War of 1812 in the Old Northwest* (East Lansing, Mich., 1958). Robert McAfee's *History of the Late War in the Western Country* (Lexington, Ky., 1816), while antiquated, is rich in detail. Horsman's *Matthew Elliott* and Sandy Antal's *Wampum Denied: Procter's War of 1812* (Ottawa, 1997) present excellent discussions of British and Indian movements during the conflict, while several essays included in Morris Zaslow, ed., *The Defended Border: Upper Canada and the War of 1812* (Toronto, 1964), focus upon various aspects of the British defense of Upper Canada. Unquestionably, the most comprehensive discussion of Procter's retreat and the death of Tecumseh can be found in John Sugden's well-written *Tecumseh's Last Stand* (Norman, Okla., 1985).

Almost all accounts of Tecumseh and his life present the Shawnee in the image of the "noble savage." Tucker's *Tecumseh: Vision of Glory* is the best (or worst) example, but Mooney's *The Ghost Dance Religion and the Sioux Outbreak of 1890,* Josephy's chapter on Tecumseh in *The Patriot Chiefs,* and even (to a much lesser extent) Sugden's *Tecumseh* all project a "lionized" image of Indian leadership. In the last section of *Tecumseh: Fact and Fiction in Early Records,* Carl Klinck includes several selections illustrating how the image of Tecumseh has grown through popular literature and drama. The most complete account of the fictitious romance between Tecumseh and Rebecca Galloway can be found in William Albert Galloway's *Old Chillicothe: Shawnee and Pioneer History* (Xenia, Ohio, 1934), while Guy St. Denis's *Tecumseh's Bones* (Montreal, 2005) examines how the mystery and confusion over Tecumseh's burial site also has added to the "Tecumseh mystique." In "Tecumseh, the Shawnee Prophet and American History: A Reassessment," *Western History Quarterly,* vol. 14 (July 1983), 261–276, R. David Edmunds evaluates all the apocrypha associated with Tecumseh and the Shawnee Prophet and assesses its appeal to the American public. In contrast, Robert Berkhofer Jr.'s *The White Man's Indian* (New York, 1978) describes the historical development of the image of Indian people in the United States, while Philip J. Deloria's *Playing Indian* (New Haven, Conn., 1998) analyzes why the image of the "noble savage" is so appealing to non-Indians.

Index